Carroll County, Tennessee

Marriages

1860 – 1873

Byron and Barbara Sistler

Carroll County, Tennessee Marriages
1860-1873

Originally published, Nashville, 1988

Reprinted by

Janaway Publishing, Inc.
732 Kelsey Ct.
Santa Maria, California 93454
(805) 925-1038
www.JanawayPublishing.com

1988, 2006, 2012

ISBN: 978-1-59641-051-5

Made in the United States of America

CARROLL COUNTY, TN MARRIAGES
1860-1873

Where two dates appear on an entry, the first one is the date license was issued, the second (in parenthese) the date marriage was solemnized. If only one date, it usually means that the date of execution was the same as the date of license issuance.

Sometimes the execution of the marriage was not reported to the courthouse, and occasionally the clerk failed to note in the marriage book that the license was returned. We would usually make a notation in the entry to indicate the non-execution of a marriage if the book so stated.

The marriages are arranged alphabetically, the first half of the book by groom--the second by bride.

The records included in this book were transcribed by us directly from microfilm of the original marriage books. Error, where it occurs, may be attributed to us, or to the clerks of the period, many of whom did an appallingly sloppy job of entering the information.

If the bride and groom were black, a B is placed at the end of the entry.

It should be remembered that this and other marriage books we have prepared are indexes, and do not include all the information to be found in the original marriage book. Such data as names of bondsmen, ministers, justices of the peace, churches, etc. are omitted. Often such information is helpful to the researcher. Consequently the serious genealogist, to obtain this additional data as well as to check on the accuracy of the transcriber, should examine the original marriage record if at all possible.

Byron Sistler
Barbara Sistler

Nashville, TN
March, 1988

Abbett, J. D. to Luellen Barksdale 1-6-1864 (no return)
Abbott, H. F. to Martha E. Norwood 10-8-1869 (10-10-1869)
Abbott, J. D. to Elizabeth Green 9-5-1870 (9-6-1870)
Abbott, John W. to Martha Jones 12-7-1863 (12-18-1863)
Abbott, L. B. to M. A. Jones 12-14-1866 (no return)
Abernathy, Josiah C. to Sarah L. Swindle 5-26-1866 (5-7?-1866)
Abinathey, S. D. to S. A. Brewer 12-11-1866 (12-16-1866)
Adams, D. R. to Catharin King 5-14-1866 (5-17-1866)
Adams, Henry to Amanda Bell 12-31-1869
Adams, J. A. to Mattie J. Houston 10-17-1871 (10-19-1871)
Adams, J. W. to S. J. Eskew 12-12-1872 (no return)
Adams, John W. to Nancy Kennon 12-19-1868 (12-20-1868)
Adams, W. S. to Elizabeth F. Mebene 4-23-1864 (4-24-1864)
Adcock, A. M. to Caroline S. Mills 5-13-1863 (5-14-1863)
Adin, Clinton to M. M. Fuqua 5-28-1865 (6-8-1865)
Adkins, H. C. to Tilda Traylor 7-30-1870 (7-31-1870)
Aikin, W. A. to Robina Brewer 8-27-1870 (8-28-1870)
Akers, Harris to Parthena Rice 1-20-1872 (1-23-1872)
Akins, Wm. to Mary Tomblinson 5-16-1871 (5-17-1871)
Albright, Austin J. to Mary Burns 2-4-1864 (no return)
Albright, Austin J. to Mary Burrus 2-4-1864 (2-7-1864)
Alexander, Benj. to Malinda Motion 12-18-1872 (12-19-1872) B
Alexander, Henry to Tisha Roach 5-3-1869 (no return)
Alexander, James to Amanda Allen 9-4-1860
Alexander, T. J. to Jennie Lanier 9-2-1865 (9-3-1865)
Algea, Jacob to Molly Shepherd 2-14-1870 (2-15-1870)
Algee, R. W. to Josephine Anderson 4-6-1863 (no return)
Algee, W. H. to M. E. Vaughter 6-28-1867
Allen, C. T. to L. A. Fletcher 6-7-1865 (6-8-1865)
Allen, Green to Hannah Bledsoe 8-31-1872 (9-1-1872)
Allen, J. J. to Martha E. Crabb 10-24-1871 (no return)
Allen, J. W. to Mary J. Pickler 7-30-1863
Allen, J. W. to Mary J. Pickles 12-5-1863
Allen, James to _____ 9-29-1871
Allen, L. P. to S. L. O. Wilson 1-12-1861
Allen, Moses R. to Mary J. Cooper 12-23-1862
Allen, Nelson to Edy Johnson 12-7-1872 (no return) B
Allgee, J. F. to M. L. J. Jones 1-1-1870 (1-2-1870)
Anderson, Henry to Dicie Jones 2-2-1871 B
Anderson, Josiah to Mary M. Pritchard 2-?-1862 (no return)
Angle, James to Louiza Grooms 7-11-1871
Antry, John C. to Mary C. Hammett 2-26-1861 (no return)
Argo, W. D. to Sarah E. Cribbs 9-8-1866 (no return)
Arington, A. P. to Martha H. McCord 8-5-1873 (8-6-1873)
Arington, B. F. to J.? A. Fussell 5-23-1861 (5-18-1861)
Arington, Eli W. to S. F. Chandler 8-23-1866
Armstrong, J. P. to Sarah Jacobs 6-7-1869
Arnett, J. M. to Lucinda P. Jackson 1-1-1869 (1-14-1869)
Arnold, J. G. to A. C. Price 10-15-1870 (10-16-1870)
Arnold, James B. to Martha L. Steele 11-5-1867 (11-7-1867)
Arrington, A. to Rebeca Price 7-3-1865 (7-6-1865)
Arvinshire, William to Frances Lightle 7-15-1864 (7-17-1864)
Atkison, George to Caroline Hillsman 12-30-1869 (1-9-1870)
Attkisson, John to Fanney Bryant 10-20-1871 (10-25-1871)
Austin, Charles to Paralee Butler 7-25-1870 (7-27-1870)
Autery, S. W. to Rilley Rogers 12-21-1863 (12-23-1863)
Autry, E. W. to M. E. McAuley 11-21-1868 (11-22-1868)
Autry, Tyson to Louiza Horn 11-26-1861 (no return)
Bailey, W. H. to J. J. McAuley 7-24-1869 (7-25-1869)
Baird, W. T. to M. C. Jones 2-4-1867 (2-12-1867)
Baker, J. F. to S. A. Snead 1-6-1873 (1-7-1873)
Baker, R. B. to L. D. Carroll 11-30-1865 (12-5-1865)
Baker, Thomas H. to Marinda James 4-22-1861 (no return)
Baker, W. D. to Emma E. Prince 12-10-1864 (12-14-1864)
Baker, William to Nancy J. Hall 6-1-1870 (6-2-1870)
Balinger, Henry C. to Lucinda J. Webb 11-21-1865 (no return)
Ballew, John G. to Mainard Mitchell 10-23-1860 (10-24-1860)
Ballew, John to Mary Scott 3-2-1863
Ballew, John to Mary Scott 3-2-1863 (no return)
Banister, Abram to Sally Herron 5-21-1869 (5-22-1869)
Barham, Andrew to Lena Fuller 8-23-1871 (8-24-1871) B
Barham, Ezekiel to Mollie McDonald 12-8-1869 (12-9-1869)
Barham, Joseph to Sarah A. Nichols 5-4-1863 (5-7-1863)
Barham, L. B. to B. E. Jones 9-16-1871 (9-17-1871)
Barham, Sim to Harriett Wright 8-5-1873 (8-6-1873) B

Barker, W. R. to N. B. Carroll 8-14-1867 (no return)
Barker, Zachary to Margaret M. A. Joyner 2-21-1861 (2-16?-1861)
Barksdale, G. T. to C. O. Barham 1-30-1871 (2-1-1871)
Barksdale, J. F. to O. V. Drake 2-20-1865 (no return)
Barksdale, N. P. to Ella Hurt 1-15-1872 (1-18-1872)
Barlow, J. H. to E. J. Campbell 12-18-1872 (12-19-1872)
Barlow, John H. to Mary Scoby 2-1-1864 (2-11-1864)
Barlow, John H. to Mary Scoby 2-1-1864 (no return)
Barlow, Robert to Manda Thogmortin 12-24-1867 (1-16-1868)
Barnes, James to Harriett Morris? 3-16-1866 (no return)
Barnes, William J. to Martha Brown 7-18-1862 (9-4-1866?)
Barnett, A. E. to Margaret Holmes 1-5-1869 (no return)
Barnett, Edward to Mollie Hampton 10-2-1869
Barnhart, J. C. to Margaret C. Rowland 4-?-1867 (4-21-1867)
Barnhart, Robert to Saphrona Palmer 7-2-1866 (7-4-1866)
Barnhart, Robt. C. to Caroline Williams 1-22-1872 (no return)
Barnhart, William to Mary E. Powel 8-19-1871 (8-21-1871)
Barns, William W. to Susan E. Cox 11-28-1868 (11-29-1868)
Barns, Wilson to Sarah Rochell 10-31-1862 (no return)
Barton, John L. to Mary J. Nichols 10-30-1867 (10-31-1867)
Barton, T.J. to Martha Rice 11-23-1872 (11-26-1872)
Bashen?, Jackson to Elizabeth Nichols 4-10-1862 (no return)
Bateman, Hugh to Penina Cantrell 9-?-1860 (9-7-1860)
Bateman, Hugh to Peronia Cantrell 9-6-1860 (9-7-1860)
Bateman, J. B. to Martha J. Polston 6-22-1869 (6-23-1869)
Bateman, J. J. to T. J. Roberson 4-4-1867
Bateman, Josiah to Caroline Singleton 9-23-1867 (no return)
Bateman, W. R. to Elizabeth R. Prewitt 6-25-1870 (6-26-1870)
Bateman, William to Rianna Parish 3-2-1871 (3-5-1871)
Bates, Bevily to Sallie Vancleive 3-8-1872 (3-10-1872)
Bates, James S. to E. J. Laycock 12-5-1872
Batten, J. R. to Sophia Butler 11-27-1869 (11-30-1869)
Baucom, Cane to Harriet Crutchfield 4-19-1871 (4-20-1871) B
Baucom, Geo. to Joann Mitchell 8-31-1872 (9-1-1872)
Baucum, Samuel to Nelly Sparks 3-8-1870
Baxter, John to Marassela C. Rollins 8-5-1865 (8-6-1865)
Baxter, Robert J. to Lou J. Hughs 8-1-1866 (no return)
Baxter, W. K.? to J. C. Algee 1-1-1861 (1-2-1861)
Beavers, J. H. to Mary Ann Rece 6-27-1863 (7-5-1863)
Belerford, Rewbin to Millie Miller 4-27-1873 B
Belew, G. T. to Martha McCollum 5-25-1870 (5-26-1870)
Belew, Giles to Martha Braswell 2-13-1864
Belew, Giles to Martha Braswell 2-13-1864 (no return)
Belew, James R. to Verona A. Hardy 12-22-1869 (12-23-1869)
Belew, James W. to N. C. Pinckley 11-9-1870 (11-10-1870)
Belew, John G. to Mamaret? Mitchell 10-?-1860 (10-24-1860)
Belew, N. H. to Currillea J. Hardy 11-23-1870 (no return)
Bell, Anderson to Emaline Carson 12-27-1870 (1-2-1871) B
Bell, Isaac to Jennie Johnson 12-24-1868 (12-28-1868)
Bell, Jonathan to Sarah Culp 10-27-1871 (no return)
Bell, R. D. to Elizabeth M. Shofner 1-10-1866
Bell, R. J. to U. J. Phillips 11-27-1868 (11-29-1868)
Bell, Robt. to Lue Clay 10-5-1870 (10-6-1870)
Bell, Samuel to Mary Beard 12-2-1869 (12-4-1869)
Bellew, J. F. to Martha C. Herron? 12-11-1865 (no return)
Bellew, John L. to Susan H. Phillips 2-9-1862 (no return)
Bellew, John W. to M. E. Black 12-26-1871 (12-27-1871)
Bellew, R. A. to Elizabeth Fuqua 9-14-1866
Bellew, R. H. to E. J. Fite 9-17-1872 (9-18-1872)
Belliew, W. H. to Vandalia Belliew 9-10-1870
Bellows?, Z. T. to Penelope E. Burrow 10-3-1860 (10-7-1860)
Bennett, A. M. to Martha A. Spellings 12-31-1872 (no return)
Bennett, Benjamine to Elizabeth McCain 12-6-1872 (12-7-1872)
Bennett, E. G. H. to Mary B. Dewhit 1-7-1866
Bennett, George W. to Lutitia P. Palmer 12-19-1860 (12-20-1860)
Bennett, Samuel H. to Martha A. Williams 10-29-1868
Bennett, William F. to Martha S. Cobb 1-28-1869
Bennett, Wm. to Elizabeth Pace 3-30-1871
Benton, B. L. to Sarah S. Brown 9-18-1869 (9-19-1869)
Benton, H. H. to Rebecca Jones 8-15-1866 (8-16-1866)
Benton, Jas. M. to Martha J. Davis 9-25-1866 (9-27-1866)
Benton, John T. to Sophronia A. Brown 11-22-1867 (11-23-1867)
Berry, M. S. to Nancy Rochell 11-21-1868 (11-22-1868)
Berry, Newton P. to Mary A. Lett 2-10-1862 (2-11-1862)
Berry, Z. H. to Andromedia Vickers 12-24-1872

Berryhill, J. J. to C. C. Gwinn 10-11-1871 (10-12-1871)
Berryhill, J. T. to N. P. Pettyjohn 2-20-1869 (2-21-1869)
Berryhill, W. J. to Jerlien Stanfield 8-9-1863
Berryhill, Wm. J. to Jerleen Stanfield 8-?-1863 (no return)
Bethewen, J. H. to D. A. Taylor 1-9-1873 (1-12-1873)
Bevell, Jerome to M. R. Leshlie 12-21-1872 (12-25-1872)
Biggart, Joseph S. to Martha E. T. Carter 3-5-1868 (no return)
Bigham, Ben to Adline Bigham 2-10-1872 B
Bigham, John M. to Cynthia Lee 9-29-1865 (10-1-1865)
Bigham, R. L. (Dr.) to Mollie D. Fly 5-22-1867 (5-23-1867)
Bigham, Robert to Fanny New 12-10-1868 (12-11-1868)
Bigham, S. Y. to Margarett Morris 5-14-1860 (5-16-1860)
Bigham, Silas to Rachel Hurt 9-27-1871 (9-28-1871) B
Bilbrey, F. M. to Nancy E. Rogers 1-17-1865
Bilbrey, W. H. to Nancy R. Wadkins 12-29-1870
Bilbry, James C. to Nancy A. Rowe 4-17-1871 (4-20-1871)
Billberry, Josiah to Martha Swain 1-1-1866 (1-10-1866)
Birdwell, Albert to Daney Ann Butler 4-5-1864 (4-6-1864)
Birdwell, V. S. to Victoria Montgomery 1-8-1872 (1-10-1872)
Birmingham, E. B. to Mary T. Carver 6-17-1871 (6-18-1871)
Bishop, G. F. to Elizabeth W. Burrow 3-27-1866 (3-29-1866)
Bitter, James to E. Burns 12-13-1861 (12-15-1861)
Blackwell, John T. to M. E. J. Kee 6-8-1872 (6-9-1872)
Blair, W. C. to Mary L. Kee 10-11-1866
Blakeny, Bery to Martha Smothers 3-9-1861 (3-10-1861)
Bledsoe, Edward to Diner Anderson 10-21-1870 (10-23-1870)
Bledsoe, Jacob D. to Mary W. Allen 11-19-1863 (no return)
Bledsoe, Ned to Earline Sweargim 7-23-1868 (7-29-1868)
Bledsoe, Peter to Amanda Brevard 12-30-1872
Bledsoe, Wm. H. to Myra T. Allen 12-8-1864 (no return)
Blount, John G. to Winnie R. King 2-24-1869
Blow, T. R.? to Sallie Mathis 2-?-1868 (2-6-1868)
Boaz, George W. to Sophia Lorance 10-13-1866 (10-14-1866)
Boaz, S. T. to Margaret M.J. (Mrs.) Tomlinson 11-13-1867 (11-14-1867)
Boaz, William J. to Martha E. Glover 2-7-1862 (no return)
Bogle, R. E. to Susan C. Giles 12-27-1868 (12-28-1868)
Bohanon, D. L. to Mary E. Bibbs 3-6-1866 (3-8-1866)
Bolin, William to Adaline Barham 10-26-1871 (10-31-1871)
Bolton, Jeremiah T. to Sarah E. Byers 9-20-1865 (9-21-1865)
Bomar, W. C. to S. E. Compton 9-7-1869
Boren, H. J. to Martha J. Edwards 12-26-1865 (12-28-1865)
Boston, Jacob to Mary Ann Jenkins 6-30-1870 (7-2-1870)
Boston, Jesse to Catharine E. Bunch 4-30-1870 (5-1-1870)
Boswell, Benjamin to Sarah P. Rowland 12-12-1860
Boswell, G. W. to Ellen Fuqua 1-23-1871 (no return)
Boswell, sJ. T. to Anne E. Rowland 3-20-1861 (no return)
Bouldin, G. W. to M. A. Mullins 4-13-1870 (4-14-1870)
Bowelen, J. W. to Mary F. Phillips 1-2-1867
Box, James H. to Harriet A. Hood 9-25-1865 (10-18-1865)
Boyd, Jabez T. to Emily M. Pinkston 8-25-1868 (8-26-1868)
Boyd, Robert S. to Martha G. Jones 7-17-1861 (7-18-1861)
Boyd, William T. to America P. Robison 4-29-1870 (5-1-1870)
Brach, Green to Mary L. Delany 3-12-1863 (no return)
Brackens, Felix H. to Lydie A. Wyatt 7-16-1869 (7-17-1869)
Brackin, Wm. A. to J. P. Butler 8-28-1872 (8-29-1872)
Bradberry, W. B. to Susan J. Pickler 1-27-1864 (1-31-1864)
Branch, J. M. to Sarah J. Johnson 12-23-1872 (12-24-1872)
Branch, Joseph to Nancy Willis 1-7-1864 (no return)
Brand, John to Ann Jones 1-4-1873 (1-5-1873)
Brandon, Allen K. to Louisa A. E. Kennon 12-2-1869
Brandon, C. S. to Rosanna A. Benton 7-3-1861 (7-4-1861)
Brandon, H. S. to Mary Webb 10-17-1866
Brandon, J. B. to Elizabeth Grogan 11-7-1872
Brandon, James M.? to Sarah C. Johnson 12-28-1861 (1-6-1862)
Brandon, Lackey to Joanna Shay 12-23-1868 (12-24-1868)
Brandon, Michael to Issabella McCluskey 11-2-1864 (no return)
Brandon, Murray A. to Margaret C. Wilson 2-2-1869
Branoch, Austin to Tenness Boyd 11-23-1871 (11-25-1871) B
Brasher, J. W. to V. R. Curren 10-22-1870 (10-23-1870)
Brasier, Westly to Matilda E. Gee 1-1-1866 (1-4-1866)
Braswell, M. D. to Araminta Delany 7-18-1860 (no return)
Bratton, Alexander to Eliza Williams 8-18-1860 (8-19-1860)
Brawner?, H. D. to Louisa Morris 1-23-1869 (1-24-1869)
Brevard, B. J. to Susan A. Henderson 12-8-1868

Brewder, Henry to Louiza Carter 6-21-1871 (6-22-1871) B
Brewer, Enoch to Polly Ann (Mrs.) Kerly 12-28-1867 (1-2-1868)
Brewer, Isaac N. to Dorthy Kirk 10-25-1865 (10-31-1865)
Brewer, J. N. to M. F. Mitchell 1-20-1872 (1-22-1872)
Brewer, Nathaniel to Nancy Bird 5-30-1867 (no return)
Brewer, P. B. to Alcy C. Horn 12-18-1865 (12-19-1865)
Brewer, Thomas to Milly Linzy 11-24-1870 (no return)
Brewer, Wm. M. to Harriett A. Abernathy 2-21-1866 (2-22-1866)
Briant, Adolphus to Lucy A. Prince 11-19-1868
Briant, Charles P. to Sarah J. Purvis 12-31-1868
Briant, Daniel M. to Mary L. McLemore 11-10-1866 (11-11-1866)
Briant, Isah to Harriett Lorate 1-1-1872 (no return) B
Briant, John jr. to Ardina Leach 10-18-1870 (10-23-1870)
Briant, John to Recca Blanks 9-2-1867 (no return)
Briant, Noah to Bell Clark 12-9-1871 (no return)
Briant, Richard H. to M. L. Mitchell 2-20-1861 (2-21-1861)
Briant, Richd. H. to M. L. Mitchell 2-20-1861 (2-21-1861)
Briant, T. J. to M. E. Noell 6-14-1866
Briant, W. B. to M. E. Edwards 2-14-1870 (2-15-1870)
Briant, Z. B. to M. A. Browney 7-22-1864 (no return)
Bridgeman, Marshall to Mary Cunagham 7-13-1871
Bridges, C. A. to D. A. Rogers 4-1-1865 (no return)
Bridges, J. T. to M. J. Stewart 12-11-1872
Bridges, Jason A. to Elizabeth S.? Cross 6-23-1860 (6-25-1860)
Bridges, John H. to Martha Taylor 2-16-1864 (no return)
Bridges, W. A. C. to L. E. Cunningham 12-16-1867 (12-18-1867)
Bridges, W. F. to Cordelia C. Smith 5-25-1865 (5-30-1865)
Briges, John H. to Martha Tayler 2-16-1864 (no return)
Brinkley, Jefferson to Texanna Manning 4-28-1868 (5-3-1868)
Brinkley, R. C. to Elizabeth Hempstead 12-24-1860 (12-31-1860)
Brinkley, Seth to America Allmon 8-27-1860 (8-28-1860)
Britt, J. Y. to N. A. Crawford 9-8-1869 (9-9-1869)
Britt, James H. to Sarah E. Oliver 10-?-1861 (10-20-1861)
Britt, Peter to Fredonia Pearson 5-29-1871 (5-30-1871)
Britt, Wiley to Martha Oliver 9-9-1864 (9-11-1864)
Britt, Wily to Martha Oliver 9-9-1864
Broach, Green to Mary L. Delaney 3-12-1863 (no return)
Broach, Sidney to Lucie Swarigen? 9-12-1867
Brown, Adam to Ritter Seymore 2-22-1869 (2-28-1869)
Brown, Charles G. to Sarah D. Thompson 10-19-1869 (10-21-1869)
Brown, E. E. B. to Sarah Perkins 12-24-1866 (1-1-1867)
Brown, Eli D. to Beanthur Crider 11-8-1862 (11-9-1862)
Brown, George W. to Mattie Palmer 10-5-1864 (10-7-1864)
Brown, J. A. to S. A. J. Hampton 5-30-1864 (5-31-1864)
Brown, J. D. to Julie A. Brown 1-17-1866
Brown, J. F. to B. F. Pope 4-9-1866 (no return)
Brown, J. W. to Martha Allen 1-11-1862 (no return)
Brown, John to Elizabeth Messer 7-16-1873 (7-17-1873)
Brown, John to Martha Hall 9-6-1862 (9-8-1862)
Brown, Joseph S. to Mary E. Crider 12-20-1866
Brown, Nathaniel to Adaline Nannie 3-30-1869
Brown, Thomas C. to Sarah E. Rushin 12-3-1860 (12-9-1860)
Browning, M. R. to Susan E. Springer 1-21-1868 (no return)
Browning, Robert C. to Caroline Holland 11-18-1861
Browning, Z. T. to M. T. Leach 8-5-1872 (8-8-1872)
Bryant, A. D. to Alethia M. Quinn 10-15-1866 (no return)
Bryant, Alfred to Amey Bishop 12-31-1870 (1-5-1871)
Bryant, Boyd to Mollie Algee 7-31-1873 (7-27?-1873)
Bryant, Wm. J. to Susan Thomas 12-20-1870 (12-22-1870)
Buchanan, J. C. to N. A. Roney 8-6-1872 (no return)
Buchannon, D. A. to Caroline Wilson 12-7-1864 (12-8-1864)
Buckannan, D. A. to Caroline Wilson 12-7-1864
Bugg, Andrew M. to Louiza M. Jacobs 10-13-1866
Bullington, D. A. to Ellen Browning 11-27-1869 (12-2-1869)
Bullington, J. C. to Mary Bullington 12-29-1865 (12-31-1865)
Bullington, J. S. to Lidy J. Meritt 12-15-1870
Bullington, M. L. to Nancy J. Stribling 12-19-1871 (no return)
Bullington, Wlilliam C. to Sarah J. Browning 12-2-1862 (12-5-1862)
Bumpass, R. E. to Elizah Mitchum 11-18-1870 (11-22-1870)
Bunch, B. F. to Mary A. Boston 3-8-1870
Burdet, John to Criddie Cody 8-31-1872 (no return) B
Burdit, Robt. to Ann Carson 12-19-1870 (12-20-1870) B
Burk, Virgil R. to Mary E. Greenwood 6-12-1863
Burk, Virgil R. to Mary E. Greenwood 6-12-1863 (no return)
Burk, W. M. to S. A. Maxwell 2-29-1872

Burks, John T. to Sarah E. Reddick 7-17-1869 (7-19-1869
Burns, A. T. to E. F. Porter 12-16-1872 (12-19-1872)
Burns, H. C. to Alice H. Newbill 12-19-1864 (no return)
Burns, James H. to Amanda J. McKiney 11-28-1866 (12-2-1866)
Burrow, Banks M. to Martha J. Mills 10-1-1867 (no return)
Burrow, Daniel to Caroline Webb 2-13-1871 (2-16-1871)
Burrow, Ephraim to Lu? Briant 2-1-1869
Burrow, Henderson to Mary Cook 11-15-1871 (no return)
Burrow, Jordan to Marry (Amey?) Smith 5-19-1871 (5-20-1871)
Burrow, Nimrod to Elizabeth Harper 11-15-1861 (no return)
Burrow, Robt. H. to Mary Richardson 5-1-1873 (no return) B
Burrow, W. E. to E. J. Porterfield 3-2-1871
Burton, George W. to Emily J. Ballew 12-30-1865 (12-31-1865)
Burton, James A. to Cordelia E. Pritchard 6-19-1871 (no return)
Burton, John to Victoria Jamerson 1-23-1861 (1-27-1861)
Busbee, G. to Sally Evans 2-14-1870 (2-17-1870)
Bush, John to Lucy Leigh 11-24-1861
Butler, A. J. to Susan Bradbery 9-30-1867 (10-1-1867)
Butler, A. T. to Nancy J. Dickenson 1-26-1866 (1-28-1866)
Butler, A. T. to Ruth Sherfield 3-28-1870 (3-30-1870)
Butler, C. K. to Nancy J. Boswell 9-13-1865 (9-15-1865)
Butler, David M. to M. P. Green 10-8-1870 (10-9-1870)
Butler, G. W. to Pinkey Kyle 10-29-1867
Butler, Granvill H. to Mary A. Scott 2-6-1872
Butler, H. H. to Susan H. Medearis 9-12-1860 (no return)
Butler, J.? P. to Narcissa Anderson 11-16-1867 (11-17-1867)
Butler, Jacob to Jane Parish 2-8-1873 (2-9-1873) B
Butler, Joel A. to Frances Rogers 1-1-1868 (1-5-1868)
Butler, Jordon to Artimisa F. Whitley 3-2-1869 (3-10-1869)
Butler, L. F. to C. J. Eason 6-8-1867
Butler, Levi to Ella Rowland 8-24-1870
Butler, Marvell to Susan Liles 8-6-1860
Butler, P. T. to Mary A. McArthur 7-21-1862 (no return)
Butler, Philip T. to Sarah C. Boyd 3-2-1864 (no return)
Butler, Phillip T. to Sarah C. Butler 3-28-1864 (3-3-1864)
Butler, S. H. to J. E. Pendygrass 9-28-1871
Butler, Thomas to Nancy E. B. Hall 10-29-1860 (10-30-1860)
Byrns?, Richard H. to Darthula Pope 1-19-1869 (1-24-1869)
Cagle, Wm. T. to Elizabeth J. Liles 4-14-1860 (4-29-1860)
Cain, William to Elizabeth Moss 12-2-1865 (no return)
Caldwell, Nelson to Rachel Shad 5-10-1870 (5-14-1870)
Calhoun, Thomas C. to T. C. Hubbard 12-11-1860 (12-13-1860)
Campbell, John to Molley Barber 4-24-1870 (no return)
Cannie, John to Mary A. McAdoo 3-18-1868
Cannon, Jas. H. to Margarett Everett 12-18-1872 (no return)
Cannon, John M. to Eliza A. McCrackin 12-26-1864 (12-27-1864)
Cannon, W. M. to Mary M. H. Everett 12-19-1866
Canon, James A. to J. M. Dickson 1-3-1861 (1-6-1861)
Capps, James S. to Sarah P. Winn (Norrod) 8-28-1868
Capps, William to Mary C. Jones 2-18-1869
Capps?, P. B. to P. A. C. Bruce? 4-20-1867 (4-21-1867)
Caps, P. B. to Sarah L. Rumage 9-13-1870
Carden, Jas. E. to Nancy A. Neighbours 12-18-1865 (12-19-1865)
Carey, Felix to Nancy Brewer 5-14-1870 (5-18-1870)
Carigton, Richard to D. P. Kerby 3-27-1867 (3-28-1867)
Carlton, John F. to Mary Ann Hall 10-28-1861 (no return)
Carlton?, James D. to Ellen H. Rollins 2-8-1871 (2-9-1871)
Carnal, J. M. to L. E. Parker 3-13-1867 (3-15-1867)
Carnal, James J. to Rachael L. Milam 1-26-1870 (1-27-1870)
Carnal, James M. to Ellen Nichols 6-28-1869 (6-29-1869)
Carnall, W. L. to S. E. Parker 1-23-1873
Carnes, A. R. to Mintie S. Rogers 3-5-1862 (3-6-1862)
Carr, R. D. to M. A. Smoot 10-14-1866 (no return)
Carray, Thomas to Della Roberts 6-1-1867 (no return)
Carroll, J. J. to N. H. Harper 2-13-1873
Carroll, W. B. to J. A. Gardner 9-4-1871
Carroll, W. R. J. to Permelia J. Nelson 7-6-1867 (no return)
Carson, John to Sallie Branoch 3-28-1872 (no return) B
Carson, Richard to Louisa Barham 8-17-1868 (8-18-1868)
Carson, Steward to Margarett Sparks 11-21-1872 B
Carson, W. M. to Sallie Ridley 1-14-1862 (no return)
Carter, Berry to Fannie Prince 12-14-1872 (12-19-1872) B
Carter, Columbus to Harriet Fuller 1-21-1870
Carter, G. N. to Martha Leech 3-14-1861 (no return)
Carter, Henry to Sarah C. French 10-30-1869 (10-31-1869)

Carter, J. W. to M. D. Williamson 1-14-1867 (no return)
Carter, John L. to Harriett F. Earls 1-28-1868 (1-30-1868)
Carter, John M. to Sarah L. Carr 11-27-1866
Carter, John to Martha R. White 11-14-1865 (11-15-1865)
Carter, Joseph to Jinnie McDonald 9-15-1869 (9-20-1869)
Carter, L. H. to Cathorin Nichols 7-14-1873
Carter, R. B. F. to M. J. Wilson 12-10-1868
Carter, R. S. to Sarah A. Wood 10-14-1862 (10-16-1862)
Carter, T. B. to S. A. Waller 2-28-1866 (3-1-1866)
Carter, Thomas H. H. to Mary F. Hardy 12-18-1869 (12-19-1869)
Carter, W. H. to L. J. Broach 12-4-1872
Carter, W. H. to Tabitha L. Kemp 12-26-1863 (no return)
Carver, W. G. to Linda Ann Eliza Steel 3-5-1870 (3-9-1870)
Caudle, W. H. to Nancy Shaver 1-11-1867 (1-17-1867)
Cawthon, John to Frances Jamerson 11-22-1866
Chamberlin, A. G. to M. E. Haywood 7-11-1872 (7-13-1872)
Chamberlin, Alexander to Margaret Bailey 12-2-1863 (12-3-1863)
Chambers, B. F. to V. V. Martin 11-1-1871 (no return)
Chambers, Wm. C. to M.J. Pinckley 2-2-1871
Chambless, H. A. to P. C. Stewart 1-18-1870
Chambless, Hinton to Mary Jane Hurt 10-11-1869 (10-13-1869)
Chambliss, Orange to Ellen Lorance 1-10-1873 (no return)
Chance, W. H. to Nannie Alexander 8-24-1870 (8-25-1870)
Chandler, Archa B. to Elizabeth Niceler 6-22-1860 (no return)
Chandler, James A. to Mary A. N. Pace 7-27-1860
Chandler, James A. to Mary A. N. Pace 7-?-1861 (7-7-1860?)
Chandler, John to Mary E. Turner 4-9-1866 (4-12-1866)
Chandler, Stephen D. to Eliza A. Chilton 3-17-1869 (3-18-1869)
Chandler, William B. to Corilla Cooper 5-21-1869
Childress, James L. to Martha L.? Turner 12-16-1867 (12-18-1867)
Chilton, Samuel L. to Martha J. Smith 2-16-1870
Christain, W. R. to Fannie E. Moore 11-20-1866 (11-23-1866)
Christerbery, J. J. to Sallie Dill 2-7-1867
Christian, A. B. to H. R. Smith 6-24-1868 (6-25-1868)
Christian, W. C. to L. A. Cawthan 12-1-1866 (no return)
Churchwell, Jas. P. to Piecia Allen 5-10-1873 (5-11-1873)
Claiborn, J. H. to C. A. Looney 4-21-1865 (no return)
Clancy, Samuel C. to Rosalia Niederegger 1-18-1868 (1-19-1868)
Clark, B. C. to Adline Griffin 4-2-1867
Clark, Bowlen to Harriett Newbill 7-4-1870 (7-7-1870)
Clark, Charles to Missouri Jamison 1-8-1870 (1-9-1870)
Clark, Felix H. to Sarah Bradford 11-10-1869 (11-14-1869)
Clark, Henry to Harriet Rhodes 12-20-1869 (12-22-1869)
Clark, Henry to Molly Clark 12-18-1869 (12-23-1869)
Clark, J. P. to Martha S. Darby 11-3-1866 (11-5-1866)
Clark, Joshua D. to Sarah J. Brimage 7-3-1871 (7-6-1871)
Clark, Lewis to Harriett Bomar 1-22-1873 (1-23-1873) B
Clark, Mitchell to Mollie Cunningham 12-5-1868 (12-6-1868)
Clark, Nelson to Frances Hammett 10-26-1861 (10-30-1861)
Clark, W. H. to E. R. Neely 1-16-1871 (no return)
Clark, William to Frances E. Warren 9-25-1867 (no return)
Clay, Henry to Varna Jones 7-22-1871 (7-23-1871) B
Clay, J. H. to E. D. Craddoc 5-21-1873 (5-22-1873)
Clay, Richard to Eliza Greer 4-19-1870 (4-20-1870)
Clay, Sancho to Martha Patterson 9-21-1868
Clements, James K. P. to M. T. Hart 8-31-1868 (9-3-1868)
Clements, Worelson to Penelopee L. Driggers 12-21-1860 (12-25-1860)
Cloid, Newton F. to Mary L. Argo 1-17-1870
Clopton, J. P. to B. C. Brown? 2-12-1868 (2-13-1868)
Clopton, R. A. to Margarett Guffee 3-4-1868 (3-15-1868)
Cobb, Marion to Elizar O. Slaton no date (8-22-1869)
Cobb, Wm. to Susan A. Grooms 9-27-1870 (10-16-1870)
Coble, Hezekiah to Martha L. Owenby? 9-20-1866 (10-3-1866)
Cockrell, J. L. to M. E. McBride 2-10-1873 (2-11-1873)
Cody, Steward to Lanah Crofford 10-27-1870 (10-28-1870) B
Cole, Geo. B. to Celester A. Bryant 10-10-1872 (10-11-1872)
Cole, Jackson to Lucy Henderson 12-27-1870 (12-28-1870)
Cole, Jasper N. to Catharine A. Pruett 11-15-1865 (11-19-1865)
Coleman, E. J. to Kate Younger 11-14-1865 (11-15-1865)
Coleman, George to Louisa Brannock 9-4-1869 (9-19-1869)
Coleman, Green to Rena Hoggard 12-9-1868 (12-10-1868)
Coleman, J. H. to Mattie H. Fowler 6-24-1870 (6-28-1870)
Coleman, James to Alabama Thomas 12-24-1867 (1-5-1868)
Coleman, Joseph to Maggie Clark 3-20-1872 (no return) B?

Coleman, Marion to Winney Higgins 4-1-1870 (4-2-1870)
Coleman, Robert to Maria Harris 12-28-1869
Collins, C. A. to Sarah Hurt 12-19-1860 (no return)
Collins, John to Nancy C. L.? King 8-2-1865 (8-4-1865)
Collins, Thomas F. to Loucy Ramsey 12-27-1866 (no return)
Colvett, James to Emmy Bennett 5-24-1864 (5-25-1864)
Colvitt, W. C. to P. F. Miller no date (8-6-1873)
Comes, Henry to A. S. Gee 1-1-1873 (1-2-1873)
Compton, Eli to E. J. Penick 2-18-1867 (2-19-1867)
Compton, John A. to Salina Anderson 3-19-1861 (no return)
Condray, William F.? to Catharine Humphry 3-10-1866 (3-11-1866)
Conley, Franklin to Martha M. Webb 12-30-1869
Connell, John H. to Selah Ann M. Smith 3-14-1864 (no return)
Connell, John H. to Selahann M. Smith 3-14-1864 (no return)
Conner, George to Alice Brinder 5-8-1869
Cook, George W. to Sopha Blair 12-16-1872 (12-19-1872)
Cook, James to Mary J. McLemore 10-5-1869 (10-7-1869)
Cook, Josiah to Temperance Dollohite 8-9-1860 (8-14-1860)
Cook, L. D. to Frances E. McKinney 1-16-1865 (1-17-1865)
Cook, R. G.? to Irene E. Dougherty 9-10-1867 (no return)
Cook, William to Sarah J. Holloway 3-2-1867 (3-3-1867)
Cooper, John to Jane Bennett 4-2-1860 (4-6-1860)
Cooper, John to Josephine Rowland 1-11-1872
Cooper, Joseph to Jane Phipps 11-20-1865 (11-31?-1866?)
Cooper, T. H. to R. E. Taylor 10-14-1868
Cooper, T. T. to E. A. Ozier 7-12-1867 (no return)
Cooper, W. F. to Margaret E. Murphy 7-4-1870 (7-5-1870)
Cooper, W. S. to Martha Utley 5-22-1865 (no return)
Cooper, Wm. F. to Amanda Parker 9-17-1862 (9-18-1862)
Corder, William to Nancy Jolly 4-25-1861
Cotton, J. M. to Ardell Mitchell 8-14-1866
Cotton, J. N. to Sophronia E. Mitchell 3-29-1870 (no return)
Cotton, J. N. to Sophronia E. Mitchell 7-25-1870
Coulter, William to Tamar Newnan? 12-27-1869 (12-28-1869)
Counts, James to Rose Burnett 11-?-1868 (11-22-1868)
Covington, Caroline to Agnes Wilson 9-16-1869 (9-18-1869)
Covington, Madison to Jeroline Cody 1-26-1870
Cox, B. F. to J. A. Butler 6-8-1867 (6-23-1867)
Cox, H. C. to Mary Ann Roper 10-24-1866 (10-25-1866)
Cox, J. A. to Bhethsheba? White 12-17-1872 (12-19-1872)
Cox, J. W. to Mary P. Matheny 1-24-1870 (1-27-1870)
Cox, Newton to Rosella Lowery 6-16-1860 (6-24-1860)
Cox, W. H. to Louisa Ezell 3-28-1865 (3-30-1865)
Cozart, John L. to Celia Enocks 12-23-1869 (12-26-1869)
Crab, John to Mary J. Walker 3-29-1873 (3-30-1873)
Crafton, John to Dulla Pearce 8-14-1871 (8-17-1871)
Craig, John to Mary Roach 3-15-1864 (3-16-1864)
Craig, John to May Roach 3-15-1865 (no return)
Crane, Christopher C. to Mary L. Wilkins 11-3-1860 (11-4-1860)
Crawford, J. T. to L. D. Young 12-20-1869 (12-22-1869)
Crawford, M. A. to S. C. Stubbs 1-6-1868 (1-9-1868)
Crawford, Robert to Martha Butler 10-19-1869 (10-24-1869)
Crawford, W. M. to Sarah F. Browning 12-3-1867
Crdier, H. C. to M. A. Steel 12-26-1871 (no return)
Crenshaw, William to Letha Burrow 1-4-1870 (1-5-1870)
Crewes, Walter C. to Mary Jane Pearman 10-24-1860 (no return)
Crews, Beverly J. to Fanny Melton 7-30-1870 (8-7-1870)
Crews, Green to Nicie Rice 8-28-1871 (8-31-1871)
Crews, J. C. M. to Eliza J. Canon 9-19-1866 (no return)
Crews, John W. to Catharine Nannie 11-4-1865 (11-5-1865)
Cribbs, Asville P. to Sarah E. Johns 4-28-1863
Cribbs, Asville P. to Sarah E. Johns 4-28-1863 (no return)
Crider, John D. to Delia A. Hilliard 2-9-1865 (no return)
Crider, Milton H. to Mary E. Freeman 1-16-1864 (no return)
Crider, Milton H. to Mary E. Freeman 1-16-1864 (no return)
Crider, R. H. to Mary L. Mitchell 3-6-1869 (3-7-1869)
Cross, J. M. to Lavina C. Lorance 12-20-1869 (12-23-1869)
Crossett, A. T. to M. A. F. Pearman 2-17-1866 (2-20-1866)
Crossett, J. B. to M. A. Pearman 1-8-1864 (no return)
Crossett, J. B. to M. A. Pearmon 1-8-1864 (no return)
Crow, J. A. to S. J. Hanna 1-16-1869 (1-20-1869)
Crumb, J. T. to H. E. Wilson 1-18-1871 (1-19-1871)
Cruse, Thomas to Annie Harper 7-7-1865 (7-10-1865)
Culee?, John to Lucinda Patterson 2-12-1867 (2-13-1867)
Culp, Jack to Mattie Gregory 10-25-1870 (10-26-1870) B

Cuningham, Add to Parlee Striblin 1-14-1873
Cuningham, Charles to Clary Walker 12-29-1871 (11-30-1871) B
Cuningham, J. J. to Josephine Leach 1-31-1871 (2-2-1871)
Cuningham, Nelson to Amanda Britt 1-7-1873 (no return) B
Cunningham, Cornelius to Amanda Caldwell 12-16-1868 (12-17-1868)
Cunningham, Shad to Eliza Guinn 12-31-1869
Cunningham, Thos. J. to Mary J. Carter 2-23-1863 (2-26-1863)
Cunningham, Thos. J. to Mary J. Carter 2-25-1863
Cunningham, Wm. F. to Mary Robinson 10-1-1860 (10-2-1860)
Dalton, Daniel H. to Catharine Crider 12-23-1867 (12-24-1867)
Dammond?, Armstead to Jenny Wingo 2-1-1870 (2-2-1870)
Dane, Joseph to Martha E. Forrest 9-17-1868 (no return)
Daniel, Samuel to Jula Ann Burrow 4-30-1873 (5-1-1873) B
Darnall, Daniel to Vilet Kirk 12-27-1870 (12-29-1870) B
Darnall, Nicholas M. to Margaret Bell 8-29-1865 (no return)
David, Wm. A. to Jackson 12-27-1868 (12-28-1868)
Davis, A. to H. E. Fite 3-18-1871 (4-11-1871)
Davis, F. M. to M. J. M. Berry 8-17-1864 (8-18-1864)
Davis, J. H. to Emily D. Rollins 2-28-1870 (2-29?-1870)
Davis, James H. to Parisett Tate 1-8-1861
Davis, Joe to Tennessee Johnson 9-30-1871 (10-9-1871) B
Davis, John to Fanny Hester 4-2-1865 (4-9-1865)
Davis, R. H. to Isabel L. Sellers 12-11-1868 (12-15-1868)
Davis, Ralph to Adaline Harris 3-19-1869 (no return)
Davis, William O. to Sarah Jane Miller 3-11-1869
Dawes, Starkey to Martha J. Herron 6-19-1869 (6-20-1869)
Deer, John F. to Josaphine F. Brashers 1-22-1868 (1-28-1868)
Delany, J. M. to Sally Patten 12-6-1865
Deleny, R. A. to Susan Morris 12-20-1860 (12-23-1860)
Demoss, H. C. to Lavina H. Edwards 11-28-1866 (11-29-1866)
Denney, Frank to Sallie Hill 12-25-1871 (no return)
Denny, B. A. to Martha Utley? 10-15-1866 (10-17-1866)
Dent, G. W. to Mollie W. Burris 10-11-1869 (10-12-1869)
Denton, Joe to Salenia Long 1-18-1873 (no return) B
Derryberry, E. H. to Charlott Shipman 8-7-1860 (8-14-1860)
Derybery, E. W. to M.A. Shipman 1-8-1868 (1-9-1868)
Deshong, William W. to Mollie E. Enloe 6-8-1869 (6-10-1869)
Deshony, L. F. to B. L. Thompson 10-28-1872 (10-29-1872)
Devine, Alfred to Paralle Whitehorn 8-19-1868 (8-21-1868)
Dewhitt, Thomas to D. M. Williams 12-31-1866 (1-1-1867)
Dickinson, J. H. to Susan E. Dickson 7-24-1869 (8-4-1869)
Dickson, John M. to Emma A. Patterson 12-18-1866 (12-20-1866)
Dickson, R. D. to Mary Ann Coble 10-5-1861 (10-6-1861)
Dickson, Richard D. to Mary Ann Coble 10-?-1861 (10-6-1861)
Diggs, Thomas F. to Mary F. Haynes 10-3-1860 (no return)
Diggs, W. M. to Elizabeth Blake 1-15-1866
Dilda, W. D. to Mary V. Pruitt 10-20-1863 (10-25-1863)
Dilda, Wm. D. to Mary V. Pruit 10-20-1864
Dilday, Charles to Winney Diggs 8-5-1869
Dilday, Henry J. to Sarah C. Capps 5-6-1861 (5-12-1861)
Dilday, William D. to Mary V. Pruitt 10-20-1863 (no return)
Dill, A. W. to Sarah M. Kee 10-25-1860
Dill, J. B. to L. V. Laycook 2-13-1873
Dill, T. J. to N. C. (Mrs.) Barham 4-9-1860
Dillon, G. N. to Sarah E. Rowland 2-3-1868 (2-5-1868)
Dinwiddie, Jackson to Susan Norvell 8-4-1870
Dinwiddie, Joseph to Victoria Guinn 12-29-1868 (1-2-1869)
Dinwiddie, M. S. to Ann Sparks 11-2-1863 (11-5-1863)
Dinwiddie, Rafe to Mary Gorden 1-15-18?? (1-27-1870)
Dinwiddie, S. A. to B. A. Province 8-29-1871 (8-31-1871)
Dinwiddie, W. A. to Lula Cooper 6-18-1872 (no return)
Dismukes, G. W. to Agness Hannah 12-10-1867 (12-11-1867)
Dodd, Benjamin to Mary C. Burkett 4-25-1860 (4-26-1860)
Dolan, Robert to Mary J. Dolan 12-22-1866 (12-23-1866)
Donaldson, Godfrey to Fannie Killan 5-25-1872 (5-26-1872) B
Donavan, D. J. to Mary H. Keaney 12-27-1869 (12-28-1869)
Dorsey, William L. to Mattie J. Loveland 5-14-1861
Dotson, William H. to Mary E. Hester 3-30-1862 (no return)
Douglass, Eli to Susan A. Beck 9-20-1869 (no return)
Douglass, M. F. H. to Nancy Burnett 12-26-1865 (12-31-1865)
Dowden, S. C. to S. L. C. Keaton 11-6-1869 (11-21-1869)
Downing, Bennett to Kate McDougal 8-25-1869
Downing, J. J. to Jane Moore 7-6-1867 (7-11-1867)
Drake, George to Esabella Gilbert 9-2-1868 (9-3-1868)
Drake, Granville to Lucy A. Bell 3-19-1873 B

Drewrey, L. N. to C. T. McAdoo 8-2-1871 (8-3-1871)
Drummonds, J. H. to Louisa Hayley 10-30-1867
Dudley, Elzey to Amanda Lansden 7-17-1869 (no return)
Dudley, John to Elizabeth Coleman 4-11-1871 (4-15-1871)
Dudley, Richard to Catherine Pate 7-18-1872 B
Duffer, H. G. to N. L. Simmons 1-26-1871 (1-29-1871)
Duke, Alexander to Ellen Williams 12-4-1869 (12-5-1869)
Duke, T. A. to Susan Y. Woods 7-15-1868
Dunkin, Stephen to Malinda Lett 12-24-1866 (12-27-1866)
Dunlap, N. J. to E. J. Perkins 2-3-1872 (2-5-1872)
Dunn, John to Ardella Freeland 4-5-1864 (4-7-1864)
Dunning, John K. to Mary L. Woodard 8-28-1864 (no return)
Dysart, W. H. H. to M. C. Holmes 8-23-1870 (8-24-1870)
Easters, Jesse C. to Sarah A. Barnhart 8-6-1866 (8-7-1866)
Edwards, A. C. to Tabitha A. Williams 11-8-1871
Edwards, Anderson to Nancy Watkins 8-9-1860 (no return)
Edwards, Frank to Nancy Adams 12-24-1869 (12-30-1869)
Edwards, G. W. to Frances P. Wilson 10-15-1866 (10-16-1866)
Edwards, J. F. to Q. L. A. Akers 1-7-1871 (1-8-1871)
Edwards, Jas. W. to Mary F. Jones 1-17-1871
Edwards, John H. to Lucinda F. Lipe 9-14-1871
Edwards, Marion to Mary Ann Shofner 3-16-1864
Edwards, Marion to Maryann Shofner 3-16-1864 (no return)
Edwards, Nathaniel J. to Mary F. Spellings 10-6-1865 (10-8-1865)
Edwards, William J. to _____ 12-8-1866 (12-11-1866)
Elbowe, Gross to Mary C. Bowden 9-13-1865 (9-17-1865)
Elder, R. F. to L. E. Patten 1-1-1866 (1-7-1866)
Elem, Richard to Julia Strayhorn 7-26-1872 (no return)
Elgin, Frank to Julia Marris 10-1-1870 (10-2-1870)
Elison, Larance to Lonezar Clark 9-26-1870 (10-9-1870)
Elkins, J. M. to Polly J. Butler 10-11-1871 (10-12-1871)
Ellender, B. F. to N. C. King 9-15-1860 (9-16-1860)
Ellis, W. A. to Annie W. Lanier 12-19-1865 (no return)
Ellsberry, B. L. to Mattie V Parnell 10-31-1870 (no return)
Ellsberry, E. M. to L. W. Barlow 7-12-1864 (7-13-1864)
Elmore, Hugh to Mary Barrett 10-23-1863 (10-25-1863)
Elmore, Hugh to Mary Barrett 10-23-1864 (no return)
Elmore, Robert H. to Drucilla Ward 2-25-1863
Elmore, Robert H. to Drucilla Ward 2-25-1863 (2-27-1863)
Elzan, James C.? to Clarinda E.? Cribbs 7-28-1860 (7-31-1860)
Enboe?, Thomas E. to Rebeca A. Spillings 9-6-1865 (9-8-1865)
Enloe, Samuel to Susan Burrow 11-2-1868 (11-8-1868)
Enochs, G. V. to Elizabeth Reed 9-11-1865 (9-12-1865)
Enochs, G. V. to Winny Read 12-28-1869 (12-30-1869)
Enocks, R. N. to M. N. Wright 12-17-1872
Eskew, Hance S. to Martha C. Fish 12-?-1861 (12-22-1861)
Eskew, J. M. to A. J. Dildy 11-1-1870
Eskew, J. W. to M. J. Larance 11-15-1871 (11-16-1871)
Estes, A. F. to Virginia Algee 9-29-1868 (10-1-1868)
Etheridge, J. H. to W. C. Sweaney 10-8-1863
Etheridge, J. H. to W. C. Sweaney 10-8-1863 (no return)
Ethridge, J. H. to W. C. Serconas 10-8-1864
Eubanks, R. B. to S. J. Boswell 3-10-1870
Evans, J. W. to Dillie Hatch 4-23-1872 (no return)
Evans, J. W. to Nancy Brigens 1-10-1871
Evans, John to Frances J. Hewey 8-29-1866 (9-2-1866)
Evans, Nelson to Sarah E. Gately 1-3-1870
Everett, Isham to Harriet Wingo 4-28-1870 (5-1-1871?)
Everett, J. E. to E. C. Matheny 4-26-1867 (5-2-1868?)
Everett, J. K. to Margaret Morgan 1-1-1871 (not executed?)
Everett, Thomas to Molly Henderson 12-24-1869 (12-25-1869)
Everett, Wm. B. to S. A. Everett 12-7-1860
Everett?, William B. to Sarah A. Everitt 12-7-1860 (12-13-1860)
Ezell, B. to Addie Williamson 9-21-1870 (9-22-1870)
Ezzell, B. G. to Ella Loving 5-4-1872 (5-5-1872)
Ezzell, D. S. to Lenora M. Roach 12-31-1872 (1-1-1873)
Ezzell, J. to Elizabeth E. White 7-17-1860 (no return)
Ezzell, Plase to Mary Pattison 5-19-1873 (5-29-1873) B
Falker, Elijah to Bettie A. Scott 2-13-1872
Faray?, Gideon to Jane Medley 2-11-1867 (2-12-1867)
Faris, Thomas H. to Nancy J. Davis 2-12-1863 (no return)
Farris, Thos. H. to Nancy J. Davis 2-12-1863
Featherston, Henry D. to Amanda L. Lusk 5-12-1862 (no return)
Felts, A. P. to D. P. Hardister 4-16-1866 (4-25-1866)
Felts, James M. to Amanda C. Price 3-11-1862

Felts, Joseph W. to Addie T. Hardister 8-31-1865 (no return)
Fields, A. J. to Perneta A. Mullin 12-4-1867
Fields, Lewis to Ann Huffman 12-31-1868 (1-3-1869)
Fields, M. A. to Martha A. Sherrell 7-13-1872 (no return)
Fields, Samuel V. to Martha J. Pinson 11-28-1865 (no return)
Fields, W. J. to Margaret D. Rothrock 5-6-1864 (5-7-1864)
Fields, William H. to Elizabeth C. Crutchfield 12-21-1864 (12-22-1864)
Finch, Edmond to Melissa J. Pinkston 10-25-1869 (10-28-1869)
Finch, Henry C. to Lucinda Hicks 8-31-1870 (9-1-1870)
Finley, Albert to Candas M. Roaney 2-3-1864 (no return)
Finley, Newton to Martha C. Jenkins 2-17-1863 (no return)
Finley, William to Paralee A. Redden 12-31-1869 (1-5-1870)
FitsJerrel, Jeremiah to Ann McNamara 1-7-1873 (1-28-1873)
Fitzgerald, Thos. to Mary Bayby 12-11-1872 (12-12-1872) B
Flake, Andrew to Edy Hampton 1-8-1872 (no return) B
Flake, James to Winnie Kee 12-19-1872 (no return)
Flake, Wm. to Espran Burnett 2-18-1865 (2-21-1865)
Fletcher, G. W. to Mollie E. Hill 2-15-1873 (2-16-1873)
Flippin, H. S. to Martha Quinn 1-6-1866 (no return)
Flippin, M. B. to J. R. Ward 4-7-1866 (4-8-1866)
Fly, James C. to Malissa A. Jacobs 9-25-1865 (10-3-1865)
Forbus, B. T. to L. Ann Bennett 10-26-1871
Forest, Wm. F. to Margaret C. Allen 9-23-1871 (9-24-1871)
Foresyth, T. D. to F. A. B. Pearce 1-15-1873
Foster, J. W. to Sarah C. George 12-11-1865 (12-31-1865)
Foster, Lee to Manerva Harris 12-24-1872 (12-26-1872) B
Foster, Thomas J. to Louisa F. Alrich? 12-18-1866 (12-19-1866)
Fowler, Adam to Eliza Patterson 11-25-1865 (4-14-1866)
Fowler, Joseph B. to Martha E. Jarrett? 10-21-1861 (no return)
Fowler, R. T. to Sallie E. Sparks 2-4-1867 (2-14-1867)
Francisco, William to Rebeca Monroe 11-21-1861 (no return)
Franklin, Thomas to Ellen Duncan 9-23-1867 (9-24-1867)
Freeland, Alphonzo to Martha E. Dill 11-15-1865 (11-16-1865)
Freeland, George W. to T. P. Pickler 8-27-1869 (8-29-1869)
Freelin, John N. to Nanc S. Pickler 12-7-1867 (12-15-1867)
Freeman, J. N. to Susan Hambleton 10-8-1870 (10-9-1870)
Freeman, T. E. to Mary V. Waters 11-7-1866
French, Coleman J. to Martha L. Arington 11-15-1860 (11-20-1860)
French, J. G. to Mary Robey 10-20-1868
French, Jesse P. to Mary B. Groom 1-6-1870
French, John W. to Latitica A. Cox 7-21-1866 (7-22-1866)
French, L. L. to Amand Garrett 2-16-1871
French, L. N. to Milly Carter 10-7-1867
French, T. H. to Martha Swinney 1-17-1872 (no return)
French, William A. to Mary M. McMackins 9-12-1865 (9-14-1865)
French, William to Sallie Swinney 8-10-1871
Frinch, W. M. to M. C. Row 2-10-1865 (3-12-1865)
Frost, B. T. to L. F. McCollum 3-4-1872 (3-5-1872)
Fry, R. D. to Elizabeth McLemore 6-13-1860 (6-14-1860)
Fuller, J. B. to Mary E. Darnall 11-16-1867 (11-17-1867)
Fuller, J. R. to M. J. Kyle 1-25-1871 (1-26-1871)
Fuqua, J. H. to Elizabeth A. Tucker 12-13-1869 (12-15-1869)
Fuqua, J. W. to M. L. Coleman 3-2-1868 (3-4-1868)
Fuqua, Jacob to Frances Knuckles 8-5-1872
Fuqua, John T. to Martha Hurt 10-21-1867 (no return)
Fuqua, W. J. to L. Cooper 9-10-1864 (9-12-1864)
Fuqua, Walter S. to Ann Pate 5-20-1863
Fuqua, Walter S. to Ann Pate 5-20-1863 (no return)
Fuqua, Walter S. to Susan Morris 11-17-1868 (11-18-1868)
Furlong, William to Allice Bird 4-29-1873 (no return)
Fussell, J. J. to M. E. Fields 4-22-1867
Gallimore, George W. to Mary E. Perkins 8-15-1870 (8-16-1870)
Gardner, G. S. to Martha F. Hamilton 2-12-1863
Gardner, Geor. to Hanah Coleman 6-10-1871
Gardner, J. H. to Nancy L. Hamilton 11-27-1860 (11-28-1860)
Gardner, J. H. to Nancy L. Hamilton 11-27-1863 (no return)
Gardner, W. R. to Emeline Vaughan 6-11-1861 (6-13-1861)
Gardner, W. S. to Mollie A. Wiles 5-16-1873 (no return)
Gardner, William R. to Catharine S. Porter 11-26-1866 (12-2-1866)
Garner, B. F. to Edney S. Hamilton 1-15-1872 (1-16-1872)
Garner, William to Mintee Diggs 11-4-1860 (not endorsed)
Garner, Wm. F. to Nancy R. Rogers 6-10-1861 (not endorsed)
Garrett, Geor. B. to Mollie L. Dickason 6-3-1872 (6-5-1872)
Garrett, J. H. to J. A. F. Harman 9-21-1871

Garrett, W. R. to Mary E. Green 9-23-1862 (9-25-1862)
Garrison, Moses to Elzira Grifin 10-30-1865
Gatland, Thomas T. to Manerva F. Vinson 12-8-1866 (no return)
Gatlin, Stephen to Priscilla Box 10-14-1867 (10-15-1867)
Gee, D. W. to J. C. Merritt 12-11-1866
Gee, James P. to Matilda C. Demoss 8-6-1861 (8-7-1861)
Gelby, R. C. to Dollie Younger 8-13-1866 (no return)
George, J. B. to Arenia Wallice 4-28-1860
Gibbon, James T. to Lamira R. Burns 8-21-1861 (8-22-1861)
Gibbons, A. B. to S. C. Moore 2-13-1863 (no return)
Gibbons, S. T. C. to Nancy A. Richardson 12-15-1869 (12-16-1869)
Gibson, Alvert to Marry Williams 6-19-1873
Gibson, B. F. to Martha G. Stubbs 11-15-1863 (no return)
Gibson, James M. to Fanlee A. McCrackin 3-21-1863 (no return)
Gibson, James M. to Paula A. McCracken 3-24-1863
Gibson, Porter to Sarah J. Bainey 5-8-1863 (5-17-1863)
Gibson, Wyley P. to Ann Dilelay? 3-12-1861
Gilbert, G. J. to Sarah J. Birmingham 9-16-1872
Gilbert, James M. to Carrie Whitten 5-18-1869
Gilbert, John to Mariah Wiggins 1-9-1871 B
Gilbert, Joseph to Emeline Gilbert 1-21-1871 (no return) B
Gilbert, Martin to Elizabeth Wingo 4-4-1871 (1-5-1871)
Gilbert, Robert to Ellen Gilbert 2-18-1870 (2-20-1870)
Gilbert, Thos. to Narcisa Wiggins 1-9-1871 B
Gilbreth, James to Mary Blaylock 1-12-1871
Giles, C. G. to Margaret McKinney 3-28-1868 (3-29-1868)
Giles, L. G. to Sarah C. Williams 11-12-1872
Giles, N. C. to Susan C. Tarply 11-7-1860
Gilkey, James T. to Sarah L. Crafter 1-11-1870 (1-13-1870)
Gilkey, S. B. to L. D. King 7-2-1863 (no return)
Givin, John to Sally Adams 12-5-1864 (no return)
Glosson, A. F. to M. C. Bennett 3-7-1872
Glosson, James to Anna Boswell 12-22-1869 (12-23-1869)
Gooch, Alfred to Lucinda Abbott 9-20-1869 (9-21-1869)
Gooch, Charles Y. to Eliza E. Mebane 10-31-1866
Gooch, Littleton O. to Mary E. Pugh 3-16-1869 (3-17-1869)
Gooch, Priestley to Elizabeth Cozart 8-13-1870 (8-14-1870)
Gooch, W. L. to Nancy Rogin 10-18-1869 (10-20-1869)
Goodin, Thomas to Susan Cunningham 5-2-1870 (no return)
Goodloe, Alexander H. to Mary E. Cunningham 12-21-1863 (no return)
Goodlow, James to P. Burns 2-4-1869
Goodman, A. R. to L. J. Burns 12-27-1860 (no return)
Goodrun, Wm. to Fanny Fisher 4-1-1869 (4-27-1869)
Gorden, P. W. to Nancy J. Smith 1-1-1866
Gordon, Jackson to Kandis Gordon 4-5-1869
Gordon, Louis to Harriet Hampton 3-21-1872 (no return)
Gorman, J. J. to Ellen Albright 8-20-1861 (8-21-1861)
Gossett, Hail to Ellen Woods 5-7-1870 (5-8-1870)
Graham, John W. to Allice Bugg 6-26-1867 (6-27-1867)
Graham, Saml. R. to Elizabeth Roberts 10-22-1866 (10-23-1866)
Granade, Wm. R. to Mary J. Cole 12-11-1865 (12-14-1865)
Grant, Archibald to Mary C. Page 12-19-1864 (no return)
Graves, G. M. to Lizzie Purdy 12-16-1865
Graves, George W. to Manerva Hamilton 6-6-1861
Graves, George W. to Minerva Hamilton 6-?-1861 (6-6-1861)
Graves, Robert B. to Josephine Murray 2-9-1870 (2-10-1870)
Graves, Wilbron H. to Elizabeth P. Hamilton 9-22-1858
Gray, Charles H. to Mary B. O'Conner 2-6-1869
Gray, John to Caroline Fields 2-17-1869 (2-18-1869)
Gray, John to T. E. Fields 1-21-1871 (1-24-1871)
Gray, Phineous to Synthia A. Rowland 1-28-1870 (2-1-1870)
Gray, W. B. W. to P. P. Bigham 3-5-1867 (no return)
Gray, W. G. to F. M. Kerr 1-21-1871
Green, A. M. to M. C. Graves 3-7-1867 (3-11-1867)
Green, D. J. to M. M. Matheny 4-23-1869 (4-25-1869)
Green, F. L. to Frances J. Gallimore 9-16-1865 (9-20-1865)
Green, J. D. R. to Elizabeth Liles 4-16-1864
Green, James C. to Sarah Neely 10-18-1860
Green, James H. to Agnes Lorance 11-14-1866 (11-16-1866)
Green, John H. to F. M. Quinn 1-19-1869 (1-22-1869)
Green, T. L. to G. V. Green 9-3-1870 (9-4-1870)
Green, Wm. H. to Szieber? C. T. Martin 1-21-1862 (no return)
Greenfield, C. F. to L. A. Cox 9-26-1870 (9-27-1870)
Greer, George to Amy Luter 4-3-1869 (4-4-1869)

Gregory, Harvy to Harriet Ezell 2-20-1869
Gregory, Peyton to Parlee Long 12-24-1869 (no return)
Gregory, W. H. to Mollie Johnson 10-6-1865 (no return)
Griffin, William to Elizabeth Burks 3-21-1864
Grissom, F. H. to Elizabeth McMackin 7-16-1873 (7-17-1873)
Grissom, John to Elizabeth Nease 9-9-1868 (9-17-1868)
Grizzard, Charles B. to Mary E. Crockett 12-17-1861 (12-18-1861)
Grizzard, Charles B. to Mary E. Crockett 12-19-1861
Grizzard, Dennis to Parlie McNeill 2-6-1872 B
Grizzard, Hulon? W. to Mary E. Flack 11-20-1860 (11-21-1860)
Grizzard, W. B. to Irene? McNeill 1-19-1871
Grogan, Joseph W. to Eliza C. Pritchard 1-12-1869 (1-13-1869)
Grogan, Nathan H. to Lila Ragland 5-21-1869
Grogan, Wm. B. to Mary Hopper 1-9-1873
Groom, J. W. to Sarah H. Rowland 12-1-1860 (12-2-1860)
Groom, James L. to Elizabeth S. Chandler 7-5-1862 (7-11-1862)
Groom, Thos. W. to Mary F. Groom 3-1-1871
Groom?, James L. to Nancy Chandler 3-20-1868
Grooms, Almus to Jane V. London 1-24-1872 (1-25-1872)
Grooms, J. M. to Elizabeth Rowland 2-19-1866
Grooms, James W. to Sarah H. Rowland 2-22-1870
Grooms, Thomas to Mary E. Green 12-13-1869 (12-14-1869)
Grooms, Thos. to Marilda Jane Russian 9-5-1867
Grun?, James C. to M. E. Neely 10-14-1864
Grundy, J. T. to Mattie Sparks 7-26-1871 B
Guffey, John to Elizabeth S. Burns 8-3-1868 (8-4-1868)
Gunter, J. W. to Martha E. Russell 8-20-1862 (no return)
Gustan, E. to Agnus S. Fox 8-8-1865 (no return)
Gwinn, John E. to Medora Alice Persons 1-6-1868 (1-8-1868)
Gwinn, Pearse to Betsey Gordan 12-23-1871 (no return) B
Haflin, Francis M. to Laura E. Henry 4-12-1866? (with 1862)
Hagler, Robert to Sarah Rice 12-17-1868 (12-18-1868)
Hale, H. C. to Rebecca T. Porter 10-14-1864 (10-16-1864)
Haley, George W. to Harriet E. Threadgill 9-20-1867 (no return)
Haley, Joseph to Dora McLemore 10-5-1869 (10-7-1869)
Hall, A. R. to Melvina George 12-13-1870 (12-15-1870)
Hall, Allen C. to Mollie E. Howard 3-22-1864 (no return)
Hall, E. A. G. to Elizabeth J. Wood 1-15-1873 (1-16-1873)
Hall, J. C. to E. B. Crider 12-17-1872 (12-18-1872)
Hall, J. R. to C. A. Russ no date (with Mar 1866)
Hall, Robert H. to A. S. Rust 4-18-1864 (4-20-1864)
Hall, Robt. P. to Mary M. Autry 11-7-1871 (11-8-1871)
Hall, W. A. to M. E. King 2-11-1867 (2-12-1867)
Hall, Wm. R. to Harriett A.? Brinley 1-19-1861 (1-24-1861)
Hallmark, W. G. to Martha J. Barnes 3-6-1872 (no return)
Hamel, James W. to Sarah C. Davis 11-27-1872
Hamett, Andy to M. A. Pearce 4-17-1872 (no return) B
Hamilton, James G. to Mary Jane Kirk 7-22-1869
Hamilton, Pete to Mary Hooper 12-30-1872 B
Hamilton, Thomas to Hannah Henning 3-12-1864 (3-16-1864)
Hamilton, Thomas to Hannah Henning 3-12-1864 (no return)
Hammett, James to Lielia Baker 7-22-1862 (no return)
Hammett, William N. to Lidia J. Robeson 11-16-1865
Hampton, Haywood to Eliza J. Robertson 1-4-1862 (1-5-1862)
Hampton, Henry A. to Nancy E. Wood 7-17-1869 (7-18-1869)
Hampton, William R. to Mary Gately 2-?-1866 (2-26-1866)
Hampton, William to Eliza Pickett 10-21-1865 (no return)
Hane, Samuel S. to Mary F. Warbrittan 10-7-1865 (10-8-1865)
Hanna, N. W. to E. C. Hanna 12-22-1864 (1-1-1865)
Hannah, Elijah to Ellen Swayne 1-6-1871 B
Hannings, Solomon to Eveline Green 12-2-1868 (12-6-1868)
Hansbro, H. J. to M. C. Weatherford 2-4-1861 (2-7-1861)
Har, Wm. to Mary Woods 5-12-1865 (6-1-1865)
Hargus, Henry to Louisa Hampton 1-27-1869 (1-29-1869)
Haris, James to Nannie Doherity 9-26-1870 (9-28-1870)
Harlin, Isaac to Eliza J. Patterson 5-25-1863 (5-27-1863)
Harlin, Isaac to Eliza Jane Patterson 5-25-1863
Harness, W. P. to W. A. Green 10-23-1869
Harper, Abram to Susan G. Buchannon 11-10-1864 (no return)
Harper, H. T. to Harriet A. McKinney 1-24-1870 (1-26-1870)
Harper, J. A. to E. J. Gilkey 3-4-1869 (3-7-1869)
Harper, Quincy A. to America J. McAdoo 2-13-1866
Harrell, Pett to Lear Hurt 9-27-1871 (9-28-1871) B
Harrell, Poke to Sarah Jones 3-12-1872 (no return) B
Harrell, W. M. to Tenney C. Swinney 7-27-1872 (7-28-1872)

Harrelson, William P. to Eliza C. Dueley 10-18-1860
Harris, C. C. to Mollie E. Towns 12-25-1865 (no return)
Harris, Charles to Ann Young 1-22-1870 (2-13-1870)
Harris, George to Helen Britt 9-26-1872
Harris, Haywood F. to Louisa J. Butler 3-2-1863
Harris, Haywood F. to Louisa J. Butler 3-2-1863 (no return)
Harris, Henry to Juda E. Jamison 7-9-1870 (no return)
Harris, M. B. (Dr.) to Elizabeth Clark 11-16-1861 (11-19-1861)
Harris, Richardson to Frances King 12-31-1868 (1-1-1869)
Harris, Robt. L. to Mary J. Wood 1-18-1873 (1-19-1873)
Harris, T. J. to Mary Briant 4-26-1867 (no return)
Harris, W. H. to Sarah P.? Parsons 11-8-1869 (11-9-1869)
Hart, John to Lizzie Hampton 3-7-1871 B
Hart, John to Tilia Patterson 8-31-1870 (no return)
Hart, Milton J. to Parilee Patterson 11-19-1860 (11-20-1860)
Hart, Milton to Parilee Patterson 11-19-1860
Hart, R. L. to L. M. Johnson 5-10-1861 (no return)
Hartman, W. B.? to Mary A. Norman 10-1-1860 (10-2-1860)
Harvy, T. K. to M. A. Leech 2-3-1866 (2-5-1866)
Hatch, B. D. to Funtrey? Williams 8-?-1861 (no return)
Hatch, Geo. T. to Ridley J. Mitchell 1-16-1872 (no return)
Hatch, Granvil L. to Winnie C. Suggs 4-7-1873 (4-9-1873)
Hatch, Harry J. to Milly Kirk 2-12-1861 (no return)
Hatch, James A. to Lucinda Suggs 4-5-1861 (no return)
Hawkins, A. G. to Susan E. Prince 11-10-1869 (11-11-1869)
Hawkins, Camillus to Joe Ann Cole 11-9-1868 (11-12-1868)
Hawkins, Carroll to Jinnie Bell 4-14-1872 (no return) B
Hawkins, Joe to Caroline Priest 12-30-1871 (no return) B
Hawkins, John C. to Persia M. Porter 5-27-1863
Hawkins, L. L. to Rebeca W. Caldwell 10-2-1861
Hawkins, Levi to Lucy Bledsoe 11-26-1871 B
Hawkins, Samuel W. to Hester? B. Gardner 3-20-1867
Hawkins, W. H. to Mary E. Blackwell 10-7-1868 (10-9-1868)
Hay, Abrom to Elizabeth Winberg 10-14-1866 (no return)
Hayley, S. M. to Evalin Poindexter 3-21-1871 (no return)
Hayley, S. S. to Mollie A. Mills 12-5-1865 (12-14-1865)
Haynes, A. J. to Sarah Oliver 10-19-1869 (10-20-1869)
Haynes, Charles H. to Susan E. Cates 1-26-1870 (1-27-1870)
Haynes, Sal W. to Nancy Rumley 11-14-1872
Haynes, Thomas Y. to Fanny A. Pickett 12-21-1869 (12-22-1869)
Hayns, Rye to Sallie Williams 1-2-1871 B
Haywood, B. Z. to Elizabeth M. Rowe 1-21-1868 (1-28-1868)
Haywood, E. W. to Mary A. Linch 11-10-1871
Haywood, E. W. to Rowann Rust 3-24-1869
Haywood, Henry H. to Marth Williams 11-14-1866 (11-18-1866)
Haywood, J. C. to L. R. Autry 6-21-1867 (6-23-1867)
Haywood, John C. to Cardilea A. King 11-22-1866 (11-24-1866)
Haywood, Jones? R. to Winfred Brinkly 1-19-1861 (1-27-1861)
Haywood, W. T. to Eliza J. Pruett 12-7-1865 (12-10-1865)
Haywood, Whitley A. to Zelvey E. Taylor 11-1-1866
Hedgecock, J. W. to M. F. Quinn 7-2-1866 (no return)
Henderson, Alfred to Ann Covington 12-8-1869 (12-9-1869)
Henderson, James to Eleira? Drake 2-3-1868 (2-6-1868)
Henderson, Prince to Clary Henderson 12-13-1870 (12-12?-1870) B
Henley, Jasper to Emily Cleaver 1-8-1870 (no return)
Henley, Newton to Martha Todd 1-11-1872
Henry, David W. to Ashley? W. Pate 7-29-1861 (no return)
Henslee, John J. to Marry E. Pierce 3-6-1868 (no return)
Hensler, J. T. to M. F. Lipe 9-1-1870
Herrell, Columbus to Penny Herrell 10-23-1868
Herrell, Humphrey to Julia Lankford 8-19-1871 B
Herron, Benjamin to Laura Smith 3-23-1869 (3-24-1869)
Herron, Hardy to Esther Strayhorn 1-19-1869 (1-21-1869)
Herron, James to Easter Moore 3-12-1873 (3-13-1873) B
Hester, Joseph to Saletha Gardner 9-11-1871 (9-12-1871)
Hester, P. W. to M. C. Harper 8-6-1865
Hickman, J. R. to A. E. Gullet 1-11-1869 (1-14-1869)
Hickman, James F. to Ursul M. Mathis 5-23-1866 (5-3?-1866)
Higdon, Thomas to Jane Mullin 11-7-1866
Higdon, W. T. to Sarah Rowe 5-27-1867 (5-29-1867)
Higgs, T. J. to Martha E. M. Fuqua 1-22-1870 (1-27-1870)
Hightower, William S. to Martha D. Palmer 4-28-1866 (5-14-1866)
Hill, David to Ellen Beavers 7-13-1867 (7-14-1867)
Hill, George W. to Fanny C. Bledsoe 2-20-1867
Hill, H. M. to Nancy Raney 5-28-1864 (no return)

Hill, J. A. to M. C. Everett 9-17-1866 (9-18-1866)
Hill, J. C. to Mary J. Worrell 5-14-1870 (5-15-1870)
Hill, J. R. to Mary E. Hall 1-1-1873 (1-2-1873)
Hill, J. W. to J. T.? Bledsoe 2-11-1871 (2-12-1871)
Hill, Jobe to Louisa Stanford 8-28-1869 (9-1-1869) B
Hill, John to Jinnie Briant 7-24-1869 (7-29-1869)
Hill, Joseph to Minnie Green 12-20-1871 (no return)
Hill, R. J. to Martha F. Enochs 10-7-1872 (10-9-1872)
Hill, Robert C. to Rebecca F. Dodd 3-27-1866 (3-29-1866)
Hill, Wm. P. to Louiza M. Null 2-24-1866
Hilliard, Frank to Orrenia Brandon 8-1-1872 (8-4-1872)
Hilliard, W. E. to M. L. Taylor 3-6-1872 (3-7-1872)
Hillsman, Norvell to Sally Hillsman 8-29-1868 (no return)
Hillsman, Stephen to Ann Stanford 12-20-1871 (12-21-1871)
Hillsman, William to Betsy Ross 11-29-1869 (no return)
Hines, John to Jane Guthrie 1-15-1872 (no return) B
Hix, James M. to E. E. Kee 8-23-1866 (no return)
Hodge, James M. to M. J. Lipe 8-14-1863 (no return)
Hodge, James M. to Martha J. Lipe no date (with Aug 1863)
Hodge, James R. to Florida Ann Stoker 7-4-1872 (no return)
Hodge, James R. to Mary A. Holmes 7-28-1866 (7-29-1866)
Holaday, R. to Josephine Brevard 12-28-1870
Holland, George to Milly Herron 8-1-1868 (8-2-1868)
Hollaway, T. A. to Mary Ann Milum 1-4-1872 (no return)
Holliday, C. L. to Lucy Bayles 3-20-1867 (3-21-1867)
Hollowell, George to Margarett Roberts 10-23-1864 (10-26-1866?)
Hollowell, S. H. to Nancy Brinkley 1-8-1866 (no return)
Holmes, A. C. to Mary L. Wall 5-1-1873
Holmes, A. H. to Nancy J. Green 10-19-1866 (10-21-1866)
Holmes, G. M. to I. J. Green 12-23-1867 (12-25-1867)
Holmes, J. R. to Frances Brandon 5-28-1873
Holmes, John F. to M. J. Holmes 11-26-1872
Holmes, W. H. to V. A. Quinn 9-8-1871 (9-9-1871)
Holmgrist, Augustus to Rebecca Brashears 8-6-1870 (no return)
Holt, R. L. to Sallie E. Wingo 8-29-1871 (9-3-1871)
Hooker, R. M. to A. E. Denton 1-28-1865 (1-29-1865)
Hooker, Thos. to Sarah Cunningham 1-13-1866 (1-21-1866)
Hopkins, James F. to Jemima Gibson 3-25-1868
Hopper, A. M. to P. A. Browning 11-25-1871 (no return)
Hopper, Duncan to Eliza McRea 12-11-1869 (12-12-1869)
Hopper, J. T. to M. M. Williams 5-22-1871 (no return)
Horn, Cannon to Mary C. Gooch 12-23-1872 (12-24-1872)
Horn, J. W. to Mary A. Suggs 1-11-1867 (1-13-1867)
Horn, S. to Mary Ann R. Green 5-18-1870
Hornbuckle, William to Mary Jane Corley 2-5-1864 (5-30-1864)
Hornbuckle, Wm. to Mary Jane Corley 2-5-1864 (no return)
Horton, Hiram to Elizabeth Adams 9-12-1871
Horton, J. L. to Mary E. Palmer 7-29-1871
Horton, W. C. to R. C. Butler 3-11-1872
Horton?, James M. to Mary Cox 8-?-1861 (8-15-1861)
House, John to Nancy Campbell 1-21-1867 (1-22-1867)
House, Samuel J. to Elnore A. Tynes 1-9-1871 (1-10-1871)
Housman, G. W. to Martha L. Ingram 11-27-1867 (12-1-1867)
Houston, William H. to Elizabeth Glover 3-17-1866 (3-18-1866)
Howard, Benjamin A. to Mollie C. Johnson 7-4-1860
Howard, Jack to Caroline Gordon 2-27-1871
Howard, James to Mahaly Clark 12-27-1870 (no return) B
Howard, John to Adaline Helms 1-30-1869 (1-31-1869)
Howard, John to Martha Allen 4-11-1871 B
Howard, L. S. to L. A. Younger 7-8-1867 (7-10-1867)
Howard, N. C. to Mattie E. Love 1-30-1865 (no return)
Howard, William to Amanda J. Thomas 1-10-1872 (no return)
Hrris, G. B. to Bettie Hannah 7-25-1868 (7-27-1868)
Hudgen, Robert to Silvia Pigel 12-26-1872 B
Hudson, Henry to Sarah Frisbee 10-22-1860
Huffman, James to Lucy Dill 11-7-1866 (11-8-1866)
Huffman, L. M. to Mary E. Cunningham 2-3-1870
Huffman, T. A. to Mary A. Medearis 10-6-1861
Hughes, Jesse A. to Manerva A. Chaney 9-2-1868 (9-6-1868)
Humble, Andrew to Angeline Owen 6-7-1873 (6-8-1873) B
Humble, Carroll to Jinnie Steele 6-20-1868 (6-21-1868)
Humphrey, David to Susan Bowland 8-24-1866
Hunt, William to Manerva White 6-21-1869
Hunter, G. H. to R. Y. Allen 2-15-1872
Hunter, Isaiah to America Thomas 2-4-1869

Hurt, Adam to Jane Clay 5-14-1870 (5-15-1870)
Hurt, Berry to Sopha Collins 10-12-1867
Hurt, Daniel to Dilsey Blackwell 10-27-1872 (11-2-1872) B
Hurt, L. A. to Annie Clay 6-28-1870 (6-30-1870)
Hurt, R. M. to Martha E. (Mrs.) Woods 4-24-1860
Hurt, Wm. to Mary Woods 5-12-1865 (no return)
Hutcheson, Daniel to Eliza Hillsman 6-28-1870 (6-30-1870)
Hutchins, C.? M. to Tabitha Watson 1-22-1868
Hutchins, Erasmus J. to Sarah A. L. Lowery 7-7-1866 (7-8-1866)
Hutchins, Isaac R. to Martha T. Allen 1-15-1872 (no return)
Hutchins, Robert to Mary York 8-6-1868
Hutchins, W. C. to Hariet J. Towery 4-4-1868 (4-6-1868)
Hutchison, John to Martha Pinkston 12-1-1871 (no return)
Hyatt, A. V. to Martha A. McNight 4-27-1867 (4-28-1867)
Ingle, J. A. to E. J. Holmes 11-20-1868 (11-22-1868)
Ingram, Thos. D. to M. J. Fletcher 11-13-1866 (11-14-1866)
Irvine, Frank to Margarett White 2-26-1866 (no return)
Jackson, Andrew to Sarah Shofner 2-25-1870 (2-26-1870)
Jackson, E. J. to Martha S. Walter 12-3-1868
Jackson, Henry to Louisa Blake 5-28-1869 (5-29-1869)
Jackson, J. W. to C. A. Strouse 12-12-1865 (12-16-1865)
Jackson, W. T. to Susan H. Crowder 10-7-1867 (10-10-1867)
Jamerson, B. B. to Mary Tayler 4-15-1861 (4-17-1861)
Jamerson, R. B. to Mary Taylor 4-15-1861 (4-17-1861)
Jameson, C. K. to Adaline Taylor 2-24-1863 (no return)
Jamison, A. T. to E. B. Williams 3-13-1869 (3-14-1869)
Jamison, Alge to Harriet Peoples 12-13-1871 (no return)
Jamison, C. K. to Adaline Taylor 2-24-1863 (no return)
Jamison, Jorden to Martha Hammett 7-6-1870 (7-10-1870)
Jamison, Robert to M. E. Johnson 11-14-1866 (11-15-1866)
Jarratt, J. F. to P. J. Graves 1-16-1864 (no return)
Jarrett, J. T. to P. J. Graves 1-16-1864 (1-17-1864)
Jarrett, S. L. to M. A. Kelley 6-4-1873
Jarrett, Wm. D. to Mary Lacy 12-22-1871 (12-23-1871)
Jenkins, D. P. to L. A. Scott 1-21-1861 (1-24-1861)
Jenkins, John W. to Nancy Ann McMackens 10-4-1869 (10-28-1869)
Jenkins, W. W. to S. E. R. Jenkins 2-10-1867
Johns, James to M. Mitchum 5-10-1872 (5-12-1872) B
Johns, R. D. to C. S. Argo 12-17-1872 (12-19-1872)
Johnson, Alex to Elen Orr 11-28-1865 (11-29-1865)
Johnson, Allen jr. to Sarah J. McKinney 9-20-1871 (9-21-1871)
Johnson, Case to Wiry? Mabon 2-13-1870 (no return)
Johnson, Dick to Henrietta Mathewson 12-23-1872 (12-27-1872) B
Johnson, Freeman to Laura Hawkins 8-5-1870 (no return)
Johnson, George W. to Mary A. Chambers 11-30-1870
Johnson, J. M. to H. M. Oliver 12-27-1871 (no return)
Johnson, J. M. to Julia N. Lemmons 2-14-1867 (no return)
Johnson, J. T. to Tobitha Barham 11-16-1866 (11-18-1866)
Johnson, James A. to Emma Cook 8-26-1863 (8-27-1863)
Johnson, James A. to Sarah A. Davis 10-30-1860
Johnson, James M. to Elizabeth J. Lay 8-28-1864 (9-4-1864)
Johnson, James M. to Elizabeth J. Lay no date
Johnson, James to Mary J. Reed 6-12-1867 (6-13-1867)
Johnson, John P. to Emma Bigham 7-23-1866 (no return)
Johnson, M. W. to Emeline Singleton 11-12-1869 (11-18-1869)
Johnson, Patrick to Julie Glancy 9-24-1866 (9-28-1866)
Johnson, R. J. to Agness Bryant 10-26-1861 (10-27-1861)
Johnson, S. T. to S. J. Rust 5-31-1867 (6-2-1867)
Johnson, Sidney A. to Manerva C. Traywick 9-26-1866 (10-4-1866)
Johnson, W. J. to Mary C. Gill 3-12-1870 (3-13-1870)
Johnson, W. P. to Melvina E. Bibb 12-21-1869 (12-24-1869)
Johnson, Washington to Ellen Palmer 7-23-1868 (no return)
Johnson, Wesley J. to Dicey Hopper 3-10-1864 (no return)
Johnson, Wiley J. to Dicey Hopper 3-10-1864 (3-12-1864)
Johnson, William S. to Molly Perkins 7-17-1868 (no return)
Johnston, Edward to Martha Chadwick 8-9-1860 (8-12-1860)
Joiner, James M. to Mary E. Williams 9-17-1860 (9-18-1860)
Joiner, N. C. to Nancy T. Pugh 11-5-1867
Jolly, Johns W. to Emma J. Fry 10-1-1861
Jones, Anderson to Eliza Newbill 9-28-1869 (9-30-1869)
Jones, B. A. to S. A. Williamson 2-7-1871 (no return)
Jones, B. H.? to M. J. Mitchell 1-1-1868 (1-2-1868)
Jones, Calvin to Susan Taylor 8-15-1860 (8-16-1860)
Jones, G. A. to Susan A. Kerby 11-22-1868 (12-10-1868)
Jones, George S. to Ann T. Kirkland 5-13-1868 (5-17-1868)

Jones, George S. to Fannie Stanly 12-19-1867 (no return)
Jones, Gip to Molba? Patterson 2-28-1871 (3-2-1871)
Jones, Henry T. to Mary A. Moore 2-6-1866 (2-8-1866)
Jones, J. C. to Frances Hurt 2-19-1872
Jones, J. R. to Mary A. Leach 10-27-1866 (no return)
Jones, J. R. to S. V. Hiatt 1-3-1867
Jones, James to Louisa Hurt 12-19-1871 (no return) B
Jones, John H. to Sarah E. Thorn 7-5-1866
Jones, John L. to M. A. Walton 7-21-1864 (7-23-1864)
Jones, John T. to Martha J. Clark 6-9-1873 (no return)
Jones, John to Judy Clay 10-4-1869 (10-9-1869)
Jones, L. M. jr. to S. E. Webb 1-7-1873 (no return)
Jones, Marsellis to Frances Cane 10-6-1869
Jones, Moses to Jennetta Stafford 1-2-1869 (1-3-1869)
Jones, R. W. to Tennessee Williams 1-22-1866 (1-25-1866)
Jones, Richard to Harriett Adkison 9-21-1867 (no return)
Jones, Sam to Callie Adams 9-13-1870 (9-15-1870) B
Jones, Spencer to Vina Younger 1-31-1871 (2-2-1871)
Jones, T. E. to Harriet L. McCarter 1-13-1866
Jones, T. J. to R. A. Jarrett 7-22-1871 (7-23-1871)
Jones, Thomas E. to Amanda M. Randall 9-30-1861 (10-1-1861)
Jones, W. D. to J. A. Porter 11-6-1861
Jones, William to Elizabeth Newbill 3-7-1866 (no return)
Jones, Wm. E. to J. B. James 11-27-1871 (no return)
Jordan, Josh to Angeline Briant 8-1-1871 B
Jordan, Mike to Amanda Clark 12-27-1870 (12-29-1870) B
Jordeen?, Jesse J. H. to Julie A. McLune? 4-2-1866 (no return)
Jordon, E. F. to Lucy A. Bevill 3-14-861
Joyner, E. Marshall to Lucy J. Morris 2-27-1866 (3-1-1866)
Joyner, N. L. to C. W. King 7-6-1865
Joyner, Nick G. to Martha E. Sellers 2-7-1866 (2-8-1866)
Kain, William to Elizabeth Moss 5-2-1866 (5-3-1866)
Kates, William to Ginny Hart 7-23-1868 (no return)
Keane, John O. to Mary Ellis 10-25-1860 (10-28-1860)
Kearney, J. K. to Florence A. Drewry 12-27-1869 (12-28-1869)
Keaton, C. L. to Sarah E. Fuqua 8-4-1868 (no return)
Keaton, J. W. to Mollie A. Keaton 1-30-1873 (1-31-1873)
Kee, G. W. to L. F. Laycock 10-27-1872
Kee, J. W. to Martha Caffrey 9-29-1860
Kee, Janes to Clery? A. Suggs 11-10-1860 (11-17-1860)
Kee, Lewis K. to M. L. V. Forsheer 8-6-1873 (8-7-1873)
Kee, Milton B. to Savanah Hicks 6-16-1866 (6-17-1866)
Kee, Thomas L. to Susan E. Pritchard 8-12-1868 (8-13-1868)
Keirman, Thomas to Ann Fergerson 4-10-1869 (4-17-1869)
Kelley, V. H. to R. J. H. Lewis 1-4-1871
Kelley, Wesley to Penelope A. Brashear 5-13-1869
Kelly, J. M. to Z. L. Tosh 12-19-1872
Kelly, J. W. to M. E. Louis 1-2-1873
Kelly, John Z. to Nancy Tosh 1-10-1866
Kemp, Basey D. to Mahulda A. Williams 3-17-1869
Kennaday, M. A. to Nancy Barnett 8-14-1866 (8-16-1866)
Kennon, John to Harritt A. Carter 12-20-1870 (12-21-1870)
Kennon, William B. to Susan A. Moore 9-14-1866 (no return)
Kerby, F. M. to Margaret J. Hord 3-29-1862 (3-30-1863?)
Kerby, Joseph T. to Rocinda Carter 12-19-1868 (12-23-1868)
Kerly, James A. to Mary Jane Cloyd 8-9-1860 (8-12-1860)
Kernan, M. T. to Laura A. Pope 5-28-1872 (no return)
Kerr, W. J. to Amanda M. Townes 12-17-1867 (12-19-1867)
Key, J. H. to N. ____ 2-?-1860 (no return)
Key, John to Mary J. Colvett 12-26-1866 (12-27-1866)
Key, Richard to Martha Morgan 3-20-1865 (3-22-1865)
Key, Robert T. to Amanda Worsham 3-25-1869
Keys, Edom to Matilda Ridley 6-14-1868
Kile, G. W. to Melvina Steele 12-6-1869
Kile, Jack to Caroline Patterson 12-31-1869 (1-1-1870)
King, Alfred to Sarah Anderson 8-10-1871
King, Benjamin to Sarah Gooch 9-20-1871 B
King, Calvin to F. Eubanks 2-12-1864 (2-14-1864)
King, Clinton to Mary J. Moore 10-24-1871 (10-25-1871)
King, J. C. to Eveline Sugs 2-20-1866 (2-25-1866)
King, J. M. to Preciller Cantrell 1-3-1871 (1-4-1871)
King, J. M. to Sarah L. Hampton 3-21-1868 (3-22-1868)
King, J. R. to M. J. Maxwell 7-30-1873 (7-31-1873)
King, J. W. to Mary A. Jones 1-1-1873 (1-2-1873)
King, J. W. to Mary E. Joyner 11-19-1866 (11-20-1866)

King, J. W. to Nancy E. Sugg 12-3-1868 (12-6-1868)
King, James C. to Susan E. Jones 12-22-1866 (12-24-1866)
King, John R. to Elizabeth B. Butler 4-18-1870 (4-19-1870)
King, John W. to Mary Parsons 11-5-1869 (11-9-1869)
King, Presley to Luisa Haywood 12-8-1865 (12-10-1865)
King, Rewbin to Pollie Cantroll 8-5-1871 (8-6-1871)
King, Thomas to Caroline Suggs 2-20-1864 (2-22-1864)
King, W. E. to Margaret A. Choate 11-2-1865 (11-5-1865)
King, W. P. to Ann Roberson 12-16-1872 (12-17-1872)
King, W. P. to Martha J. Parish 11-3-1868 (11-4-1868)
King, W. T. to S. A. Wassey 10-17-1871 (10-19-1871)
King, William to Caroline Reed 12-14-1860 (12-19-1860)
King, Wilson to Eviline Rhodes 5-11-1865 (5-14-1865)
Kirby, Berry to Mary McVey 8-24-1870 (8-25-1870)
Kirby, D. W. to Ruth A. Carter 12-11-1869 (12-12-1869)
Kirby, Joseph C. to Nancy A. Murphy 5-15-1862 (5-18-1862)
Kirby, Joseph to Mary Smith 12-14-1871 (12-15-1871)
Kirk, J. M. to A. E. Roberts 9-16-1869
Kirk, Nathan to Mary Jane Warbritton 1-24-1870 (1-29-1870)
Knight, Robert F. to Frances E. Robison 5-25-1869
Kyle, E. R. to Angeline Butler 5-17-1866 (5-13-1866)
Kyle, L. C. to M. C. King 2-6-1873
Lacy, John M. to Ella C. Herron 11-20-1872 (11-21-1872)
Lacy, W. S. B. to Ritter K. Snowden 4-4-1866 (4-5-1866)
Laddamare, Hugh to Lidda Brunsull? 1-10-1867 (1-13-1867)
Lambert, John to Alice Cunningham 3-11-1870 (3-13-1870)
Lammond, Thomas to Laura Heflin 11-16-1869 (11-17-1869)
Landrum, L. T. to Callie Guthrie 6-3-1872 (6-5-1872)
Landrum, W. E. to M. A. Newbill 12-3-1870 (12-6-1870)
Lane, Monroe to Amanda Forrest 4-8-1869
Lanear, J. H. to M. E. Christian 12-18-1866 (12-20-1866)
Lankford, D. M. to M. C. Coble 4-9-1867 (4-10-1867)
Lankford, Smith to Anna E. Oliver 9-10-1872 (9-11-1872)
Lannum, Wm. D. to Molly Harrell 11-28-1864 (no return)
Laster, H. to Susan King 6-23-1863
Laster, J. P. to Susan E. King 1-24-1863 (1-25-1863)
Latham, R. Wilson to Parthena Butler 6-1-1872 (6-2-1872)
Laurence, H. M. to Jane Brashers 4-20-1867 (4-21-1867)
Lawhorn, Isaac to Jane Shaw 1-3-1872 (no return)
Lawrence, John G. to Nancy Parale Key 11-14-1869
Lawrence, Wm. H. to Lucinda Monroe no date (with 10-1867)
Laycock, Francis M. to Mary J. Forluss 7-28-1860 (7-29-1860)
Laycock, John S. to |illy E. Wilks 12-27-1866
Laycook, John C. to N. C. Dill 12-31-1868
Leach, J. F. to J. M. McCollum 1-?-1867 (1-15-1867)
Leach, J. W. to S. C. House 12-27-1870 (12-28-1870)
Leach, Thomas W. to Delila M. Burrow 1-31-1866 (2-1-1866)
Leach, Thos. A. to Mollie A. Hurt 10-27-1865
Leach, W. J. to M. W. Ballew 3-31-1865 (no return)
Lee, J. W. to Mary J. Lemons 10-2-1865 (10-3-1865)
Lee, William S. to Martha E. Jackson 2-23-1867 (2-27-1867)
Leech, A. to Elizabeth (Mrs.) Branch 10-8-1861
Leech, Aliner to Elizabeth Branch 10-1-1861 (10-8-1861)
Leech, James B. to Nancy Jane Crowel 12-12-1868 (12-15-1868)
Leech, Thomas A. to Malissa A. Hurt no date (10-31-1865)
Leek, Bolivar to Elizabeth Crews 6-4-1860 (6-5-1860)
Leflore, S. P. to Julia Crosswell 10-20-1869 (10-21-1869)
Leigh, James D. to Emeritter Smith 3-13-1867 (3-14-1867)
Lemmons, A. H. to Mary White 2-11-1867 (2-12-1867)
Lemons, H. C. to N. S. White 12-7-1871 (no return)
Lemons, W. C. to L. F. White 4-4-1872
Leslie, S. G. to T. H. Bevill 11-26-1872 (11-27-1872)
Lesslie, James to M. J. McAuley 9-6-1871 (9-7-1871)
Lewis, J. F. to E. A. Glover 12-2-1871 (no return)
Lewis, Richard to Eliza J. Forrest 1-28-1868 (1-30-1868)
Liles, David A. to July Ann Chandler 8-7-1866 (8-8-1866)
Liles, Henry to Martha Herron 12-9-1869
Liles, Sherwood L. to Elizabeth Phelps 7-3-1866 (12-27-1866)
Linch, Ansil to Frances Horn 7-13-1863
Lingo, James T. to D. A. Greenwood 9-11-1860 (9-13-1860)
Lingo, James T.? to D. A. Greenwood 9-11-1860 (9-13-1860)
Linsey, W. J. to Harriet Spain 11-22-1871 (no return)
Lipe, George to Ann Jordan 4-25-1871 (4-27-1871)
Lipe, J. W. to Mary E. Hodge 11-30-1872 (12-1-1872)
Lissenberry, M. E. to E. T. Johnson 2-1-1873 (no return)

Lissey, John B. to Caroline Tucker 5-3-1860
Listen, L. B. to S. B. Field 12-22-1870
Little, A. J. to M. J. Walker 5-14-1864 (no return)
Little, Adam to Ellen Duncan 7-30-1870 (7-31-1870)
Little, Austin P. to Fannie Barksdale 5-14-1863 (no return)
Little, David to Willy Clark 8-7-1868 (8-12-1868)
Little, G. M. to M. A. Merrett 12-7-1872 (12-8-1872)
Little, Harvy T. to Nancy C. Williams 1-12-1867 (1-13-1867)
Little, Thomas to Ana Liza Rual? 12-26-1861
Little, Thomas to Sarah J. Cunningham 3-11-1863
Little, Thomas to Sarah J. Cunningham 3-11-1863 (no return)
Little, William to Mary Williams 4-7-1866 (4-15-1866)
Livingston, M. to Rebecca Owensbey 12-1-1863 (no return)
Livingston, Mark to Mary J. Jarret 2-17-1860 (2-18-1860)
Logue, F. M. to Eliza Spain 12-15-1869 (12-22-1869)
Long, John to Polly Walker 3-8-1865 (3-10-1865)
Long, S. S. to M. Cuningham 8-21-1872 (no return) B
Looney, B. H. to America Griffin 1-17-1870 (1-18-1870)
Looney, J. F. to E. C. Henderson 12-19-1865
Lorance, J. A. to L. H. Lusk 1-11-1867 (1-16-1867)
Love, A. G. to Rosy Patton 11-22-1870 (11-24-1870)
Loveless, P. C. to Mollie G. Deshong 12-27-1865 (12-28-1865)
Lovin, Austin to Mary J. Horn 1-24-1872
Lowder, Wm. J. to Mary Ann K. Bell 2-16-1864 (no return)
Lowder, Wm. J. to Maryann K. Bell 2-16-1864
Lowrey, Elijah M. to Virginia E. Butler 2-24-1870 (2-25-1870)
Lowrey, W. H. to Ennis Rowland 12-31-1872 (1-1-1873)
Lurence, James C. to Lowtica? Leigh 12-19-1867
Lush, John D. to Fannie Heards 12-11-1860 (12-13-1860)
Lutsinger, G. L. to Rebecca Everett 11-26-1870 (11-27-1870)
Mack, Barney to Araminta Wallace 10-27-1860
Madison, James to Lucy Foster 11-13-1871 (no return) B
Mainard, Israel E. to Rutha A. Petty 8-7-1866
Malear, G. W. to Mary E. Rogers 1-20-1866 (3-4-1866)
Malone, James N. to Louisa C. Lodgins 4-28-1865 (4-29-1865)
Malone, Jefferson to Bell (Mrs.) Lane ?-?-1863 (with Aug 1863)
Malone, L. H. to E. C. Turner 10-4-1867 (10-6-1867)
Mann, C. G. to Julie E. Mann 5-19-1860 (5-20-1860)
Mann, J. W. to N. C. Edmerson 3-23-1872 (3-24-1872)
Mann, Johnathan to Mary Langlie 3-28-1872 (no return)
Mann, Robert to Susan J. Connell 9-15-1871 (9-20-1871)
Mann, Thos. J. to Dicey H. Mann 8-7-1862
Mann, William A. to Mary F. Nelson 8-10-1870 (8-11-1870)
Mann, William L. to Martha Carver 1-12-1870
Manning, J. M. to Emily M. Green 7-10-1871 (7-12-1871)
Manning, Thomas B. to Mattie E. McLemore 4-13-1870 (4-24-1870)
Manuel, Alexander to Martha J. Rogers 4-21-1864 (4-23-1864)
Manuel, H. K. to Victoria Owen 3-15-1869 (3-16-1869)
Marshall, D.? to Susan A. Pearman 1-5-1863 (1-7-1863)
Marshall, M. D. to Susan A. Pearman 1-5-1863 (no return)
Martin, A. W. M. to D. M. A. Spain 8-7-1871
Martin, Allen to Angeline McMackens 12-25-1868 (12-27-1868)
Martin, C. H. to Sarah Burns 7-22-1861 (7-24-1861)
Martin, George H. to Martha E. Gowan 11-14-1868 (11-12?-1868)
Martin, H. P. to E. J. Freeman 6-19-1869 (6-20-1869)
Martin, James F. to Martha M. Martin 11-20-1866 (11-21-1866)
Martin, James M. to Mary S. Cox 8-14-1861 (8-15-1861)
Martin, L. L. to M. J. Lewis 8-5-1868
Martin, M. S. to Fannie R. Jordan 3-9-1869 (3-11-1869)
Martin, Newton H. to Matilda D. Pinson 2-20-1865 (2-25-1865)
Martin, Wm. P. to Mary A. Rogers 12-15-1860 (not endorsed)
Massey, J. R. to P. C. Pinson 2-25-1870 (2-28-1870)
Massey, James to Virenna Shepherd 12-17-1868 (12-18-1868)
Massey, John to Judiath S. Rogers 4-22-1871 (4-26-1871)
Massey, W. H. H. to Mary E. Russel 9-26-1870 (9-28-1870)
Matheny, James W. to Judith L. Craft 2-23-1870 (no return)
Matheny, W. A. to P. A. Tucker 9-29-1868 (10-1-1868)
Mathews, Quincy J. to Elizabeth Lewellen 3-11-1862
Mathis, M. R. to Margaret Biggart 10-20-1866 (10-21-1866)
May, James S. to Nancy French 3-5-1870
May, James to Ann Edwards 1-12-1863 (no return)
May, William S. to Sarah Dilday 2-10-1863
May, William to Lucy Mooney 2-16-1871
May, Wm. S. to C. S. Revel 8-29-1864 (9-1-1864)
Mayes, Stephen to Amand Darnall 9-2-1872 (no return) B

Maynard, J. M. to Mary E. Graham 6-28-1871
Maynard, Samuel to Mary Jane Ritchie 7-21-1869 (7-22-1869)
Maynard, William to Catharine E. Ellis 4-15-1870 (4-17-1870)
Mays, C. B. to Sarah L. Cook 7-11-1866 (7-19-1866)
Mays, Robert J. to America J. Jacobs 12-14-1866 (12-18-1866)
McAdoo, Alonzo to Martha Merrett 1-13-1872 (no return)
McAdoo, Austin to Margaret A. Davis 9-?-1862 (9-14-1866?)
McAdoo, J. R. to M. L. Britt 12-22-1868 (12-23-1868)
McAdoo, Leonedas to Mary Key 12-3-1864
McAdoo, Wm. to Laura Jones 2-2-1866 (2-4-1866)
McAdoo, Wm. to Mahala Mathis 8-6-1864 (no return)
McAlexander, J. R. to S. E. Leach 2-5-1866 (2-8-1866)
McAlexander, Nelson to M. E. Hickman 3-17-1871 (3-18-1871)
McAlister, W. T. to F. E. Kenady 12-4-1868
McAllexander, Jesse to Rebecah F. Hickman 2-24-1868
McAnley, B. S. to Mary J. Hill 12-17-1866 (12-20-1866)
McArnally, James R. to Emma C. Warbritton 3-11-1867 (3-13-1867)
McArthur, H. V. to E.L. Jones 2-25-1867 (2-27-1866?)
McAulay, J. M. to L. W. Butler 12-29-1870
McAuley, A. G. to Jane Bell 9-20-1872 (9-22-1872) B
McAuly, E. T. to M. J. Hall 2-4-1868 (2-5-1868)
McBride, G. A. to M. C. Nelson 1-4-1872 (no return)
McCain, Dennis to Mary Ann Prichard 8-21-1869 (8-22-1869)
McCall, W. A. to Nannie Royall 10-?-1867 (10-29-1867)
McCall, W. T. to Janie Snead 5-20-1872 (no return)
McCall, William S. to Rachel J. Crawford 6-3-1861 (no return)
McCally, James B. to Mary E. Hall 2-13-1870
McCane, Amos to Margaret Robinson 12-25-1860 (12-27-1860)
McCargo, Oscar to Sarah McCracken 1-22-1869 (1-28-1869)
McCarter, D. L. to H. M. E. Carter 3-10-1873 (no return)
McCaslin, Thomas J. to Caroline Richars? 12-18-1866 (12-19-1866)
McClintock, J. M. to Narcissa C. McKinzie 8-11-1866 (no return)
McCloud, David to Martha White 1-31-1870 (no return)
McClusky, J. M. to P. Delany 1-5-1866 (1-6-1866)
McCollom, Benjamin C. to Martha E. Leach 12-29-1868 (12-31-1868)
McCollom, Jesse to Sarah Ann Howard 12-21-1868 (12-22-1868)
McCollum, Arch to Sina Gregory 2-3-1872 (no return) B
McCollum, Arch to Sinia Gregory 1-7-1870 (not endorsed)
McCollum, J. C. to M. C. Giles 12-28-1872 (12-29-1872)
McCollum, Jesse to Mary M. (Mrs.) Putman 7-3-1860 (7-5-1860)
McCollum, Jessy to Mary M. Putman 7-3-1860 (7-5-1860)
McCollum, John H. to Ellen Warpooll 1-?-1867 (1-16-1867)
McCollum, Samuel to Mary Hassell 12-14-1869 (12-16-1869)
McColum, Allen G. to Harriet V. Crews 1-6-1868 (1-7-1868)
McCracken, J. R. to Mattie A. Brown 11-19-1866 (no return)
McCracken, Lycurgus to Susan A. Rothrock 11-10-1863
McCracken, Saml. to Margaret Rogers 7-25-1868 (7-28-1868)
McCracken, William L. to Martha L. Thomas 10-22-1861
McCrackin, J. R. to A. Newbill 12-15-1864 (no return)
McCullough, J. W. to Flora A. Hawkins 9-25-1869 (9-26-1869)
McCullough, S. J. to Susan Corder 12-3-1872 (12-5-1872)
McDonal, Milton to Ann Fulks 3-12-1872 B
McDonald, George to Mollie Price 1-19-1871 B
McDonald, Richard to Emma Algee 2-1-1872 B
McDugal, James A. to Mary S. Adams 1-8-1861 (1-10-1861)
McDugal, Wm. W. to Mary A. Adams 4-6-1868 (4-8-1868)
McEwen, J. D. to S. C. Johnson 12-26-1872
McGill, James A. to Perina J. Mizzell 10-16-1869 (10-20-1869)
McHood, J. R. to Norah J. Reece 9-5-1872
McHood, James to D. Robertson 1-1-1866
McKelsey, John C. to Julia A. (Mrs.) Henning 1-30-1861 (no return)
McKiney, J. H. to Caladonia J. Darnell 9-17-1861 (9-23-1861)
McKiney, J. H. to Mary L. Evans 11-2-1865 (11-5-1865)
McKiney, John C. to Mary E. McCaslin 12-17-1866 (12-18-1867?)
McKing, John J. to M. E. Britton 1-27-1866 (2-1-1866)
McKinney, J. R. to Sallie Johnson 2-20-1867 (2-22-1867)
McKinney, T. C. to E. V. Terry 6-27-1868 (7-1-1868)
McKinzie, T. D. to S. E. Travis 10-20-1868 (10-22-1868)
McLemore, King to Lizzy Herron 4-16-1870 (4-17-1870)
McLemore, Sugars to Mary J. Taylor 7-28-1862 (no return)
McLevee, N. H. to O. M. Bibbs 3-7-1867
McMackin, Andrew to Lucinda McMackin 10-9-1867 (10-10-1867)
McMackin, David to Amanda Ruff 12-24-1866
McMackins, David to Susan R. Lowery 3-18-1863 (3-19-1863)
McMackins, E. A. to F. P. Smith 1-5-1872 (1-7-1872)

McMackins, L. F. to Randy J. Rust 12-23-1869 (12-29-1869)
McNeill, Abraham to Patience Randle 1-20-1871 (1-22-1871) B
McNeill, Alfred to Emma Gaines 4-20-1870 (4-21-1870)
McNeill, Thos. A. to Rachel M. Coldwell 8-11-1862 (no return)
McShane, P. to Mary Shadwick 11-7-1868 (11-8-1868)
Meador, W. J. to S. A. (Mrs.) Carroll 12-10-1867
Meadows, Foster to Eliza Wingo 12-24-1870 (12-27-1870)
Meals, Wm. M. to Julia A. Pearcy 7-22-1865 (7-25-1866?)
Meals?, L. H. to M. J. Flake 1-6-1873
Mebane, J. G. to L. J. Gooch 2-4-1868 (2-5-1868)
Mebane, W. E. to Louisa Eason 1-29-1867 (1-30-1867)
Mebene, Sidny A. to Tennessee R. Briggance 2-12-1861
Medlin, J. P. to Lovey A. French 11-11-1864 (11-12-1864)
Medlin, James T. to Evelin Allen 6-15-1872 (no return)
Medlin, James to Catharine Allen 4-22-1865 (4-23-1865)
Melton, E. W. to Serrilda Manuel 8-2-1872 (8-3-1872)
Melton, R. R. H. to M. L. Bradford 9-5-1866? (9-8-1867)
Melton, W. T. J. to Mily A. Reader 12-27-1867 (12-28-1867)
Merrett, J. C. to Arytine Holms 4-28-1873 (4-29-1873)
Merrett, J. C. to Parilla Jarrett 7-30-1869 (8-1-1869)
Merrett, J.H. to M. W. Gee 1-17-1871 (1-20-1871)
Merritt, Hadley to Kezziah Finly? 1-16-1861
Merritt, J. C. to Nancy Merritt 4-28-1866 (4-29-1866)
Metheny, Eli S. to Quixanna Jones 8-31-1871 (9-3-1871)
Meyers, Louis P. to Callie D. Bigham 6-3-1872 (6-6-1872)
Midlin, G. M. to T. S. Henley 6-17-1870 (6-19-1870)
Milam, Joseph G. to Susan L. Stubbs 9-3-1870 (no return)
Miller, A. H. to F. M. Elenor 9-25-1872 (9-26-1872)
Miller, S. A. to M. C. Mathis 1-24-1867
Milligan, Lewis J. to Mary E. Bogle 10-1-1860 (10-4-1860)
Mills, B. D. to E. J. Lenea? 10-7-1871 (10-9-1871)
Mills, G. W. to C. J. Adams 12-14-1871 (no return)
Mills, J. W. to Margarett L. Gibbons 9-18-1865 (9-20-1865)
Mills, S. C. to M. A. Burrow 1-27-1873
Mills, W. W. to Sarah F. Threadgill 11-18-1865 (no return)
Mitchel, Jerry to Martha McCutchin 10-23-1872 (10-24-1872)
Mitchel, Thomas to Sarah P. Hill 3-30-1867 (3-31-1867)
Mitchell, J. R.? to Sarah A. Ray? 12-6-1860
Mitchell, J. W. to Mary L. Gardner 1-21-1868 (1-22-1868)
Mitchell, Joseph to Esper An T. Mann 11-12-1870 (11-13-1870)
Mitchell, Joseph to Margaret Edmison 2-8-1869 (no return)
Mitchell, Nathan to Callie Holt 4-13-1869 (4-14-1869)
Mitchell, William to Angeline Morris 9-5-1868 (9-6-1868)
Mitchell, William to Mollie Nesitt 2-4-1869
Mitchum, Harvy to Hellen Patterson 6-1-1866 (6-7-1866)
Mitchum, J. M. to M. A. Newbill 2-9-1871 (no return)
Mitchum, Nelson to Marsha Scates 12-5-1870 (no return)
Mizell, A. J. to Amanda J. Rogers 11-28-1867 (1-6-1868)
Modlin, J. C. to M. J. Compton 3-4-1865 (3-5-1865)
Mohan, James to Ann Murry 5-15-1861 (5-16-1861)
Montgomery, George W. to M. E. Carter 1-3-1870 (1-5-1870)
Montgomery, J. L. to Mollie B. Fry 10-18-1870 (10-19-1870)
Montgomery, Jess to Rebeca Crow 7-1-1867
Montgomery, S. J. to L. A. Neely 1-13-1869
Montgomery, W. B. to M.L. Spain 2-8-1873 (2-9-1873)
Montgomery, Wm. to Emeline C. Robeson 1-28-1864 (2-1-1864)
Montgomery, Wm. to Emeline C. Robeson 1-29-1864 (no return)
Moore, Abriham to Deliah Strayhorn 3-10-1873 (3-13-1873) B
Moore, Benjamin to Betsy Jane Bradford 2-8-1868 (2-10-1868)
Moore, Carroll to Vira Gilbert 12-25-1871 (no return) B
Moore, Elwood to Mary H. King 9-25-1861 (9-29-1861)
Moore, F. M. to G. A. Kesbitt 3-24-1866 (3-29-1866)
Moore, G. D. to N. A. Rodgers 1-23-1867
Moore, George S. to Ann Jones 2-3-1869 (2-4-1869)
Moore, George to Ama Smith 12-25-1872 (12-26-1872) B
Moore, Henry N. to Sarah P. Rogers 11-14-1868
Moore, Hezekiah to Elizabeth Abernathy 10-10-1861
Moore, J. B. to L. D. Yancy 2-5-1868 (1?-11-1868)
Moore, J. Dennis to Mary Townes 5-4-1866 (5-6-1866)
Moore, James to Sarrah E. Rowland 10-6-1870
Moore, Joseph to Eliza Gilbert 9-25-1868 (9-27-1868)
Moore, N. M. to Tenness King 12-3-1866 (11?-6-1866)
Moore, R. G. to Roxanna F. Williams 2-9-1864 (3-10-1864)
Moore, R. G. to Roxanna F. Williams 2-9-1864 (no return)
Moore, Richard B. to Lou J. Goodwin 11-10-1870 (11-24-1870)

Moore, Robt. to Martha Vinson 2-19-1872 (2-20-1872)
Moore, Thompson to Martha E. Hill 10-5-1869
Moore, W. C. to Harriett Bledsoe 12-3-1860 (12-6-1860)
Moppin, Harrison to Mary Blackwell 6-1-1868 (no return)
Morgan, Benjamin to Mahala A. Cannon 11-28-1860
Morgan, E. W. to Susan Gatland 12-15-1862 (12-16-1862)
Morgan, Felix G. to Mary Mathis 10-15-1861
Morgan, G. H. to M. L. Coleman 12-29-1866 (12-20-1866)
Morgan, Joseph to Emma Moss 1-20-1872 (1-21-1872)
Morgan, Pleasant G. to Mary P. Mathis 8-1-1866 (8-2-1866)
Morgan, Ralph to Caroline Younger 12-16-1868 (12-17-1868)
Morgan, T. T. to Bettie Sampson 1-3-1872 (no return)
Morris, Isarah to Sarah A. Barbrey Leigh 11-3-1866
Morris, M. M. to Louisa Robeson 3-31-1865 (4-6-1865)
Morris, Milton to L. A. Jones 3-6-1871 (no return)
Morris, N. M. to Martha Ann Robinson 1-22-1864
Morris, N. M. to Martha Ann Robinson 1-22-1864 (no return)
Morris, Nathan to Margaret Barlow 7-23-1862
Morris, Thomas J. to Louisa Stewart 2-26-1862 (2-27-1862)
Moss, Eli S. to Lucinda McMackins 3-28-1870 (3-31-1870)
Moss, J. A. to Virginia H. Fuqua 1-18-1865
Moss, W. E. to Nancy A. Allen 8-12-1864 (no return)
Moten, James to Susan Burrow 8-5-1871 (8-13-1871)
Mull, James to Cilla Murry 5-4-1872 (no return) B
Mulligan, L. J. to M. L. J. Branch 12-23-1872 (12-24-1872)
Mullin, James to Jane Malone 7-1-1861 (7-7-1861)
Mullins, Lewis J. to Mary E. Bogle 10-?-1860 (10-4-1860)
Murphee, David D. to Mary C. Ward 9-23-1867
Murphey, Jery to Effarilla Pearson 5-25-1872 (5-26-1872) B
Murphy, Henry to Susan O'Conner 4-8-1868
Murphy, John R. to Sarah E. Stewart 9-14-1868 (9-20-1868)
Murphy, Tilson to Martha A. Ross 6-24-1870 (6-25-1870)
Murray, John L. to Adaline Neely 8-28-1869 (8-29-1869)
Murray, W. W. to Mary Henry Strange 1-4-1869
Murry, Peter to Jinnie Jamison 6-24-1872 (no return) B
Muzzall, N. G. to P. C. Compton 1-2-1871 (1-5-1871)
Myer, Henry S. to Susan Cathey 4-22-1861
Myers, Moses to Missouria A. Cooper 12-12-1864 (12-13-1864)
Myers, Phillip to Virinda C. Swayne 9-7-1862 (9-8-1862)
Myers, Robert E. to Elizabeth C. Cooper 2-11-1863
Myers, Robert E. to Elizabeth Cooper 2-11-1863
Myrack, W. D. to Elizabeth Vancleave 3-22-1867 (3-24-1867)
Myrick, George W. to Julia Ann Berry 8-11-1868 (8-12-1868)
Nance, P. H. to Martha T. Davis 10-5-1864 (10-9-1864)
Nash, J. Z. to Newty L. Cobb 1-30-1869 (1-31-1869)
Neal, J. B. to Josephine Boles 2-25-1871 (2-26-1871)
Neal, Samuel to Jane Traywick 5-18-1869 (5-20-1869)
Nease, G. H. to Arcenoe Barnett 7-18-1871
Neely, A. S. J.? to Martha A. Algee 5-23-1860 (no return)
Neely, C. C. to S. M. Brown 12-28-1865
Neely, James M. to Mary E. Hester 10-25-1865
Neely, John B. to R. H. Brown 3-26-1864
Neely, Thomas to Annie Humphrey 8-5-1862 (no return)
Neenan, Patric to Nancy E. Jenkins 9-21-1861
Neighbours, Harvey to Nancy A. E. Brecheen 11-27-1860
Nelson, William S. to Sarah H. Bird 11-23-1867 (11-24-1867)
Nesbett, Ed to Sarah E. Dolron 1-25-1871 (1-26-1871)
Nesbett, Fed to Sarah Barker 10-20-1870 B
Nesbitt, Andrew to Mary Ann Shoffner 2-19-1870 (2-20-1870)
Nesbitt, Jerry to Harriett Milam 2-3-1873 (2-6-1873) B
Nesbitt, N.? B. to S. F. Mebane 2-27-1867
Nesbitt, S. S. to Sarah Harris 12-26-1864 (12-27-1864)
Nesbitt, Sidney B. to Jinnie Mitchell 9-12-1872 B
Nesbitt, Toney to Silvey Strayhorn 2-27-1869
Nevill, W. B. to Emily Manning 12-20-1869 (12-23-1869)
Newbill, John A. to Sarah Pearce 12-8-1869 (12-9-1869)
Newbill, N. T. to Caroline E. Sweany 6-23-1866 (no return)
Newbill, Nathaniel to Nancy Popkins 7-26-1866 (no return)
Newbill, R. A. to Bettie S. Upton 8-26-1868 (no return)
Newbill, Richard to Allice Harper 12-28-1872 (12-24?-1872)
Newbill, W. G. to M. M. Brown 11-30-1872 (no return)
Newbill, Wm. to Emily Harper 12-4-1863 (no return)
Newell, R. A. to Mollie Jones 1-7-1867 (no return)
Newlett?, William D. to Elnora Purslay 11-8-1865 (11-11-1865)
Newman, Patrick to Nancy E. Jenkins 9-21-1861

Newman, Wm. C. to Mary A. Pinkston 8-6-1861 (8-9-1861)
Newson, Patrick to Arabella C. Owens 9-19-1860 (9-20-1860)
Newson, Thomas H. to Lucy A. Bowslon? 12-1-1865 (12-4-1865)
Nichols, A. R. to Sarah Jane Burrow 5-26-1865 (no return)
Nichols, Daniel W. to Mary T. House 11-9-1868 (11-12-1868)
Nicler, Albert to H. S. Aurenchine 6-26-1873 (no return)
Night, Presly to Mary Cruise 10-5-1870 (10-6-1870)
Noell, James H. to Eliza J. Dill 12-20-1865
Norman, John B. to Fanny Ragland 10-31-1865 (11-1-1865)
Northcut, William J. to Elizabeth F. Spain 7-16-1868
Norwood, Lewis to Mary A. (Mrs.) Brooks 7-20-1860 (7-22-1860)
Norwood, Thos. to Elizabeth Pinkston 1-2-1866
Nowlin, Briant to Mollie Denton 11-27-1871 (no return)
Nowlin, G. W. to Mary A. Yonger 1-5-1867 (no return)
Nowlin, Wade H. to Emma Henderson 10-17-1870 (10-20-1870)
Nunnery, Nathaniel to Frances Brewer 10-31-1860 (11-10-1860)
O'Kane, A. A. to Milissia A. Gibson 8-8-1873 (9-3-1873)
O'Malley, M. J. C. to F. E. Williams 3-7-1870 (3-8-1870)
O'Neill, Samuel M. to Mary Bigham 11-1-1869
O'Neill, W. C. to L. L. Woollen 10-25-1870 (10-26-1870)
Offenshine, John to Mary J. Pace 4-14-1869 (4-15-1869)
Olive, James to Elizabeth Flake 9-9-1865 (9-13-1866?)
Oliver, J. M. to Tabitha C. Haynes 5-5-1866 (5-9-1866)
Oliver, T. J. to Adelia C. Ridley 10-17-1866 (10-18-1866)
Oliver, W. T. to Martha A. Thredgill 12-2-1867 (12-4-1867)
Oneil, J. A. to Mattie Younger 2-28-1871
Orr, John to Margarett Falkner 10-18-1865
Orr, Thomas to M. J. Johnson 1-13-1870
Osborne, C. F. to Addie Bigham 2-4-1868 (2-5-1868)
Owen, J. R. to S. E. Cawthon 10-19-1870 (10-20-1870)
Owen, Nathaniel to Martha J. Boswell 10-4-1871 (10-5-1871)
Owen?, P. R. to S. C. Cauthern 1-13-1868 (1-16-1868)
Owenby, Cahl P. to Orpha J. Malcar 12-13-1866
Owenby, E. P. to Martha E. Joiner 1-?-1867 (1-23-1867)
Owenby, J. G. to Ida Chandler 12-17-1872 (12-18-1872)
Owenby, W. D. to Dilla Huffman 8-14-1867 (8-15-1867)
Owens, George to Sarah J. Morgan 11-29-1871 (11-30-1871) B
Owens, Samuel A. to F. A. Cawthon 4-23-1866 (4-26-1866)
Ownby, C. R. to N. H. Cannon 10-9-1868 (10-11-1868)
Ozier, J. R. to N. A. Moore 3-21-1871
Ozier, James H. to E. A. Tate 11-25-1862
Ozier, James W. to Narcissa H. Hamilton 10-15-1867 (no return)
Ozier, Levi to Martha E. Taylor 11-5-1870 (11-6-1870)
Ozier, Loyd to Jane Bobitt 11-7-1861 (no return)
Pace, J. P. to Susan A. Ware 2-15-1866 (no return)
Page, Wily E. H. to Caroline Blake 8-10-1861 (no return)
Palmer, E. B. to Tennessee B. Carrington 1-24-1861
Palmer, Harvey to Harriett Butler 1-13-1872 (1-14-1872)
Palmer, J. H. to Permelia W. Clark 11-23-1863 (no return)
Palmer, James F. to Mary J. Allen 2-24-1866 (2-26-1866)
Palmer, Jesse W. to Martha J. Ross 11-14-1867 (11-17-1867)
Palmer, Jessie to Mollie Jones 6-22-1871
Palmer, Levin to Lettie Shofner 12-20-1869 (1-10-1870)
Palmer, Tilman to Margarett J. Blair 12-20-1866
Palmer, W. A. to M. A. Belew 10-27-1868 (10-28-1868)
Palmer, W. G. to Sarah A. Spoon 1-14-1870 (1-16-1870)
Palmer, W. H. to Mary A. Green 11-1-1871 (no return)
Parham, L. G. to Louiza Smith 5-27-1871 (6-7-1871)
Parish, E. F. to S.? M. Clark 3-14-1872
Parish, Elijah to Rianna Kates 12-18-1865
Parish, G. F. to Sarah A. Miller 9-17-1872 (9-19-1872)
Park, George W. to ElizabethJ. Bowland 11-3-1860 (11-4-1860)
Park, H. O. to Susan F. Duncan 3-30-1861 (4-5-1861)
Park, James P. to Amada Horton 3-1-1861 (no return)
Park, John H. to Flenda Finch 2-9-1861 (2-10-1861)
Parker, G. W. to Mary A. Robison 1-13-1868 (1-14-1868)
Parker, Manuel to Susan Vinson 12-25-1869 (no return)
Parkinson, G. M. to Corsicana? Swift 12-8-1863 (no return)
Parnell, H. R. to M. E. Wray 12-19-1868 (12-20-1868)
Parnell, James to Martha Jones 9-29-1869 (9-30-1869)
Parnell, S. D. to G. W. James 12-19-1870 (12-21-1870)
Parnell, Wiley M. to Harriet J. Jones 10-24-1860
Parrish, George to Elizabeth Wallace 11-3-1863
Parrish, Mark to Elizabeth Brinkly 6-27-1866 (no return)
Parrish, Syron? to Eliza J. Montgomery 12-10-1866 (12-13-1866)

Partete, Richd. T. to Manerva F. Rollins 9-24-1861 (9-29-1861)
Pary, Malone to Lucy J. Bridges 8-31-1866 (9-2-1866)
Pate, F. H. to Emma G. Fletcher 5-15-1869 (5-17-1869)
Pate, J. D. to S. V. Turner 10-8-1867 (10-10-1867)
Pate, J. K. to S. V. Pate 2-27-1873 (3-2-1873)
Patterson, A. H. to Frances A. Wilder 10-3-1864 (no return)
Patterson, F. M. to M. F. Liston 12-23-1868
Patton, J. H. to M. E. Fox 1-23-1869 (1-26-1869)
Patton, Monro to Millie Clemons 9-5-1870 (no return)
Patton, Thomas M. to Molly Terry 12-18-1866 (no return)
Pearce, A. C. (Dr.) to Mattie E. Barham 12-8-1866 (12-11-1866)
Pearce, Isaac to S. A. Browning 1-9-1871 (1-12-1871) B
Pearce, J. C. to Harriett Thompson 12-18-1866 (12-20-1866)
Pearce, Latent to Any (Mrs.) Pickler 8-20-1860 (8-24-1860)
Pearce, Wm. M. to M. M. Rome 1-4-1862
Pearson, Antina to Lucinda Duglas 6-14-1872 (no return) B
Pearson, John to Eviline Parker 1-25-1865 (1-26-1865)
Pearson, Peter to L. E. Milon 10-6-1866 (10-11-1866)
Pearson, Shadrick to Eliza Liffsy 9-19-1864 (9-21-1864)
Peel, J. P. to N. M. McHood 2-12-1872 (2-14-1872)
Peel, N. J. to Mary E. Scarlett 1-12-1871 (1-13-1871)
Peeples, Wm. C. to Harriet McAdoo 10-26-1863 (no return)
Pendergrass, J. W. to Elizabeth Kirly 3-27-1872
Pendigrass, William to Mary Murphy 1-27-1866 (1-28-1866)
Perminter, Henry to Adaline Rhodes 9-20-1867 (9-22-1867)
Perrett, Johnson to Martha E. Hardy 10-16-1872
Perry, B. J. to Canellis E. Moore 11-21-1867 (11-22-1867)
Perry, Elvis to Amanda Hopper 10-6-1870
Perry, Jesse to E. M. Hopper 9-1-1870
Petty, H. C. to Nancy A. Williams 12-26-1865 (12-27-1865)
Pettyjohn, A. J. to F. A. Jordan 9-13-1864 (9-14-1864)
Phelps, John F. to Sarah M. Liles 11-25-1864 (11-26-1864)
Phelps, Joseph N. to Elizabeth Price 12-15-1870 (no return)
Phelps, R. to Susan E. Malone 1-27-1869 (1-30-1869)
Phillips, Benjamin Taylor to Sarah E. Hampton 12-8-1866 (12-12-1866)
Phillips, Charles to Malissa Atkison 8-27-1869
Phillips, David to Amanda Little 7-3-1864
Phillips, James to Martha Ann Hampton 2-17-1866
Phillips, Jasper to Julia Hawkins 6-22-1872 (no return) B
Phillips, Lagrand P. to M. F. (Mrs.) Rowland 8-25-1860 (8-26-1860)
Phillips, R. D. to Sarah A. Carter 12-16-1862 (no return)
Phillips, William to Mourning E. Pritchard 9-11-1860
Phipps, E. D. to Caroline Ezell 7-17-1860 (no return)
Pickett, W. R. to Mary E. Benton 1-14-1862
Pickler, J. M. to Margaret Rowland 12-29-1866 (12-31-1867?)
Pickler, Jesse to Lucy Butler 8-2-1865 (8-3-1865)
Pickler, John H. to Sallie spears 7-11-1871 (no return)
Pierce, Martin to Mary E. Moore 4-20-1867 (4-21-1867)
Piger, Nathan to Mollie Green 6-26-1869 (6-27-1869)
Piggue, Elizah to Zora Montgomery 7-14-1871 (7-15-1871)
Pinckley, A. A. to M. L. Rose 7-12-1872 (no return)
Pinckley, Andrew to Susan F. Comer 12-18-1869 (12-19-1869)
Pinckley, R. K. to Elizabeth Lawrance 10-13-1865 (10-15-1865)
Pinckley, Scott to Burnetta Springer 3-29-1869 (3-31-1869)
Pinckley, Simpson to Araminta B. Moore 3-9-1870 (3-10-1870)
Pinckston, Green C. to N. A. Morris 4-15-1872 (no return)
Pinckston, Napoleon B. to Matilda Killbreath 12-31-1869 (1-4-1870)
Pinkston, J. D. to Manerva Butler 4-29-1870 (5-7-1870)
Pinkstone, Wm. P. to Julia A. Newnan 6-23-1865 (6-25-1865)
Pinson, Isaac to Eliza Shofner 11-7-1864 (11-8-1864)
Pinson, Thomas W. to Martha Massey 10-24-1860 (10-25-1860)
Pinson, W. L. to Martha C. Loveall 11-2-1870 (11-6-1870)
Piper, Erasmus to Martha T. Green 8-9-1860
Pitman, L. W. to M. A. Holmes 3-31-1869 (4-1-1869)
Plummer, J. R. to Lizzie Bigham 7-14-1869 (no return)
Pollard, Wallis to Macilda E. Cunningham 4-22-1870 (4-24-1870)
Polston, J. W. to Polley Worlds? 12-22-1866 (12-23-1866)
Pope, John W. to Nancy Blair 4-14-1863 (4-15-1863)
Pope, John W. to Nancy Blair 4-14-1864 (no return)
Pope, S. N. J. to Martha Jones 7-19-1861 (no return)
Pope, W. H. to Harriett Perkins 2-28-1866 (3-1-1866)
Pope, W. H. to M. Jane Maynard 9-21-1870 (9-22-1870)
Porter, D. G. to Nancy E. Spain 12-10-1868 (12-11-1868)
Porter, J. J. to Elizabeth Reaves 1-17-1871 (1-18-1871)

Porter, J. R. to Easter J. Jones 12-6-1866 (12-5?-1866)
Porter, J. W. to Harriet A. Southerel 8-29-1868 (8-30-1868)
Porter, J. W. to Nannie Bryant 8-2-1873 (no return)
Porter, Jas. J. to Margaret C. Moore 2-25-1873 (2-26-1873)
Porter, Perry to Martha Porter 2-14-1870 (2-15-1870)
Porter, W. A. to E. J. Hickman 9-5-1870 (9-8-1870)
Pounds, John H. to Christiana E. Morris 12-24-1866 (12-25-1866)
Prat, W. to S. C. Belew 9-13-1870
Presson, R. A. to M. E. Turner 10-9-1871 (no return)
Presson, T. H. H. to Elizabeth Liles 12-?-1861 (12-15-1861)
Presson, T. H. W. to Elizabeth Tiles 12-13-1861 (12-15-1861)
Prewett, J. N. to Elizabeth Walker 12-8-1871 (no return)
Price, James to Betty Sparks 9-16-1869 (9-18-1869)
Prince, Frank to Nannie Edwards 12-15-1872 B
Prince, Samuel to Margaret Hawkins 12-25-1868 (12-30-1868)
Pritchard, Bemin to Nancy C. Key 12-26-1869
Pritchard, H. M. to Sallie Ann McClame 8-12-1873
Pritchard, Jason to Frances E. Hanfred? 3-24-1866? (3-25-1868)
Pritchard, Jonathan to C. M. Thomas 5-4-1867 (5-8-1867)
Pritchard, William to Issabel Brandon 10-14-1867 (10-15-1867)
Pritchett, J. W. to Mary S. Martin 5-20-1869
Pruett, Ferrell to Mary S. Rowe 12-6-1870 (12-8-1870)
Pruett, James W. to Nancy Dilday 8-9-1865 (8-10-1865)
Pruett, James to B. L. King 3-8-1871
Pruett, John to M. J. Chambers 2-7-1871
Pruett, Robert M. to Nancy C. Rowe 10-2-1865 (10-8-1865)
Pugh, Davis J. to Susan F. Nichols 9-6-1867 (9-11-1867)
Pugh, Walter C. to Tensy E. Kee 11-13-1860 (11-14-1860)
Quinn, Lawson to Nancy Smith 4-12-1861 (no return)
Quinn, Mitchell to Frances Hutchison 3-6-1871 (no return)
Quinn, William P. to Martha Jackson 2-24-1864 (no return)
Quinn, Wm. P. to Martha Jackson 2-24-1864 (2-26-1864)
Ragland, John T. to H. J. Williamson 2-14-1861
Ragland, W. H. to Lenora Williamson 4-27-1870 (4-28-1870)
Rainey, James H. to Martha J.? Burch 12-21-1867 (12-24-1867)
Ramsey, R. W. to Lucy J. Lankford 10-16-1860 (10-15?-1860)
Randle, Maston to Caroline Mayberry 4-11-1865 (4-12-1865)
Rawls, R. H. to Cordelia Wolff 2-11-1869
Ray, James W. to Luvica W. David 8-6-1860 (8-8-1860)
Ray, L. P. to Mollie Cannon 12-18-1872 (12-19-1872)
Reaves, J. N. to R. J. McCullough 10-18-1870 (10-19-1870)
Redden, H. J. to M. C. Britt 7-24-1872 (no return)
Reddin, William A. to Josephine Allen 1-16-1866 (1-18-1866)
Reece, James S. to Narcissa A. Phipps 5-7-1867 (no return)
Reece, John to Susan E. Travis 1-26-1867 (1-30-1867)
Reece, Samuel P. to Mary E. King 1-7-1861 (1-9-1861)
Reed, Washington C. to Mary A. Barton 9-14-1866
Reives, Alfred to Telia Patterson 9-7-1872 B
Reynolds, H. P. to M. S. Jacobs 12-13-1870 (no return)
Reynolds, Henry to Mima Brown 3-31-1871 (4-2-1871)
Reynolds, J. M. to Mary Perritt? 5-15-1869 (5-16-1869)
Reynolds, James M. to Elizabeth Ann V. Reynolds 2-18-1864
Reynolds, James M. to Elizabeth ann V. Reynolds 2-18-1864 (no return)
Reynolds, R. B. to P. L. Williams 5-14-1870 (5-15-1870)
Reynolds, W. T. to M. J. Garner 6-22-1861 (8-1-1861)
Rhoads, James H. to Mary E. Massey 11-30-1870 (12-1-1870)
Rhoads, W. B. to Sarah Sampson 10-27-1870
Rhodes, Joseph C. C. to Nancy C. Laycock 1-5-1870
Rhodes, Wilson B. to Nancy Bumbley 11-10-1861 (11-17-1861)
Rhodes, Wilson B. to Nancy Rumly 11-16-1861 (11-11?-1861)
Rhodes, Z. T. to Lucinda Benton 2-19-1869 (2-23-1869)
Rial, T. J. to Clarkie Ruff 12-29-1868 (12-30-1868)
Rice, E. L. to Mollie P. Fletcher 2-6-1871 (no return)
Rice, N. L. to Nancy A. Green 3-27-1868 (3-29-1868)
Rich, Nathan G. to Martha H. Berry 10-15-1866 (10-17-1866)
Richardson, Hiram to Mattie Shad 12-15-1869 (12-16-1869)
Richardson, W. G. to W. F. Towns 11-26-1872 (11-27-1872)
Richardson, Willie C. to Virginia C. Gibbons 11-29-1871 (11-30-1871)
Richardson, Wm. B. to E. C. Rainey 8-9-1864 (8-12-1864)
Richardson, Wm. to Levina Fuller 4-9-1873 B
Ridley, C. H. to N. L. Oliver 3-7-1870 (3-9-1870)
Ridley, Julius to Frances Sparks 12-31-1868 (1-7-1869)
Ridley, Robt. to Charity Haynes 12-22-1870 (12-29-1870) B
Ridley, Willie to Sallie Cole 1-11-1871 (1-12-1871)

Rieves, J. W. to C. A. Haze? 5-29-1872
Riggins, Henry to Lucy Green 10-9-1872
Riggs, J. M. to Mary Q. Haynes 12-27-1869 (12-29-1869)
Rigsby, D. L. to Sarah Lammond 12-5-1868 (12-7-1868)
Rigsby, Moses M. to Hanna R. Phelps 8-12-1862 (no return)
Ritter, James to Elzy Burns 12-13-1861 (12-15-1861)
Roach, J. C. to L. E. Younger 5-20-1872 (5-21-1872)
Roach, T.? to Mary Winters 1-21-1862
Roach, W. H. to Alice Lansdon 9-23-1867 (10-1-1867)
Roark, W. D. to Rienia Brandon 7-23-1872 (no return)
Roaz, E. H. to Sarah P. Gateley 1-11-1865 (1-14-1865)
Roberson, Silvestis to July Ann Jordan 11-23-1870 (12-1-1870)
Roberson, Wm. R. to Sarah F. Butler 11-27-1872
Roberts, Amos to Eliza Shaver 8-26-1868
Roberts, Fantry to Martha J. Petty 12-12-1867
Roberts, George N. to Luzana C. Bevill 10-16-1869 (10-17-1869)
Roberts, J. M. to L. B. McCollum 8-10-1872 (8-13-1872)
Roberts, J. M. to Mary M. Thomason 8-23-1864 (8-24-1864)
Roberts, John N. to Harriet A. Roberts 5-19-1871 (5-21-1871)
Roberts, Miles J. to Nancy C. Green 9-6-1860 (9-19-1860)
Roberts, S. W. to Elizabeth A. Parish 9-17-1861 (9-18-1861)
Roberts, William to Amea? E. Rogers 1-2-1862 (no return)
Roberts, William to Anna E. Rogers 1-1-1862 (1-2-1862)
Roberts, William to Anna Rogers 12-31-1861 (1-1-1862)
Roberts, Willis to Artemissa Butler 12-8-1869 (12-9-1869)
Robins, M. N. C. to H. L. Grant 12-13-1867 (12-16-1867)
Robinson, Anderson to ____ Haywood 10-21-1866 (10-23-1866)
Robinson, Isom to Lucinda Furgerson 1-17-1871 (2-4-1871) B
Robinson, Samuel A. to L. E. Martin 2-2-1870 (2-13-1870)
Robison, G. T. to Sarah Bridges 2-14-1870 (2-15-1870)
Robison, Jacob to Louisa Anderson 5-23-1867 (no return)
Robison, L. C. to Everline King 12-5-1871 (no return)
Robison, L. C. to Mary Loving 4-22-1866 (no return)
Robison, Nelson to Massely? Browning 10-4-1870 (10-6-1870)
Rochell, J. J. to Amanda J. Cloid 1-15-1873 (no return)
Rodgers, J. R. to E. Y.? Rodgers no date (with Aug 1866)
Rogers, A. E. to Mary J. Brinkly 10-9-1865 (no return)
Rogers, A. J. to M. L. Duning 12-2-1872 (12-5-1872)
Rogers, C. A. to Mary E. Elkins 1-22-1873 (1-23-1873)
Rogers, Elijah G. to Martha L. Butler 1-21-1868 (1-22-1868)
Rogers, George H. to Mary E. Null 10-13-1863 (no return)
Rogers, Green C. to Martha J. Smith 7-31-1866 (8-2-1866)
Rogers, J. A. W. G. to Mary Jane Grisson 7-31-1861 (8-1-1861)
Rogers, J. F. to Sarahann M. Williams 6-16-1871 (6-18-1871)
Rogers, J. H. to Nancy M. Bennett 8-19-1871 (8-20-1871)
Rogers, J. T. to F. A. Joiner 5-14-1864
Rogers, James K. P. to Georgiann Litle 8-3-1869
Rogers, James K. to Elizaeth L. Hull? 8-8-1867 (8-9-1867)
Rogers, James M. to Eliza Liles 8-27-1860 (9-7-1860)
Rogers, John D. to Beda A. Jones 5-23-1865 (5-24-1865)
Rogers, N. J. to Sarah E. Phelps 5-15-1873
Rogers, W. A. to Mary J. Fussell 9-2-1861 (9-3-1861)
Rollins, James H. to Mary P. Humphrey 2-10-1869
Roney, M. F. to M. J. Finley 12-31-1862 (1-1-1863)
Roney, M. F. to Nelly Bernard 10-26-1872 (10-27-1872)
Roper, G. L. to M. A. Vaughter 5-18-1868 (5-19-1868)
Roper, Norwood to Leanna Longmyre 8-14-1868 (8-16-1868)
Roper, Thomas G. to Elizabeth Pritchard 7-15-1868 (7-16-1868)
Rose, W. H. to Martha E. Hardy 3-4-1861 (3-19-1861)
Rose, Z. B. to Julie E. King 1-2-1867 (no return)
Rosebery, Thomas to Susan M. Gardner 4-14-1866 (4-15-1866)
Ross, Charles M. to Ellen E. Cobb 6-10-1863
Ross, Charles M. to Ellen E. Cobb 6-10-1863 (6-14-1863)
Ross, Charles M. to Ellen E. Cobb 6-10-1863 (no return)
Ross, Chas. M. to Lucy A. Harder 4-22-1871 (4-27-1871)
Ross, Jacob to Martha Harris 5-13-1863 (5-16-1863)
Ross, William C. to Orfrey M. Palmer 12-8-1860 (12-9-1860)
Rossom, W. C. to Latitia Riggs 10-17-1861 (10-11?-1861)
Rowe, E. G. to Alice B. Wood 3-29-1869 (3-30-1869)
Rowe, J. W. to S. F. Butler 8-10-1872 (8-12-1872)
Rowe, John M. to Josephine J. Jordan 10-1-1868
Rowland, Eben to Eliza A. Park 3-13-1866
Rowland, John M. to Nancy A. Moore 4-25-1861
Rowland, Moses to Adaline Massey 1-23-1869 (1-27-1869)
Rowland, Pinkney B. to Martha E. Bailess 11-25-1865 (11-26-1865)

Rowland, Robt. N. to Elizabeth F. McMackins 11-25-1872 (11-26-1872)
Rowland, Sam to Della Cumpton 7-29-1868 (7-30-1868)
Rowland, T. B. to Nancy Rowland 1-24-1867
Rowland, Thos. L. to Anna Butler 9-18-1872
Royal, William C. to Elizabeth D. Butler 8-26-1866 (8-27-1866)
Royall?, E. N. to F. C. Ozier 8-15-1867
Ruse, Baher to Jane Beavers 5-23-1864 (5-27-1864)
Rushing, John W. to Tennessee Pate 9-25-1865 (9-28-1865)
Russel, Henry to Matilda Norvell 1-7-1870 (1-8-1870)
Russel, James to Sarah Busey 1-6-1872 (no return)
Russell, David H. to Saphronia C. Blake 1-?-1866 (1-11-1866)
Russell, J. A. to Permelia C. Nevills 8-27-1869 (8-29-1869)
Russell, Lewis to Esther Doherty 6-1-1870 (6-5-1870)
Russell, Thos. to Ellen Arrington 6-8-1863 (6-11-1863)
Russell, William to Julia Ann Williams 2-17-1870
Rust, C. T. to Martha J. Ellinor 8-1-1867 (8-2-1867)
Rust, J. G. to M. J. Elliner 7-27-1863 (7-27-1866?)
Rust, J. T. to Arminta Parish 9-10-1870 (9-11-1870)
Rust, John R. to Bettie (Mrs.) Giles 10-12-1867 (10-13-1867)
Rust, John Y. to M. J. Ellmor 7-27-1862 (no return)
Rust, William L. to Mary E. Churchwell 12-16-1871 (no return)
Sales, J. L. to M. J. Algee 1-19-1861 (1-21-1861)
Sanders, J. E. to L. A. Munn 1-21-1872
Sanders, John M. to Mary A. McAnley 4-10-1867
Sanders, M. A. to S. L. Blount 1-15-1872 (1-17-1872)
Saunders, Benj. A. to Mary E. Butler 9-19-1860 (9-20-1860)
Saunders, William C. to Elizabeth D. Boyd 3-18-1869
Sayle, William A. to N. J. Baxter 1-23-1861 (1-24-1861)
Sayles, J. G. to Santefee B. Coleman 7-9-1862 (no return)
Sayles, John to Elizabeth Shoeterick? 3-16-1866 (3-23-1866)
Sayles, Wm. A. to Mary Morris 2-14-1865 (2-15-1865)
Scalbrough, Wm. H. to Charlott Holmes 8-9-1860 (8-11-1860)
Scales, Ellis to Amanda E. Cox 1-23-1863 (1-29-1863)
Scales, John to Amanda Patterson 2-26-1872 (2-27-1872)
Scarbro, R. P. to E. P. Ross 12-3-1866 (12-5-1866)
Scarlott, Norwood to Rebeca (Mrs.) Marshall 7-18-1860
Scates, John to Amanda Patterson 3-4-1870 (no return)
Scoby, W. A. to Elizah Bayley 10-25-1870 (10-26-1870)
Scott, Abner T. to Elizabeth J. Roark 1-8-1870 (1-9-1870)
Scott, H. C. to D. J. Gulledge 6-22-1867 (6-23-1867)
Scott, J. M. to Mary Susan Little 2-2-1867 (2-4-1867)
Scott, J. R. to T. E. Erocker 12-14-1865 (12-21-1865)
Scott, James to Frances J. Chamberlin 11-4-1870
Scott, James to Mary F. Johnson 6-23-1866 (no return)
Scott, Saml. T. to Josie P. Holmes 2-13-1872
Scott, W. J. to M. E. Scoby 10-25-1860
Searingen, George B. to Mary M. Herron 11-28-1866 (11-29-1866)
Sellers, Jesse L. to Rebecca Neigbors? 8-?-1867 (8-11?-1867)
Sellers, Jno. R. to Margarett Holmes 1-18-1872 (1-19-1872)
Sellers, Wm. D. to L. F. Taylor 5-24-1873 (5-25-1873)
Selmons, Thos. A. to M. J. Butler 6-25-1864 (7-3-1864)
Seymore, Geo. to Rachel McClintock 11-17-1863 (no return)
Seymore, W. F. to Elizabeth Ann Leach 2-23-1863 (no return)
Seymore, W. F. to Elizabeth ann Leach 2-23-1863
Shad, Levi to Vandalia Dickson 1-24-1870 (1-27-1870)
Shaffin, S. B. to M. S. Stroud 3-29-1869 (3-31-1869)
Shaw, J. P. to Cornelia A. Mayar 12-24-1866 (12-26-1866)
Shaw, J. P. to M. C. Ledsinger 12-21-1869
Shaw, S. R. to E. J. Comer 12-1-1861 (12-2-1865?)
Shaw, S. R. to E. J. Comer 12-?-1861 (12-2-1861)
Shaw?, James A. to N. D. Caldwell 11-24-1866 (11-27-1866)
Shawl, Alexander to Ellen Shelly 10-3-1865
Shephard, W. M. to Cora A. Roach 4-26-1872 (no return)
Sherwood, William to Permelia Rumley 12-14-1871 (5-23-1871?)
Shoffner, Isaac to Deliar A. Rust 9-5-1871 (9-6-1871) B
Shoffner, Robert D. to E. T. Spellings 9-20-1869 (9-23-1869)
Shofner, Cain to Dosha Shofner 10-9-1869 (10-10-1869)
Shofner, D. J. to Jane Clarke 5-15-1861
Simmonds, B. B. to Mary Massey 11-9-1863 (11-10-1863)
Simmonds, James to Clara Abbott 5-7-1870 (5-8-1870)
Simmons, John to Folly Ann Bragden 8-24-1864 (no return)
Simmons, Richd. to Elizabeth Pate 12-11-1870 (12-15-1870) B
Simpson, Asher to S. C. Dollar 1-3-1871
Simpson, Harrison to Wilmoth C. Philps 12-11-1860

Simpson, J. R. to G. A. Pasteur 2-19-1866 (2-20-1866)
Simpson, W. F. to R. E. Revel 11-8-1866 (11-9-1866)
Simpson, William to Henrietta Sellers 1-29-1861
Singleton, J. D. to A. V. Green 12-12-1871 (12-14-1871)
Sipe, James D. to Nancy Bradley 3-11-1862
Sloan, James F. to Rebecca Sweney 12-29-1869 (1-6-1870)
Smith, B. C. to Sopha A. Hatch 1-24-1872 (1-25-1872)
Smith, Benj. F. to Harriet Jo Smith 5-20-1868 (5-24-1868)
Smith, Cyrus to Mary E. Rollins 8-5-1865 (8-6-1865)
Smith, E. H. to Aramissa Wiley 2-17-1868 (2-19-1868)
Smith, Edward to Frances Lemmons 6-7-1867 (6-9-1867)
Smith, G. L. to Mary J. Scrobrough 8-4-1866 (8-5-1866)
Smith, Henry P. to Mary J. Leslie 11-9-1872 (11-10-1872)
Smith, Hiram to M. C. Carroll 7-20-1872 (no return)
Smith, J. W. to E. F. Harris 5-29-1866 (6-3-1866)
Smith, J. W. to J. N. Walters 12-2-1869
Smith, John T. to Ann E. Lafloore 12-11-1868 (12-13-1868)
Smith, Philip to Adline Blan? 1-13-1872 (no return) B
Smith, R. E. D. to Bettie C. Carson 1-28-1868
Smith, S. E. to Sarah E. Scarbrough 2-4-1865
Smith, T. C. to Susan Ray 10-17-1868 (10-21-1868)
Smith, Thomas to Sarah Ann Lowell 1-?-1862 (1-13-1862)
Smith, W. M. to L. E. Butler 11-11-1872 (11-13-1872)
Smith, W. P. to E. H. Bevill 2-4-1867 (2-7-1867)
Smith, W. S. to A. T. Bevell 8-12-1867 (8-13-1867)
Smothers, Sebrom to Sarah E. Laycock 6-11-1870 (6-12-1870)
Smothers, Sebron to Frances McCoy 12-18-1868 (12-22-1868)
Smothers, Wiley to Catharine Dillion? 6-30-1869
Smothers, Z. T. to S. E. Crockett 4-25-1872 (no return)
Sneed, A. J. to Elizabeth Sneed 1-11-1871 (1-12-1871)
Sneed, Garland to Lydia Keting 6-21-1869 (6-22-1869)
Snowden, J. L. to Vina A. Petty 11-14-1867
Spain, A. H. to Frances L. Morris 11-26-1869 (11-28-1869)
Spain, David T. to Mary E. Hickman 2-4-1869
Spain, J. H. to M. R. House 10-14-1871 (10-15-1871)
Spain, J. H. to M. T. Porter 2-19-1873
Spain, T. C. to M. J. Adams 2-25-1873 (2-27-1873)
Spalding, Arthur to Culine? Barns 7-22-1860
Sparks, Benjamin to Betsy Carson 7-3-1869 (7-4-1869)
Sparks, James to Clara Baucum 3-8-1870
Sparks, James to Dorah Carson 12-31-1872 (1-2-1873) B
Sparks, Mitchel to Nannie Swayne 12-23-1872 (12-24-1872) B
Sparks, Ross to Margaret Lankford 1-18-1869 (1-21-1869)
Sparks, W. R. to Susan G. Harper 3-8-1873 (3-28-1873)
Spears, Thomas to Elizabeth Everett 3-22-1869 (3-23-1869)
Spelling, John to E. T. O. Hamilton 9-19-1867 (no return)
Spellings, William to A. P. Jordon 3-22-1871 (3-23-1871)
Spoon, Wm. B. to Elizabeth Towsend 1-2-1866 (1-5-1866)
Springer, H. T. to Nancy E. Sellars 12-7-1871 (no return)
Springer, Hosea to Nancy C. Settles 11-8-1865 (11-8-1865)
Springer, J. M. to M. E. Laws 11-13-1867
Springer, R. B. to Clementine Sellers 12-9-1865 (12-19-1865)
Springer, Thos. to Lucy C. Brandon 12-5-1872 (12-6-1872)
Springer, Urias to Elizabeth Gullage 12-13-1870
Stacy, Thomas W. to Nancy C. Leigh 8-23-1871 (8-24-1871)
Stanford, Thomas L. to Mary L. Massey 10-8-1865 (10-12-1865)
Stanly, Newton C. to Martha C. Gullage 9-12-1860
Stayton, E. F. to N. P. Robertson 3-1-1873 (3-3-1873)
Steel, John to Nancy Mathis 6-14-1860
Steele, John S. to G. A. Moore 10-4-1869 (10-6-1869)
Steele, John T. to Mary J. Smith 5-29-1867 (5-30-1867)
Stell, John T. to Lucinda Johnson 4-1-1861 (4-2-1861)
Stephenson, James to Delia M. Hall 11-7-1868 (11-8-1868)
Stewart, Andrew to Triona L. Springer 12-5-1865 (12-6-1865)
Stewart, Benager to Lydia B. Dill 4-4-1868 (4-5-1868)
Stewart, James D. to Jarusha Jane (Mrs) Taylor 11-3-1867
Stewart?, Andrew to Triona L. Springer 12-5-1865 (12-6-1865)
Stoker, Haywood C. to Jimmie Ann Cox 4-18-1870 (4-19-1870)
Stoker, W. W. to M. A. Townsel 2-8-1867
Stokes, Loyd to Adline Cole 10-26-1870 (10-27-1870)
Stone, Henry C. to N. C. Harvy 8-29-1866 (no return)
Stone, Samuel to Elizabeth Rogers 8-3-1863 (no return)
Strayhorn, Hudson to Elizabeth McLemore 10-7-1871 (no return) B
Stroud, John D. to Emarilla J. Hallum 9-20-1869 (9-22-1869)
Stubbs, N. J. to E. K. Anderson 11-26-1870 (12-1-1870)

Stubbs, Thomas J. to Jane C. Anderson 1-3-1870 (1-20-1870)
Sugg, J. D.? to T. J. King 9-7-1866 (9-9-1866)
Suggs?, Wm. A. to Mary C. Bridges 8-18-1860
Suiter, W. J. to L. M. Nelson 11-1-1871 (11-2-1871)
Sullivan, Thomas to Mary Holcomb 9-20-1866 (9-3?-1866)
Surber, R. H. to N. E. Fussell 3-4-1872 (3-7-1870?)
Sutton, Wiley to Letha Mebane 10-24-1868
Swaringin, W. T. to M. J. Crawford 12-3-1864 (12-5-1864)
Swayne, John to Jane Huffman 4-27-1872 (no return) B
Swearengin, Champ to M. E. Blalock 10-12-1871
Swindell, Robert H. to Sarah C. Abernathy 3-14-1864 (no return)
Swindell, Robt. H. to Sarah C. Abernathy 3-14-1864 (3-20-1864)
Swindle, Moses B. to Clarissa L. Westmoreland 9-11-1868 (9-12-1868)
Swinney, J. A. to Sallie Bolton 6-14-1871 (6-15-1871)
Swinney, Samuel L. to Sarah Harris 4-17-1868 (no return)
Tarply, F. P. to Margrarett? J. McMullin 9-24-1860 (9-25-1860)
Tate, Thos. S. to Mollie C. Alexander 2-9-1865 (no return)
Tayler, T. L. to Mary A. King 6-18-1873
Taylor, Andrew to Reny Perkins 10-31-1871 (no return) B
Taylor, Arden to Sylvia Bledsoe 5-7-1870 (5-8-1870)
Taylor, George to Margarett M. Gray 1-21-1864 (no return)
Taylor, Henry C. to Dorothy A. Read 2-16-1864 (no return)
Taylor, J. A. to L. C. Briant 2-28-1872 (3-1-1872)
Taylor, J. H. to L. E. Edwards 9-21-1871
Taylor, J. H. to Mary E. Allen 7-8-1871 (7-9-1871)
Taylor, James F. to A. C. Cox 9-21-1869 (9-23-1869)
Taylor, James to Louza Green 9-4-1865 (no return)
Taylor, Jarrett to Nancy French 6-4-1864
Taylor, R. C. to Mary E. Browning 7-22-1864 (no return)
Taylor, Thos. L. to S. A. Fowler 5-28-1873 (no return)
Taylor, W. M. to R. C. Ruse 10-7-1862 (10-12-1862)
Tesh, John to Elizabeth Gist 9-26-1861
Thomas, D. M. to Levinia Mount 10-9-1862 (no return)
Thomas, E. A. to M. Ella Shofner 2-17-1873 (2-19-1873)
Thomas, E. S. to Mary McAskille 2-26-1873 (2-27-1873)
Thomas, H. B. to S. A. Roach 10-31-1867 (11-5-1867)
Thomas, Louis to Allis Hudson 7-13-1871 (7-14-1871) B
Thomas, Luke to Mary E. Covington 11-19-1870 (11-24-1870)
Thomas, Luke to Rachel Williams 12-16-1870 (12-28-1870) B
Thomas, Mack to Amanda Hillman 1-25-1873 (1-26-1873)
Thomas, Marshall to Lavenia Mount 3-3-1863 (no return)
Thomas, Polk to Angaline Barker 1-22-1873 (1-23-1873) B
Thomas, W. T. to E. F. (Mrs.) Todd 10-19-1869
Thomas, W. T. to Malinda Hedgecock 10-9-1862 (no return)
Thomason, J. W. to Louisa Parish 12-24-1869 (12-28-1869)
Thomason, R. C. A. to Nancy C. Taylor 2-13-1861 (2-16-1861)
Thompson, A. J. to Mary C. F. Thompson 12-19-1871 (no return)
Thompson, B. F. to S. E. Webb 12-20-1871 (no return)
Thompson, C. K. to Maryann King 12-16-1865 (12-18-1865)
Thompson, Calvin L. to Angeline E. Johnston 2-8-1870 (2-9-1870)
Thompson, Edward to Elizabeth Oliver? 11-1-1866
Thompson, J. C. C. to Mary F. Gowen 12-12-1865 (12-14-1865)
Thompson, J. D. to E. J. Hamilton 10-17-1867 (no return)
Thompson, James J. to Elizabeth A. Rollens 7-13-1863 (no return)
Thompson, James R. to Arabella Thomas 12-30-1868 (12-31-1868)
Thompson, W. E. to Susan Adams 5-12-1873 (5-13-1873)
Thompson, W. H. H. to Ellen Sneed 1-19-1871 (1-20-1871)
Thompson, Wm. A. to Martha J. Heelly 1-6-1865 (no return)
Threadgill, Wm. A. to Harriet A. Mills 11-28-1860 (no return)
Tidwell, Charles W. to Sarah J. Richardson 3-26-1868
Tippitt, Sanford to Elizabeth Mathis 12-14-1866 (12-16-1866)
Todd, Benjamin to Sarah F. Drinkard 10-21-1865 (10-29-1865)
Todd, F. H. to Josephine Brewer 12-3-1866 (12-5-1866)
Todd, Fleming C. to Eliza F. Gee 10-21-1861 (10-22-1861)
Todd, Harey to Amanda C. Demoss 8-16-1865 (no return)
Todd, Hugh S. to Nancy Bailey 2-16-1864 (no return)
Todd, J. M. to S. E. Denning 9-10-1869 (9-12-1869)
Todd, John B. to Mary Margaret Hendly 11-8-1867 (11-10-1867)
Tomlinson, N. C. to Tempey Everett 7-17-1872 (no return)
Tood?, M. L. to Susan C. Alexander 1-?-1866 (1-17-1866)
Tosh, H. H. to M. E. Eskew 11-30-1871 (12-15-1871)
Tosh, J. G. to Frances Scott 3-1-1866
Tosh, James M. to Elizabeth C. Dodd 1-9-1871 (1-10-1871)
Tosh, L. M. to L. J. Louis 3-11-1868
Tosh, R. H. to Evaline Scott 12-11-1870 (12-13-1870)

Totty, James E. to Josie (Mrs.) Hope 4-14-1873 (4-24-1873)
Townes, Beverly to Eveline Shoffner 8-1-1868 (8-3-1868)
Townes, Henry C. to Alice C. Crockett 12-17-1868
Towns, Bevily to Nancy Davis 11-1-1871 (11-15-1871)
Towns, James M. to Anna T. Persons 4-5-1865 (no return)
Townsend, Albert to Abigail (Mrs) Butler 6-25-1862 (no return)
Townsend, George to Mary A. Hallmark 7-29-1871
Townsend, James to Henrietta L. Sellers 6-3-1871 (6-11-1871)
Townsend, Nathaniel to Lanna Butler 9-18-1871
Townsend, Sy to N. P. Berchun 3-12-1873 (3-16-1873)
Townsend, William J. to Ortha A. Butler 8-27-1868 (8-28-1868)
Towsend, George W. to Amanda Townsend 4-8-1864 (4-9-1864)
Towson, John W. to M. Walker 2-2-1865 (2-6-1865)
Trainer, J. C. to E. C. Towns 3-7-1871 (3-8-1871)
Trap, Samuel to Sally A. Burchit 1-16-1864 (1-18-1864)
Trat, Samuel to Sally Ann Burchit 1-16-1864 (no return)
Travis, T. M. to Susan Jonett 12-30-1872 (1-1-1873)
Travis, William to M. J. Bobo 1-3-1868 (1-6-1868)
Traywick, Elvis R. to Nannie B. Coleman 12-26-1872
Traywick, H. A. to Martha J. Moore 1-1-1867
Trotter, William to Angeline McNeill 9-4-1871 (9-7-1871) B
Tucker, A. C. to M. B. G. Palmer 12-7-1864 (12-8-1864)
Tucker, John W. to Amanda C. Guffe 1-2-1869
Tucker, Joseph H. to Caroline Black 2-22-1866 (2-25-1866)
Tucker, Richard to Betty Crider 4-2-1872 (4-3-1872) B
Turner, F. W. to S. A. Wren 6-27-1870 (6-29-1870)
Turner, J. T. to M. J. Gowan 2-8-1873 (2-18-1873)
Turner, Jacob to L. S. Mizell 5-21-1873 (5-22-1873)
Turner, James F. to Mary J. Cunningham 3-23-1868 (3-24-1868)
Turner, R. to Mary H. Bunn 10-19-1870 (10-20-1870)
Turner, Thomas A. to Mary Massey 10-10-1868 (10-11-1868)
Umpstead, Edgmere? to Catharine Adams 1-24-1868 (no return)
Utley, George to Bettie Clay 8-29-1872
Utley, J. A. R. to M. J. Lee 11-24-1870
Utley, J. B. to M. P. Scruggs 5-30-1873 (no return)
Utley, Ned to Amy Lucas 1-4-1869 (1-8-1869)
Vancleave, James E. to Amanda P. Carver 7-24-1868 (7-26-1868)
Vancleave, Wm. H. to Mary J. Carver 4-1-1869
Vaughan, Henry to Mary Houseman 4-1-1866 (no return)
Vauters, Thomas D. to Elen Priest 1-18-1865
Vawter, A. J. to Frances P. Rhodes 1-2-1866 (no return)
Vawter, Robert to Sarah M. Crossett 1-11-1870 (no return)
Vawter, T. D. to Nancy E. Coffman 12-24-1870 (12-25-1870)
Vawter, Wm. H. to M. J. Harrell 1-2-1866 (1-3-1866)
Vawton, R. L. to A. J. Rhodes 11-15-1869 (no return)
Viar, John N. to Nancy M. E. Younger 10-24-1860 (10-25-1860)
Vickers, David C. to Mary A. Darnall 3-4-1863
Vickers, David C. to Mary A. Darnall 3-4-1863 (no return)
Vickers, John S. to L. A. Humphreys 4-9-1873 (4-10-1873)
Vickers, Thomas J. to Mary E. McCaslin 12-7-1867 (12-12-1867)
Vincent, Benjamin D. to Elizabeth Felps 1-29-1868 (no return)
Vinson, Andrew to Margarett Moore 1-17-1872 (1-18-1872)
Vinson, James R. to Elizabeth Diggs 1-31-1872
Waddill, John E. to Fannie E. James 10-6-1869 (10-7-1869)
Waddle, W. M. to Elizabeth A. Smith 2-8-1868
Waddle, Wm. E. to Susan H. Brach 2-4-1868 (2-5-1868)
Wadkins, G. H. to M. A. Comton 6-1-1868 (6-4-1868)
Wahls, George to Elizabeth P. Bagby 3-1-1871 (3-2-1871)
Walker, Andrew to Silvia Wilson 1-4-1873 (1-9-1873) B
Walker, G. G. to Nannie Seymore 12-21-1868 (12-22-1868)
Walker, George W. to Alice Mitchell 3-12-1870 (3-13-1870)
Walker, George W. to Mary E. Longworth 1-2-1861 (1-3-1861)
Walker, H. A. to A. E. Holmes 9-13-1866 (9-16-1866)
Walker, James D. to Mary E. Garrison 2-?-1862 (no return)
Walker, James to Martha Long 6-30-1866 (7-1-1866)
Walker, John to Elizabeth Dildy 1-30-1867 (no return)
Walker, Milton to Allice Hughs 12-23-1872 (12-26-1872) B
Walker, R. S. to J. P. Sampson 11-7-1861
Walker, Z. R. to Julia A. S. Fisher 4-21-1866 (no return)
Wall, Henry C. to Delpha A. Flake 10-20-1871 (10-22-1871)
Wall, John O. to Martha J. Grogan 1-6-1870 (1-7-1870)
Wallick, P. M. to Virginia C. Towns 10-14-1867 (10-16-1867)
Walters, A. J. to I. N. Moore 2-19-1873 (2-20-1873)
Walters, J. W. to Anna Cole 2-22-1872
Walters, Joell W. to Martha J. Hinson 2-1-1868 (2-5-1868)

Walton, L. M. to Mattie L. Swinney 1-1-1866 (1-4-1866)
Walton, P. T. to Martha Pate 5-23-1865 (no return)
Warbriton, N. G. to Frances A. Gee 12-12-1864
Warbritten, B. F. to Mary Harris 12-21-1864 (12-22-1864)
Warbritton, J. N. to S. F. Traywick 2-5-1870 (2-6-1870)
Warlick, P. D. to M. E. Mitchiner 7-15-1867 (no return)
Warlick, Walton to Filbis Moore 1-5-1871 B
Warner, Wm. E. to C. P. Terry 5-8-1863 (5-10-1863)
Warner, Wm. E. to C. R. Terry 5-8-1863 (no return)
Warpool, B. F. to Emily Keaton 12-4-1865 (12-17-1865)
Warren, W. M. to Mary L. Evans 10-10-1860 (not executed)
Watkins, Joseph H. to Parilee J. Crews 12-5-1870 (12-6-1870)
Watson, J. H. to Rebeca Surber 12-20-1867 (12-22-1867)
Watson, John W. to Rebecca J. Parker 12-18-1860
Watts, Benjamin to Mary J. Younger 10-16-1860 (10-6?-1860)
Weams, J. W. to Mathe Houston 1-20-1868 (1-21-1868)
Weatherford, Charles to Mollie Hogan 11-29-1866 (11-2?-1866)
Webb, Henry to Martha Foster 10-17-1867
Webb, James J. to Louisa K. Taylor 8-23-1867 (8-25-1867)
Webb, James to Elizabeth Foster 8-4-1865 (8-6-1865)
Webb, R. F. to N. M. Foster 8-15-1871 (no return)
Webb, W. G. to Susan Webb 12-12-1860 (12-13-1860)
Webb, William to Eliza Perrett 9-27-1860
Welch, Patrick J. to Louiza Cunningham 5-28-1873
White, A. to Dora Walker 3-18-1861
White, Abe to Ellen W. Denton 11-10-1869 (11-11-1869)
White, E. to Rebecca Shaw 2-22-1861 (no return)
White, Ed to Amand Porter 2-21-1873 (2-23-1873)
White, Edward to Elizabeth Culp 8-11-1869 (8-12-1869)
White, George to Mary J. Gardner no date (with Feb 1863)
White, J. C. to Ann Kelly 7-20-1872 (no return)
White, J. M. to N. J. Wilcox 11-9-1870 (11-10-1870)
White, J. W. to Jennie Plummer 7-25-1871 (7-13?-1871)
White, Jessie to Janie Jones 9-4-1871
White, R. H. to S. C. Wyatt 11-28-1870 (11-30-1870)
White, T. A. to Emma J. Dozier 6-12-1871
White, W. C. to Nancy B. Bibbs 1-19-1871
White, William to Maria J. McMacken 9-21-1869 (9-23-1869)
White, William to Mary E. Shankle 3-3-1869
White, Wilson to Ellen Palmer 7-2-1869 (7-4-1869)
White, Z. R. to A. A. Stone 11-7-1866 (no return)
Whitehorn, Elvis B. to A. P. Williams 8-10-1867 (8-11-1867)
Whitehorn, James S. to Sarah F. Parsons 11-27-1869 (11-28-1869)
Widdis, William to Charlotte Grant 4-12-1869 (4-13-1869)
Wilborn, E. B. to Malissa Jane Rowland 8-14-1868 (8-16-1868)
Wilder, C. to F. J. Sayles 1-11-1867
Wilder, J. C. to Fannie Jones 6-25-1872 (no return)
Wilder, James W. to Corar Guthrie 9-24-1867 (no return)
Wilds, Columbus J.? to Ellen C. Colvet 10-15-1872 (10-6?-1872)
Wiles?, W. Z.? to Susan Webb? no date (with 12-1860)
Wiliamson, Louis to Bettie Adkisson 12-26-1871 (12-28-1871) B
Wilk, G. W. to Margaret A. Lacy 1-4-1866 (1-14-1866)
Wilkins, W. P. to L. S. Burns 10-8-1860 (10-9-1860)
Wilkins, W. P. to M. E. Patton 10-12-1869 (10-13-1869)
Wilks, E. B. to Julia A. Mitchell 3-25-1869
Wilks, Yancy E. to Mary E. Rhodes 12-16-1869
Williams, B. M. to Didema Abernathy 10-13-1862 (no return)
Williams, Benjamin A. to Jobie A. Wright 6-26-1861 (6-27-1861)
Williams, D. H. to M. J. Pritchard 1-28-1868 (1-30-1868)
Williams, Edwin to Mary E. Caudle 9-25-1865
Williams, F. A. to M. E. Winn 8-10-1867 (8-11-1867)
Williams, F. G. to Anna E. Priest 10-19-1871 (no return)
Williams, G. H. to Nancy C. Huffman 7-14-1866 (7-15-1866)
Williams, G. P. to M. L. Benton 1-11-1873 (1-12-1873)
Williams, G. W. to M. J. Ledsinger 10-7-1871 (10-8-1871)
Williams, J. W. to Elvira M. Burrow 12-4-1865 (12-6-1865)
Williams, James M. to M. B. P. Peler 11-10-1870
Williams, James T. to Sarah T. Gray 1-29-1870 (2-3-1870)
Williams, John J. to Canely? M. Norvell 3-27-1864 (3-27-1864)
Williams, John to Dinarza M. Jones 9-2-1862
Williams, John to Rebeccah Roberts 8-21-1866
Williams, John to Sarah Scales 12-24-1868 (12-25-1868)
Williams, Jon F. to Rebeca C. Bennett 2-28-1867
Williams, Joseph A. to Elizabeth Palmer 2-3-1863 (2-4-1863)
Williams, L. D. to Louisa Roberts 1-8-1865

Williams, L. F. to C. J. McCall 11-16-1866 (11-21-1866)
Williams, L. T. to Elizabeth Walls 8-13-1872 (8-15-1872)
Williams, Livra? to Martitia Ray 2-28-1868 (3-1-1868)
Williams, R. T. to Bethe Taylor 12-25-1861 (no return)
Williams, Samuel to Susan A. Pucker 8-19-1867 (8-20-1867)
Williams, T. T. to M. E. Mebane 10-26-1870
Williams, Thomas P. to Narcissa Roberts 9-25-1861 (no return)
Williams, W. A. to L. P. Huffman 1-24-1873 (1-30-1873)
Williams, W. F. to V. P. Churchwell 10-24-1871
Williams, Westly to Darthula Cravens 11-21-1865
Williams, William A. to Emeritta Tosh 12-11-1865 (12-12-1865)
Williams, William R. to M. E. Rees 7-27-1863 (7-28-1863)
Williams, William R. to Martha E. Rees 7-27-1863
Williamson, Ed to Elvora Smith 11-27-1868
Williamson, G. W. to Elizabeth J. Williamson 9-7-1864 (no return)
Williamson, Henry to Eliza Robison 5-3-1870 (no return)
Williamson, J. M. to Mary J. McCollum 4-26-1866
Williamson, Jas. A. to Cyntha C. Stone 4-21-1863 (no return)
Williamson, Jesse to Ann Smith 12-11-1869 (12-12-1869)
Williamson, John M. to Billie Anders 3-27-1872 (3-28-1872)
Williamson, John N. to Mary E. H. McClure 1-6-1868 (1-7-1868)
Williamson, Lewin? to F. E. Carter 7-21-1873 (7-22-1873)
Williamson, S. E. to Cordelia Hammer 4-1-1871 (4-4-1871)
Williamson, S. W. to M. J. Huddle 9-15-1869 (no return)
Williamson, Samuel B. to Mary E. Abernathy 10-26-1869 (10-31-1869)
Williamson, Wm. K.? to Mary J. Vincent 7-9-1861 (7-10-1861)
Willson, James T. to Mary S. Butler 2-22-1871
Willson, T. C. to Margaret D. Allen 8-21-1866 (8-23-1866)
Wilson, David N. to Mary F. Cooper 12-25-1869 (12-26-1869)
Wilson, G. H. to Amanda Owens 2-15-1865 (2-20-1865)
Wilson, George N. to Amanda Todd 8-5-1868
Wilson, J. T. to Elizabeth L. Berger 12-18-1866 (no return)
Wilson, James G. to Elizaeth C. French 2-24-1870
Wilson, Joseph to Amanda L.? Carter 12-17-1867 (12-18-1867)
Wilson, Richard to Frances Sneed 3-4-1870
Wilson, Samuel to Adeline Bledsoe 10-13-1865 (10-24-1865)
Wilson, William B. to Artamissa J. Smith 9-18-1865
Wingo, John J. to Mary A. Cooper 5-8-1864
Wingo, T.? R. to Mary J. C. Jones 2-18-1867 (no return)
Witt, Silas D. to Nancy G. Palmore 2-23-1861 (2-24-1861)
Wood, G. W. to N. C. Palmer 2-20-1869 (2-21-1869)
Wood, H. to A. G. Algee 10-1-1869 (10-3-1869)
Wood, J. L. to N. E. Hall 12-12-1865 (12-15-1865)
Wood, John T. to Catharine T. Taylor 2-5-1869
Wood, Marion to Sarah A. Penick 12-18-1866 (12-19-1866)
Woodall, B. F. to Martha S. Harrell 9-16-1861 (no return)
Woodard, James E. to Susan A. Shuford 3-17-1868 (3-18-1868)
Woodard, James M. to Lucy Jane Smith 8-3-1869 (no return)
Woodard, W. P. to Cintha J. Graham 1-8-1868 (1-9-1868)
Woods, J. M. to T. B. Butler 2-1-1868 (2-5-1868)
Woods, R. J. to J. B. Standfield 7-27-1871
Woods, Robert P. to Louiza J. Willson 12-31-1861 (1-5-1862)
Woods, S. P. to Harriett Moore 12-31-1868 (1-1-1869)
Woods, W. H. to H. E. Cawthan 1-27-1868 (1-29-1868)
Woodson, Doctor to Betty Cunningham 6-28-1871 (6-29-1871) B
Woodson, Ned to Alice Cunningham 1-22-1869 (1-23-1869)
Woolen, A. T. M. to M. C.? Rogers 4-2-1860 (4-10-1860)
Worel?, John M. to Martha A. Cawthan 1-9-1863 (no return)
Worrel, Jesse to Lenora Foshee 1-1-1870 (1-2-1870)
Wren, J. B. to M. A. Cooper 10-22-1868
Wren, N. J. to Julie Edwards 11-18-1867 (11-20-1867)
Wren, Robert to Mary A. Smith 8-1-1865 (no return)
Wright, C. H. to Mary Jane Turner 8-30-1860 (9-4-1860)
Wright, Columbus to Nancy Moore 2-24-1869
Wright, G. W. to Nancy L. Ruce? 1-31-1870 (2-10-1870)
Wright, H. W. to Lucinda McCane 11-16-1865
Wright, J. A. to Winna R. Rogers 8-22-1864 (8-25-1864)
Wright, J. P. to Nancy Tilmon 3-5-1867 (3-10-1867)
Wright, John H. to Mahala McCollum 11-10-1863 (11-12-1863)
Wright, Pleasant to Mary Grizzard 8-23-1870 (8-24-1870)
Wright, Robert to Martha G. Jolly 9-21-1861 (no return)
Wyatt, George to Prudence Clark 9-25-1871 (10-2-1871) B
Wyatt, Pinkney to California Stokes 12-28-1866 (12-29-1866)
Wyatt, R. S. to Mary A. Chambers 9-13-1870 (9-14-1870)
Wyatt, Silas R. to Susan A. Vawter 1-13-1866 (1-15-1866)

Wyatt, Zachariah to Margaret T. Sullivan 5-20-1869 (no return)
Yarbrough, G. W. to Margarett Turner 5-13-1873 (5-14-1873)
Yarbrough, N. R. to Mary T. Anderson 12-20-1865 (12-2-1865)
Yarbrough, W. J. to Sarah Ann Turner 12-18-1865 (12-20-1866?)
Yergan, A. G. to Clementine Barnes 11-17-1869 (11-18-1869)
Young, A. to Catharine Cobb 11-27-1867 (11-28-1867)
Young, Doremus N. to Martha Mebane 9-26-1865
Young, John A. to Elizabeth Parsons 4-10-1866
Younge, Jas. M. to Pining B. O'Neill 11-7-1865 (11-9-1865)
Younger, J. T. to M. F. Walpole 7-21-1864 (7-25-1864)
Younger, T. W. to H. M. Haynes 2-10-1865 (2-12-1865)
Younger, Thomas A. to Tamer J. North 10-1-1860 (no return)
Younger, W. T. to Callie T. Hansbro 1-16-1869 (no return)
Zellner, J. A. to E. J. Robinson 2-26-1872 (2-27-1872)

Abbott, Clara to James Simmonds 5-7-1870 (5-8-1870)
Abbott, Lucinda to Alfred Gooch 9-20-1869 (9-21-1869)
Abernathy, Didema to B. M. Williams 10-13-1862 (no return)
Abernathy, Elizabeth to Hezekiah Moore 10-10-1861
Abernathy, Harriett A. to Wm. M. Brewer 2-21-1866 (2-22-1866)
Abernathy, Mary E. to Samuel B. Williamson 10-26-1869 (10-31-1869)
Abernathy, Sarah C. to Robert H. Swindell 3-14-1864 (no return)
Abernathy, Sarah C. to Robt. H. Swindell 3-14-1864 (3-20-1864)
Adams, C. J. to G. W. Mills 12-14-1871 (no return)
Adams, Callie to Sam Jones 9-13-1870 (9-15-1870) B
Adams, Catharine to Edgmere? Umpstead 1-24-1868 (no return)
Adams, Elizabeth to Hiram Horton 9-12-1871
Adams, M. J. to T. C. Spain 2-25-1873 (2-27-1873)
Adams, Mary A. to Wm. W. McDugal 4-6-1868 (4-8-1868)
Adams, Mary S. to James A. McDugal 1-8-1861 (1-10-1861)
Adams, Nancy to Frank Edwards 12-24-1869 (12-30-1869)
Adams, Sally to John Givin 12-5-1864 (no return)
Adams, Susan to W. E. Thompson 5-12-1873 (5-13-1873)
Adkison, Harriett to Richard Jones 9-21-1867 (no return)
Adkisson, Bettie to Louis Wiliamson 12-26-1871 (12-28-1871) B
Akers, Q. L. A. to J. F. Edwards 1-7-1871 (1-8-1871)
Albright, Ellen to J. J. Gorman 8-20-1861 (8-21-1861)
Alexander, Mollie C. to Thos. S. Tate 2-9-1865 (no return)
Alexander, Nannie to W. H. Chance 8-24-1870 (8-25-1870)
Alexander, Susan C. to M. L. Tood? 1-?-1866 (1-17-1866)
Algee, A. G. to H. Wood 10-1-1869 (10-3-1869)
Algee, Emma to Richard McDonald 2-1-1872 B
Algee, J. C. to W. K.? Baxter 1-1-1861 (1-2-1861)
Algee, M. J. to J. L. Sales 1-19-1861 (1-21-1861)
Algee, Martha A. to A. S. J.? Neely 5-23-1860 (no return)
Algee, Mollie to Boyd Bryant 7-31-1873 (7-27?-1873)
Algee, Virginia to A. F. Estes 9-29-1868 (10-1-1868)
Allen, Amanda to James Alexander 9-4-1860
Allen, Catharine to James Medlin 4-22-1865 (4-23-1865)
Allen, Evelin to James T. Medlin 6-15-1872 (no return)
Allen, Josephine to William A. Reddin 1-16-1866 (1-18-1866)
Allen, Margaret C. to Wm. F. Forest 9-23-1871 (9-24-1871)
Allen, Margaret D. to T. C. Willson 8-21-1866 (8-23-1866)
Allen, Martha T. to Isaac R. Hutchins 1-15-1872 (no return)
Allen, Martha to J. W. Brown 1-11-1862 (no return)
Allen, Martha to John Howard 4-11-1871 B
Allen, Mary E. to J. H. Taylor 7-8-1871 (7-9-1871)
Allen, Mary J. to James F. Palmer 2-24-1866 (2-26-1866)
Allen, Mary W. to Jacob D. Bledsoe 11-19-1863 (no return)
Allen, Myra T. to Wm. H. Bledsoe 12-8-1864 (no return)
Allen, Nancy A. to W. E. Moss 8-12-1864 (no return)
Allen, Piecia to Jas. P. Churchwell 5-10-1873 (5-11-1873)
Allen, R. Y. to G. H. Hunter 2-15-1872
Allmon, America to Seth Brinkley 8-27-1860 (8-28-1860)
Alrich?, Louisa F. to Thomas J. Foster 12-18-1866 (12-19-1866)
Anders, Billie to John M. Williamson 3-27-1872 (3-28-1872)
Anderson, Diner to Edward Bledsoe 10-21-1870 (10-23-1870)
Anderson, E. K. to N. J. Stubbs 11-26-1870 (12-1-1870)
Anderson, Jane C. to Thomas J. Stubbs 1-3-1870 (1-20-1870)
Anderson, Josephine to R. W. Algee 4-6-1863 (no return)
Anderson, Louisa to Jacob Robison 5-23-1867 (no return)
Anderson, Mary T. to N. R. Yarbrough 12-20-1865 (12-2-1865)
Anderson, Narcissa to J.? P. Butler 11-16-1867 (11-17-1867)
Anderson, Salina to John A. Compton 3-19-1861 (no return)
Anderson, Sarah to Alfred King 8-10-1871
Argo, C. S. to R. D. Johns 12-17-1872 (12-19-1872)
Argo, Mary L. to Newton F. Cloid 1-17-1870
Arington, Martha L. to Coleman J. French 11-15-1860 (11-20-1860)
Arrington, Ellen to Thos. Russell 6-8-1863 (6-11-1863)
Atkison, Malissa to Charles Phillips 8-27-1869
Aurenchine, H. S. to Albert Nicler 6-26-1873 (no return)
Autry, L. R. to J. C. Haywood 6-21-1867 (6-23-1867)
Autry, Mary M. to Robt. P. Hall 11-7-1871 (11-8-1871)
Bagby, Elizabeth P. to George Wahls 3-1-1871 (3-2-1871)
Bailess, Martha E. to Pinkney B. Rowland 11-25-1865 (11-26-1865)
Bailey, Margaret to Alexander Chamberlin 12-2-1863 (12-3-1863)
Bailey, Nancy to Hugh S. Todd 2-16-1864 (no return)
Bainey, Sarah J. to Porter Gibson 5-8-1863 (5-17-1863)
Baker, Lielia to James Hammett 7-22-1862 (no return)
Ballew, Emily J. to George W. Burton 12-30-1865 (12-31-1865)

Ballew, M. W. to W. J. Leach 3-31-1865 (no return)
Barber, Molley to John Campbell 4-24-1870 (no return)
Barham, Adaline to William Bolin 10-26-1871 (10-31-1871)
Barham, C. O. to G. T. Barksdale 1-30-1871 (2-1-1871)
Barham, Louisa to Richard Carson 8-17-1868 (8-18-1868)
Barham, Mattie E. to A. C. (Dr.) Pearce 12-8-1866 (12-11-1866)
Barham, N. C. (Mrs.) to T. J. Dill 4-9-1860
Barham, Tobitha to J. T. Johnson 11-16-1866 (11-18-1866)
Barker, Angaline to Polk Thomas 1-22-1873 (1-23-1873) B
Barker, Sarah to Fed Nesbett 10-20-1870 B
Barksdale, Fannie to Austin P. Little 5-14-1863 (no return)
Barksdale, Luellen to J. D. Abbett 1-6-1864 (no return)
Barlow, L. W. to E. M. Ellsberry 7-12-1864 (7-13-1864)
Barlow, Margaret to Nathan Morris 7-23-1862
Barnes, Clementine to A. G. Yergan 11-17-1869 (11-18-1869)
Barnes, Martha J. to W. G. Hallmark 3-6-1872 (no return)
Barnett, Arcenoe to G. H. Nease 7-18-1871
Barnett, Nancy to M. A. Kennaday 8-14-1866 (8-16-1866)
Barnhart, Sarah A. to Jesse C. Easters 8-6-1866 (8-7-1866)
Barns, Culine? to Arthur Spalding 7-22-1860
Barrett, Mary to Hugh Elmore 10-23-1863 (10-25-1863)
Barrett, Mary to Hugh Elmore 10-23-1864 (no return)
Barton, Mary A. to Washington C. Reed 9-14-1866
Baucum, Clara to James Sparks 3-8-1870
Baxter, N. J. to William A. Sayle 1-23-1861 (1-24-1861)
Bayby, Mary to Thos. Fitzgerald 12-11-1872 (12-12-1872) B
Bayles, Lucy to C. L. Holliday 3-20-1867 (3-21-1867)
Bayley, Elizah to W. A. Scoby 10-25-1870 (10-26-1870)
Beard, Mary to Samuel Bell 12-2-1869 (12-4-1869)
Beavers, Ellen to David Hill 7-13-1867 (7-14-1867)
Beavers, Jane to Baher Ruse 5-23-1864 (5-27-1864)
Beck, Susan A. to Eli Douglass 9-20-1869 (no return)
Belew, M. A. to W. A. Palmer 10-27-1868 (10-28-1868)
Belew, S. C. to W. Prat 9-13-1870
Bell, Amanda to Henry Adams 12-31-1869
Bell, Jane to A. G. McAuley 9-20-1872 (9-22-1872) B
Bell, Jinnie to Carroll Hawkins 4-14-1872 (no return) B
Bell, Lucy A. to Granville Drake 3-19-1873 B
Bell, Margaret to Nicholas M. Darnall 8-29-1865 (no return)
Bell, Mary Ann K. to Wm. J. Lowder 2-16-1864 (no return)
Bell, Maryann K. to Wm. J. Lowder 2-16-1864
Belliew, Vandalia to W. H. Belliew 9-10-1870
Bennett, Emmy to James Colvett 5-24-1864 (5-25-1864)
Bennett, Jane to John Cooper 4-2-1860 (4-6-1860)
Bennett, L. Ann to B. T. Forbus 10-26-1871
Bennett, M. C. to A. F. Glosson 3-7-1872
Bennett, Nancy M. to J. H. Rogers 8-19-1871 (8-20-1871)
Bennett, Rebeca C. to Jon F. Williams 2-28-1867
Benton, Lucinda to Z. T. Rhodes 2-19-1869 (2-23-1869)
Benton, M. L. to G. P. Williams 1-11-1873 (1-12-1873)
Benton, Mary E. to W. R. Pickett 1-14-1862
Benton, Rosanna A. to C. S. Brandon 7-3-1861 (7-4-1861)
Berchun, N. P. to Sy Townsend 3-12-1873 (3-16-1873)
Berger, Elizabeth L. to J. T. Wilson 12-18-1866 (no return)
Bernard, Nelly to M. F. Roney 10-26-1872 (10-27-1872)
Berry, Julia Ann to George W. Myrick 8-11-1868 (8-12-1868)
Berry, M. J. M. to F. M. Davis 8-17-1864 (8-18-1864)
Berry, Martha H. to Nathan G. Rich 10-15-1866 (10-17-1866)
Bevell, A. T. to W. S. Smith 8-12-1867 (8-13-1867)
Bevill, E. H. to W. P. Smith 2-4-1867 (2-7-1867)
Bevill, Lucy A. to E. F. Jordon 3-14-861
Bevill, Luzana C. to George N. Roberts 10-16-1869 (10-17-1869)
Bevill, T. H. to S. G. Leslie 11-26-1872 (11-27-1872)
Bibb, Melvina E. to W. P. Johnson 12-21-1869 (12-24-1869)
Bibbs, Mary E. to D. L. Bohanon 3-6-1866 (3-8-1866)
Bibbs, Nancy B. to W. C. White 1-19-1871
Bibbs, O. M. to N. H. McLevee 3-7-1867
Biggart, Margaret to M. R. Mathis 10-20-1866 (10-21-1866)
Bigham, Addie to C. F. Osborne 2-4-1868 (2-5-1868)
Bigham, Adline to Ben Bigham 2-10-1872 B
Bigham, Callie D. to Louis P. Meyers 6-3-1872 (6-6-1872)
Bigham, Emma to John P. Johnson 7-23-1866 (no return)
Bigham, Lizzie to J. R. Plummer 7-14-1869 (no return)
Bigham, Mary to Samuel M. O'Neill 11-1-1869
Bigham, P. P. to W. B. W. Gray 3-5-1867 (no return)

Bird, Allice to William Furlong 4-29-1873 (no return)
Bird, Nancy to Nathaniel Brewer 5-30-1867 (no return)
Bird, Sarah H. to William S. Nelson 11-23-1867 (11-24-1867)
Birmingham, Sarah J. to G. J. Gilbert 9-16-1872
Bishop, Amey to Alfred Bryant 12-31-1870 (1-5-1871)
Black, Caroline to Joseph H. Tucker 2-22-1866 (2-25-1866)
Black, M. E. to John W. Bellew 12-26-1871 (12-27-1871)
Blackwell, Dilsey to Daniel Hurt 10-27-1872 (11-2-1872) B
Blackwell, Mary E. to W. H. Hawkins 10-7-1868 (10-9-1868)
Blackwell, Mary to Harrison Moppin 6-1-1868 (no return)
Blair, Margarett J. to Tilman Palmer 12-20-1866
Blair, Nancy to John W. Pope 4-14-1863 (4-15-1863)
Blair, Nancy to John W. Pope 4-14-1864 (no return)
Blair, Sopha to George W. Cook 12-16-1872 (12-19-1872)
Blake, Caroline to Wily E. H. Page 8-10-1861 (no return)
Blake, Elizabeth to W. M. Diggs 1-15-1866
Blake, Louisa to Henry Jackson 5-28-1869 (5-29-1869)
Blake, Saphronia C. to David H. Russell 1-?-1866 (1-11-1866)
Blalock, M. E. to Champ Swearengin 10-12-1871
Blan?, Adline to Philip Smith 1-13-1872 (no return) B
Blanks, Recca to John Briant 9-2-1867 (no return)
Blaylock, Mary to James Gilbreth 1-12-1871
Bledsoe, Adeline to Samuel Wilson 10-13-1865 (10-24-1865)
Bledsoe, Fanny C. to George W. Hill 2-20-1867
Bledsoe, Hannah to Green Allen 8-31-1872 (9-1-1872)
Bledsoe, Harriett to W. C. Moore 12-3-1860 (12-6-1860)
Bledsoe, J. T.? to J. W. Hill 2-11-1871 (2-12-1871)
Bledsoe, Lucy to Levi Hawkins 11-26-1871 B
Bledsoe, Sylvia to Arden Taylor 5-7-1870 (5-8-1870)
Blount, S. L. to M. A. Sanders 1-15-1872 (1-17-1872)
Bobitt, Jane to Loyd Ozier 11-7-1861 (no return)
Bobo, M. J. to William Travis 1-3-1868 (1-6-1868)
Bogle, Mary E. to Lewis J. Milligan 10-1-1860 (10-4-1860)
Bogle, Mary E. to Lewis J. Mullins 10-?-1860 (10-4-1860)
Boles, Josephine to J. B. Neal 2-25-1871 (2-26-1871)
Bolton, Sallie to J. A. Swinney 6-14-1871 (6-15-1871)
Bomar, Harriett to Lewis Clark 1-22-1873 (1-23-1873) B
Boston, Mary A. to B. F. Bunch 3-8-1870
Boswell, Anna to James Glosson 12-22-1869 (12-23-1869)
Boswell, Martha J. to Nathaniel Owen 10-4-1871 (10-5-1871)
Boswell, Nancy J. to C. K. Butler 9-13-1865 (9-15-1865)
Boswell, S. J. to R. B. Eubanks 3-10-1870
Bowden, Mary C. to Gross Elbowe 9-13-1865 (9-17-1865)
Bowland, ElizabethJ. to George W. Park 11-3-1860 (11-4-1860)
Bowland, Susan to David Humphrey 8-24-1866
Bowslon?, Lucy A. to Thomas H. Newson 12-1-1865 (12-4-1865)
Box, Priscilla to Stephen Gatlin 10-14-1867 (10-15-1867)
Boyd, Elizabeth D. to William C. Saunders 3-18-1869
Boyd, Sarah C. to Philip T. Butler 3-2-1864 (no return)
Boyd, Tenness to Austin Branoch 11-23-1871 (11-25-1871) B
Brach, Susan H. to Wm. E. Waddle 2-4-1868 (2-5-1868)
Bradbery, Susan to A. J. Butler 9-30-1867 (10-1-1867)
Bradford, Betsy Jane to Benjamin Moore 2-8-1868 (2-10-1868)
Bradford, M. L. to R. R. H. Melton 9-5-1866? (9-8-1867)
Bradford, Sarah to Felix H. Clark 11-10-1869 (11-14-1869)
Bradley, Nancy to James D. Sipe 3-11-1862
Bragden, Folly Ann to John Simmons 8-24-1864 (no return)
Branch, Elizabeth (Mrs.) to A. Leech 10-8-1861
Branch, Elizabeth to Aliner Leech 10-1-1861 (10-8-1861)
Branch, M. L. J. to L. J. Mulligan 12-23-1872 (12-24-1872)
Brandon, Frances to J. R. Holmes 5-28-1873
Brandon, Issabel to William Pritchard 10-14-1867 (10-15-1867)
Brandon, Lucy C. to Thos. Springer 12-5-1872 (12-6-1872)
Brandon, Orrenia to Frank Hilliard 8-1-1872 (8-4-1872)
Brandon, Rienia to W. D. Roark 7-23-1872 (no return)
Brannock, Louisa to George Coleman 9-4-1869 (9-19-1869)
Branoch, Sallie to John Carson 3-28-1872 (no return) B
Brashear, Penelope A. to Wesley Kelley 5-13-1869
Brashears, Rebecca to Augustus Holmgrist 8-6-1870 (no return)
Brashers, Jane to H. M. Laurence 4-20-1867 (4-21-1867)
Brashers, Josaphine F. to John F. Deer 1-22-1868 (1-28-1868)
Braswell, Martha to Giles Belew 2-13-1864
Braswell, Martha to Giles Belew 2-13-1864 (no return)
Brecheen, Nancy A. E. to Harvey Neighbours 11-27-1860
Brevard, Amanda to Peter Bledsoe 12-30-1872

Brevard, Josephine to R. Holaday 12-28-1870
Brewer, Frances to Nathaniel Nunnery 10-31-1860 (11-10-1860)
Brewer, Josephine to F. H. Todd 12-3-1866 (12-5-1866)
Brewer, Nancy to Felix Carey 5-14-1870 (5-18-1870)
Brewer, Robina to W. A. Aikin 8-27-1870 (8-28-1870)
Brewer, S. A. to S. D. Abinathey 12-11-1866 (12-16-1866)
Briant, Angeline to Josh Jordan 8-1-1871 B
Briant, Jinnie to John Hill 7-24-1869 (7-29-1869)
Briant, L. C. to J. A. Taylor 2-28-1872 (3-1-1872)
Briant, Lu? to Ephraim Burrow 2-1-1869
Briant, Mary to T. J. Harris 4-26-1867 (no return)
Bridges, Lucy J. to Malone Pary 8-31-1866 (9-2-1866)
Bridges, Mary C. to Wm. A. Suggs? 8-18-1860
Bridges, Sarah to G. T. Robison 2-14-1870 (2-15-1870)
Brigens, Nancy to J. W. Evans 1-10-1871
Briggance, Tennessee R. to Sidny A. Mebene 2-12-1861
Brimage, Sarah J. to Joshua D. Clark 7-3-1871 (7-6-1871)
Brinder, Alice to George Conner 5-8-1869
Brinkley, Nancy to S. H. Hollowell 1-8-1866 (no return)
Brinkly, Elizabeth to Mark Parrish 6-27-1866 (no return)
Brinkly, Mary J. to A. E. Rogers 10-9-1865 (no return)
Brinkly, Winfred to Jones? R. Haywood 1-19-1861 (1-27-1861)
Brinley, Harriett A.? to Wm. R. Hall 1-19-1861 (1-24-1861)
Britt, Amanda to Nelson Cuningham 1-7-1873 (no return) B
Britt, Helen to George Harris 9-26-1872 B
Britt, M. C. to H. J. Redden 7-24-1872 (no return)
Britt, M. L. to J. R. McAdoo 12-22-1868 (12-23-1868)
Britton, M. E. to John J. McKing 1-27-1866 (2-1-1866)
Broach, L. J. to W. H. Carter 12-4-1872
Brooks, Mary A. (Mrs.) to Lewis Norwood 7-20-1860 (7-22-1860)
Brown, Julie A. to J. D. Brown 1-17-1866
Brown, M. M. to W. G. Newbill 11-30-1872 (no return)
Brown, Martha to William J. Barnes 7-18-1862 (9-4-1866?)
Brown, Mattie A. to J. R. McCracken 11-19-1866 (no return)
Brown, Mima to Henry Reynolds 3-31-1871 (4-2-1871)
Brown, R. H. to John B. Neely 3-26-1864
Brown, S. M. to C. C. Neely 12-28-1865
Brown, Sarah S. to B. L. Benton 9-18-1869 (9-19-1869)
Brown, Sophronia A. to John T. Benton 11-22-1867 (11-23-1867)
Brown?, B. C. to J. P. Clopton 2-12-1868 (2-13-1868)
Browney, M. A. to Z. B. Briant 7-22-1864 (no return)
Browning, Ellen to D. A. Bullington 11-27-1869 (12-2-1869)
Browning, Mary E. to R. C. Taylor 7-22-1864 (no return)
Browning, Massely? to Nelson Robison 10-4-1870 (10-6-1870)
Browning, P. A. to A. M. Hopper 11-25-1871 (no return)
Browning, S. A. to Isaac Pearce 1-9-1871 (1-12-1871) B
Browning, Sarah F. to W. M. Crawford 12-3-1867
Browning, Sarah J. to Wlilliam C. Bullington 12-2-1862 (12-5-1862)
Bruce?, P. A. C. to P. B. Capps? 4-20-1867 (4-21-1867)
Brunsull?, Lidda to Hugh Laddamare 1-10-1867 (1-13-1867)
Bryant, Agness to R. J. Johnson 10-26-1861 (10-27-1861)
Bryant, Celester A. to Geo. B. Cole 10-10-1872 (10-11-1872)
Bryant, Fanney to John Attkisson 10-20-1871 (10-25-1871)
Bryant, Nannie to J. W. Porter 8-2-1873 (no return)
Buchannon, Susan G. to Abram Harper 11-10-1864 (no return)
Bugg, Allice to John W. Graham 6-26-1867 (6-27-1867)
Bullington, Mary to J. C. Bullington 12-29-1865 (12-31-1865)
Bumbley, Nancy to Wilson B. Rhodes 11-10-1861 (11-17-1861)
Bunch, Catharine E. to Jesse Boston 4-30-1870 (5-1-1870)
Bunn, Mary H. to R. Turner 10-19-1870 (10-20-1870)
Burch, Martha J.? to James H. Rainey 12-21-1867 (12-24-1867)
Burchit, Sally A. to Samuel Trap 1-16-1864 (1-18-1864)
Burchit, Sally Ann to Samuel Trat 1-16-1864 (no return)
Burkett, Mary C. to Benjamin Dodd 4-25-1860 (4-26-1860)
Burks, Elizabeth to William Griffin 3-21-1864
Burnett, Espran to Wm. Flake 2-18-1865 (2-21-1865)
Burnett, Nancy to M. F. H. Douglass 12-26-1865 (12-31-1865)
Burnett, Rose to James Counts 11-?-1868 (11-22-1868)
Burns, E. to James Bitter 12-13-1861 (12-15-1861)
Burns, Elizabeth S. to John Guffey 8-3-1868 (8-4-1868)
Burns, Elzy to James Ritter 12-13-1861 (12-15-1861)
Burns, L. J. to A. R. Goodman 12-27-1860 (no return)
Burns, L. S. to W. P. Wilkins 10-8-1860 (10-9-1860)
Burns, Lamira R. to James T. Gibbon 8-21-1861 (8-22-1861)
Burns, Mary to Austin J. Albright 2-4-1864 (no return)

Burns, P. to James Goodlow 2-4-1869
Burns, Sarah to C. H. Martin 7-22-1861 (7-24-1861)
Burris, Mollie W. to G. W. Dent 10-11-1869 (10-12-1869)
Burrow, Delila M. to Thomas W. Leach 1-31-1866 (2-1-1866)
Burrow, Elizabeth W. to G. F. Bishop 3-27-1866 (3-29-1866)
Burrow, Elvira M. to J. W. Williams 12-4-1865 (12-6-1865)
Burrow, Jula Ann to Samuel Daniel 4-30-1873 (5-1-1873) B
Burrow, Letha to William Crenshaw 1-4-1870 (1-5-1870)
Burrow, M. A. to S. C. Mills 1-27-1873
Burrow, Penelope E. to Z. T. Bellows? 10-3-1860 (10-7-1860)
Burrow, Sarah Jane to A. R. Nichols 5-26-1865 (no return)
Burrow, Susan to James Moten 8-5-1871 (8-13-1871)
Burrow, Susan to Samuel Enloe 11-2-1868 (11-8-1868)
Burrus, Mary to Austin J. Albright 2-4-1864 (2-7-1864)
Busey, Sarah to James Russel 1-6-1872 (no return)
Butler, Abigail (Mrs) to Albert Townsend 6-25-1862 (no return)
Butler, Angeline to E. R. Kyle 5-17-1866 (5-13-1866)
Butler, Anna to Thos. L. Rowland 9-18-1872
Butler, Artemissa to Willis Roberts 12-8-1869 (12-9-1869)
Butler, Daney Ann to Albert Birdwell 4-5-1864 (4-6-1864)
Butler, Elizabeth B. to John R. King 4-18-1870 (4-19-1870)
Butler, Elizabeth D. to William C. Royal 8-26-1866 (8-27-1866)
Butler, Harriett to Harvey Palmer 1-13-1872 (1-14-1872)
Butler, J. A. to B. F. Cox 6-8-1867 (6-23-1867)
Butler, J. P. to Wm. A. Brackin 8-28-1872 (8-29-1872)
Butler, L. E. to W. M. Smith 11-11-1872 (11-13-1872)
Butler, L. W. to J. M. McAulay 12-29-1870
Butler, Lanna to Nathaniel Townsend 9-18-1871
Butler, Louisa J. to Haywood F. Harris 3-2-1863
Butler, Louisa J. to Haywood F. Harris 3-2-1863 (no return)
Butler, Lucy to Jesse Pickler 8-2-1865 (8-3-1865)
Butler, M. J. to Thos. A. Selmons 6-25-1864 (7-3-1864)
Butler, Manerva to J. D. Pinkston 4-29-1870 (5-7-1870)
Butler, Martha L. to Elijah G. Rogers 1-21-1868 (1-22-1868)
Butler, Martha to Robert Crawford 10-19-1869 (10-24-1869)
Butler, Mary E. to Benj. A. Saunders 9-19-1860 (9-20-1860)
Butler, Mary S. to James T. Willson 2-22-1871
Butler, Ortha A. to William J. Townsend 8-27-1868 (8-28-1868)
Butler, Paralee to Charles Austin 7-25-1870 (7-27-1870)
Butler, Parthena to R. Wilson Latham 6-1-1872 (6-2-1872)
Butler, Polly J. to J. M. Elkins 10-11-1871 (10-12-1871)
Butler, R. C. to W. C. Horton 3-11-1872
Butler, S. F. to J. W. Rowe 8-10-1872 (8-12-1872)
Butler, Sarah C. to Phillip T. Butler 3-2-1864 (3-3-1864)
Butler, Sarah F. to Wm. R. Roberson 11-27-1872
Butler, Sophia to J. R. Batten 11-27-1869 (11-30-1869)
Butler, T. B. to J. M. Woods 2-1-1868 (2-5-1868)
Butler, Virginia E. to Elijah M. Lowrey 2-24-1870 (2-25-1870)
Byers, Sarah E. to Jeremiah T. Bolton 9-20-1865 (9-21-1865)
Caffrey, Martha to J. W. Kee 9-29-1860
Caldwell, Amanda to Cornelius Cunningham 12-16-1868 (12-17-1868)
Caldwell, N. D. to James A. Shaw? 11-24-1866 (11-27-1866)
Caldwell, Rebeca W. to L. L. Hawkins 10-2-1861
Campbell, E. J. to J. H. Barlow 12-18-1872 (12-19-1872)
Campbell, Nancy to John House 1-21-1867 (1-22-1867)
Cane, Frances to Marsellis Jones 10-6-1869
Cannon, Mahala A. to Benjamin Morgan 11-28-1860
Cannon, Mollie to L. P. Ray 12-18-1872 (12-19-1872)
Cannon, N. H. to C. R. Ownby 10-9-1868 (10-11-1868)
Canon, Eliza J. to J. C. M. Crews 9-19-1866 (no return)
Cantrell, Penina to Hugh Bateman 9-?-1860 (9-7-1860)
Cantrell, Peronia to Hugh Bateman 9-6-1860 (9-7-1860)
Cantrell, Preciller to J. M. King 1-3-1871 (1-4-1871)
Cantroll, Pollie to Rewbin King 8-5-1871 (8-6-1871)
Capps, Sarah C. to Henry J. Dilday 5-6-1861 (5-12-1861)
Carr, Sarah L. to John M. Carter 11-27-1866
Carrington, Tennessee B. to E. B. Palmer 1-24-1861
Carroll, L. D. to R. B. Baker 11-30-1865 (12-5-1865)
Carroll, M. C. to Hiram Smith 7-20-1872 (no return)
Carroll, N. B. to W. R. Barker 8-14-1867 (no return)
Carroll, S. A. (Mrs.) to W. J. Meador 12-10-1867
Carson, Ann to Robt. Burdit 12-19-1870 (12-20-1870) B
Carson, Betsy to Benjamin Sparks 7-3-1869 (7-4-1869)
Carson, Bettie C. to R. E. D. Smith 1-28-1868
Carson, Dorah to James Sparks 12-31-1872 (1-2-1873) B

Carson, Emaline to Anderson Bell 12-27-1870 (1-2-1871) B
Carter, Amanda L.? to Joseph Wilson 12-17-1867 (12-18-1867)
Carter, F. E. to Lewin? Williamson 7-21-1873 (7-22-1873)
Carter, H. M. E. to D. L. McCarter 3-10-1873 (no return)
Carter, Harritt A. to John Kennon 12-20-1870 (12-21-1870)
Carter, Louiza to Henry Brewder 6-21-1871 (6-22-1871) B
Carter, M. E. to George W. Montgomery 1-3-1870 (1-5-1870)
Carter, Martha E. T. to Joseph S. Biggart 3-5-1868 (no return)
Carter, Mary J. to Thos. J. Cunningham 2-23-1863 (2-26-1863)
Carter, Mary J. to Thos. J. Cunningham 2-25-1863
Carter, Milly to L. N. French 10-7-1867
Carter, Rocinda to Joseph T. Kerby 12-19-1868 (12-23-1868)
Carter, Ruth A. to D. W. Kirby 12-11-1869 (12-12-1869)
Carter, Sarah A. to R. D. Phillips 12-16-1862 (no return)
Carver, Amanda P. to James E. Vancleave 7-24-1868 (7-26-1868)
Carver, Martha to William L. Mann 1-12-1870
Carver, Mary J. to Wm. H. Vancleave 4-1-1869
Carver, Mary T. to E. B. Birmingham 6-17-1871 (6-18-1871)
Cates, Susan E. to Charles H. Haynes 1-26-1870 (1-27-1870)
Cathey, Susan to Henry S. Myer 4-22-1861
Caudle, Mary E. to Edwin Williams 9-25-1865
Cauthern, S. C. to P. R. Owen? 1-13-1868 (1-16-1868)
Cawthan, H. E. to W. H. Woods 1-27-1868 (1-29-1868)
Cawthan, L. A. to W. C. Christian 12-1-1866 (no return)
Cawthan, Martha A. to John M. Worel? 1-9-1863 (no return)
Cawthon, F. A. to Samuel A. Owens 4-23-1866 (4-26-1866)
Cawthon, S. E. to J. R. Owen 10-19-1870 (10-20-1870)
Chadwick, Martha to Edward Johnston 8-9-1860 (8-12-1860)
Chamberlin, Frances J. to James Scott 11-4-1870
Chambers, M. J. to John Pruett 2-7-1871
Chambers, Mary A. to George W. Johnson 11-30-1870
Chambers, Mary A. to R. S. Wyatt 9-13-1870 (9-14-1870)
Chandler, Elizabeth S. to James L. Groom 7-5-1862 (7-11-1862)
Chandler, Ida to J. G. Owenby 12-17-1872 (12-18-1872)
Chandler, July Ann to David A. Liles 8-7-1866 (8-8-1866)
Chandler, Nancy to James L. Groom? 3-20-1868
Chandler, S. F. to Eli W. Arington 8-23-1866
Chaney, Manerva A. to Jesse A. Hughes 9-2-1868 (9-6-1868)
Chilton, Eliza A. to Stephen D. Chandler 3-17-1869 (3-18-1869)
Choate, Margaret A. to W. E. King 11-2-1865 (11-5-1865)
Christian, M. E. to J. H. Lanear 12-18-1866 (12-20-1866)
Churchwell, Mary E. to William L. Rust 12-16-1871 (no return)
Churchwell, V. P. to W. F. Williams 10-24-1871
Clark, Amanda to Mike Jordan 12-27-1870 (12-29-1870) B
Clark, Bell to Noah Briant 12-9-1871 (no return)
Clark, Elizabeth to M. B. (Dr.) Harris 11-16-1861 (11-19-1861)
Clark, Lonezar to Larance Elison 9-26-1870 (10-9-1870)
Clark, Maggie to Joseph Coleman 3-20-1872 (no return) B?
Clark, Mahaly to James Howard 12-27-1870 (no return) B
Clark, Martha J. to John T. Jones 6-9-1873 (no return)
Clark, Molly to Henry Clark 12-18-1869 (12-23-1869)
Clark, Permelia W. to J. H. Palmer 11-23-1863 (no return)
Clark, Prudence to George Wyatt 9-25-1871 (10-2-1871) B
Clark, S.? M. to E. F. Parish 3-14-1872
Clark, Willy to David Little 8-7-1868 (8-12-1868)
Clarke, Jane to D. J. Shofner 5-15-1861
Clay, Annie to L. A. Hurt 6-28-1870 (6-30-1870)
Clay, Bettie to George Utley 8-29-1872
Clay, Jane to Adam Hurt 5-14-1870 (5-15-1870)
Clay, Judy to John Jones 10-4-1869 (10-9-1869)
Clay, Lue to Robt. Bell 10-5-1870 (10-6-1870)
Cleaver, Emily to Jasper Henley 1-8-1870 (no return)
Clemons, Millie to Monro Patton 9-5-1870 (no return)
Cloid, Amanda J. to J. J. Rochell 1-15-1873 (no return)
Cloyd, Mary Jane to James A. Kerly 8-9-1860 (8-12-1860)
Cobb, Catharine to A. Young 11-27-1867 (11-28-1867)
Cobb, Ellen E. to Charles M. Ross 6-10-1863
Cobb, Ellen E. to Charles M. Ross 6-10-1863 (6-14-1863)
Cobb, Ellen E. to Charles M. Ross 6-10-1863 (no return)
Cobb, Martha S. to William F. Bennett 1-28-1869
Cobb, Newty L. to J. Z. Nash 1-30-1869 (1-31-1869)
Coble, M. C. to D. M. Lankford 4-9-1867 (4-10-1867)
Coble, Mary Ann to R. D. Dickson 10-5-1861 (10-6-1861)
Coble, Mary Ann to Richard D. Dickson 10-?-1861 (10-6-1861)
Cody, Criddie to John Burdet 8-31-1872 (no return) B

Cody, Jeroline to Madison Covington 1-26-1870
Coffman, Nancy E. to T. D. Vawter 12-24-1870 (12-25-1870)
Coldwell, Rachel M. to Thos. A. McNeill 8-11-1862 (no return)
Cole, Adline to Loyd Stokes 10-26-1870 (10-27-1870)
Cole, Anna to J. W. Walters 2-22-1872
Cole, Joe Ann to Camillus Hawkins 11-9-1868 (11-12-1868)
Cole, Mary J. to Wm. R. Granade 12-11-1865 (12-14-1865)
Cole, Sallie to Willie Ridley 1-11-1871 (1-12-1871)
Coleman, Elizabeth to John Dudley 4-11-1871 (4-15-1871)
Coleman, Hanah to Geor. Gardner 6-10-1871
Coleman, M. L. to G. H. Morgan 12-29-1866 (12-20-1866)
Coleman, M. L. to J. W. Fuqua 3-2-1868 (3-4-1868)
Coleman, Nannie B. to Elvis R. Traywick 12-26-1872
Coleman, Santefee B. to J. G. Sayles 7-9-1862 (no return)
Collins, Sopha to Berry Hurt 10-12-1867
Colvet, Ellen C. to Columbus J.? Wilds 10-15-1872 (10-6?-1872)
Colvett, Mary J. to John Key 12-26-1866 (12-27-1866)
Comer, E. J. to S. R. Shaw 12-1-1861 (12-2-1865?)
Comer, E. J. to S. R. Shaw 12-?-1861 (12-2-1861)
Comer, Susan F. to Andrew Pinckley 12-18-1869 (12-19-1869)
Compton, M. J. to J. C. Modlin 3-4-1865 (3-5-1865)
Compton, P. C. to N. G. Muzzall 1-2-1871 (1-5-1871)
Compton, S. E. to W. C. Bomar 9-7-1869
Comton, M. A. to G. H. Wadkins 6-1-1868 (6-4-1868)
Connell, Susan J. to Robert Mann 9-15-1871 (9-20-1871)
Cook, Emma to James A. Johnson 8-26-1863 (8-27-1863)
Cook, Mary to Henderson Burrow 11-15-1871 (no return)
Cook, Sarah L. to C. B. Mays 7-11-1866 (7-19-1866)
Cooper, Corilla to William B. Chandler 5-21-1869
Cooper, Elizabeth C. to Robert E. Myers 2-11-1863
Cooper, Elizabeth to Robert E. Myers 2-11-1863
Cooper, L. to W. J. Fuqua 9-10-1864 (9-12-1864)
Cooper, Lula to W. A. Dinwiddie 6-18-1872 (no return)
Cooper, M. A. to J. B. Wren 10-22-1868
Cooper, Mary A. to John J. Wingo 5-8-1864
Cooper, Mary F. to David N. Wilson 12-25-1869 (12-26-1869)
Cooper, Mary J. to Moses R. Allen 12-23-1862
Cooper, Missouria A. to Moses Myers 12-12-1864 (12-13-1864)
Corder, Susan to S. J. McCullough 12-3-1872 (12-5-1872)
Corley, Mary Jane to William Hornbuckle 2-5-1864 (5-30-1864)
Corley, Mary Jane to Wm. Hornbuckle 2-5-1864 (no return)
Covington, Ann to Alfred Henderson 12-8-1869 (12-9-1869)
Covington, Mary E. to Luke Thomas 11-19-1870 (11-24-1870)
Cox, A. C. to James F. Taylor 9-21-1869 (9-23-1869)
Cox, Amanda E. to Ellis Scales 1-23-1863 (1-29-1863)
Cox, Jimmie Ann to Haywood C. Stoker 4-18-1870 (4-19-1870)
Cox, L. A. to C. F. Greenfield 9-26-1870 (9-27-1870)
Cox, Latitica A. to John W. French 7-21-1866 (7-22-1866)
Cox, Mary S. to James M. Martin 8-14-1861 (8-15-1861)
Cox, Mary to James M. Horton? 8-?-1861 (8-15-1861)
Cox, Susan E. to William W. Barns 11-28-1868 (11-29-1868)
Cozart, Elizabeth to Priestley Gooch 8-13-1870 (8-14-1870)
Crabb, Martha E. to J. J. Allen 10-24-1871 (no return)
Craddoc, E. D. to J. H. Clay 5-21-1873 (5-22-1873)
Craft, Judith L. to James W. Matheny 2-23-1870 (no return)
Crafter, Sarah L. to James T. Gilkey 1-11-1870 (1-13-1870)
Cravens, Darthula to Westly Williams 11-21-1865
Crawford, M. J. to W. T. Swaringin 12-3-1864 (12-5-1864)
Crawford, N. A. to J. Y. Britt 9-8-1869 (9-9-1869)
Crawford, Rachel J. to William S. McCall 6-3-1861 (no return)
Crews, Elizabeth to Bolivar Leek 6-4-1860 (6-5-1860)
Crews, Harriet V. to Allen G. McColum 1-6-1868 (1-7-1868)
Crews, Parilee J. to Joseph H. Watkins 12-5-1870 (12-6-1870)
Cribbs, Clarinda E.? to James C.? Elzan 7-28-1860 (7-31-1860)
Cribbs, Sarah E. to W. D. Argo 9-8-1866 (no return)
Crider, Beanthur to Eli D. Brown 11-8-1862 (11-9-1862)
Crider, Betty to Richard Tucker 4-2-1872 (4-3-1872) B
Crider, Catharine to Daniel H. Dalton 12-23-1867 (12-24-1867)
Crider, E. B. to J. C. Hall 12-17-1872 (12-18-1872)
Crider, Mary E. to Joseph S. Brown 12-20-1866
Crockett, Alice C. to Henry C. Townes 12-17-1868
Crockett, Mary E. to Charles B. Grizzard 12-17-1861 (12-18-1861)
Crockett, Mary E. to Charles B. Grizzard 12-19-1861
Crockett, S. E. to Z. T. Smothers 4-25-1872 (no return)
Crofford, Lanah to Steward Cody 10-27-1870 (10-28-1870) B

Cross, Elizabeth S.? to Jason A. Bridges 6-23-1860 (6-25-1860)
Crossett, Sarah M. to Robert Vawter 1-11-1870 (no return)
Crosswell, Julia to S. P. Leflore 10-20-1869 (10-21-1869)
Crow, Rebeca to Jess Montgomery 7-1-1867
Crowder, Susan H. to W. T. Jackson 10-7-1867 (10-10-1867)
Crowel, Nancy Jane to James B. Leech 12-12-1868 (12-15-1868)
Cruise, Mary to Presly Night 10-5-1870 (10-6-1870)
Crutchfield, Elizabeth C. to William H. Fields 12-21-1864 (12-22-1864)
Crutchfield, Harriet to Cane Baucom 4-19-1871 (4-20-1871) B
Culp, Elizabeth to Edward White 8-11-1869 (8-12-1869)
Culp, Sarah to Jonathan Bell 10-27-1871 (no return)
Cumpton, Della to Sam Rowland 7-29-1868 (7-30-1868)
Cunagham, Mary to Marshall Bridgeman 7-13-1871
Cuningham, M. to S. S. Long 8-21-1872 (no return) B
Cunningham, Alice to John Lambert 3-11-1870 (3-13-1870)
Cunningham, Alice to Ned Woodson 1-22-1869 (1-23-1869)
Cunningham, Betty to Doctor Woodson 6-28-1871 (6-29-1871) B
Cunningham, L. E. to W. A. C. Bridges 12-16-1867 (12-18-1867)
Cunningham, Louiza to Patrick J. Welch 5-28-1873
Cunningham, Macilda E. to Wallis Pollard 4-22-1870 (4-24-1870)
Cunningham, Mary E. to Alexander H. Goodloe 12-21-1863 (no return)
Cunningham, Mary E. to L. M. Huffman 2-3-1870
Cunningham, Mary J. to James F. Turner 3-23-1868 (3-24-1868)
Cunningham, Mollie to Mitchell Clark 12-5-1868 (12-6-1868)
Cunningham, Sarah J. to Thomas Little 3-11-1863
Cunningham, Sarah J. to Thomas Little 3-11-1863 (no return)
Cunningham, Sarah to Thos. Hooker 1-13-1869 (1-21-1869)
Cunningham, Susan to Thomas Goodin 5-2-1870 (no return)
Curren, V. R. to J. W. Brasher 10-22-1870 (10-23-1870)
Darby, Martha S. to J. P. Clark 11-3-1866 (11-5-1866)
Darnall, Amand to Stephen Mayes 9-2-1872 (no return) B
Darnall, Mary A. to David C. Vickers 3-4-1863
Darnall, Mary A. to David C. Vickers 3-4-1863 (no return)
Darnall, Mary E. to J. B. Fuller 11-16-1867 (11-17-1867)
Darnell, Caladonia J. to J. H. McKiney 9-17-1861 (9-23-1861)
David, Luvica W. to James W. Ray 8-6-1860 (8-8-1860)
Davis, Margaret A. to Austin McAdoo 9-?-1862 (9-14-1866?)
Davis, Martha J. to Jas. M. Benton 9-25-1866 (9-27-1866)
Davis, Martha T. to P. H. Nance 10-5-1864 (10-9-1864)
Davis, Nancy J. to Thomas H. Faris 2-12-1863 (no return)
Davis, Nancy J. to Thos. H. Farris 2-12-1863
Davis, Nancy to Bevily Towns 11-1-1871 (11-15-1871)
Davis, Sarah A. to James A. Johnson 10-30-1860
Davis, Sarah C. to James W. Hamel 11-27-1872
Delaney, Mary L. to Green Broach 3-12-1863 (no return)
Delany, Araminta to M. D. Braswell 7-18-1860 (no return)
Delany, Mary L. to Green Brach 3-12-1863 (no return)
Delany, P. to J. M. McClusky 1-5-1866 (1-6-1866)
Demoss, Amanda C. to Harey Todd 8-16-1865 (no return)
Demoss, Matilda C. to James P. Gee 8-6-1861 (8-7-1861)
Denning, S. E. to J. M. Todd 9-10-1869 (9-12-1869)
Denton, A. E. to R. M. Hooker 1-28-1865 (1-29-1865)
Denton, Ellen W. to Abe White 11-10-1869 (11-11-1869)
Denton, Mollie to Briant Nowlin 11-27-1871 (no return)
Deshong, Mollie G. to P. C. Loveless 12-27-1865 (12-28-1865)
Dewhit, Mary B. to E. G. H. Bennett 1-7-1866
Dickason, Mollie L. to Geor. B. Garrett 6-3-1872 (6-5-1872)
Dickenson, Nancy J. to A. T. Butler 1-26-1866 (1-28-1866)
Dickson, J. M. to James A. Canon 1-3-1861 (1-6-1861)
Dickson, Susan E. to J. H. Dickinson 7-24-1869 (8-4-1869)
Dickson, Vandalia to Levi Shad 1-24-1870 (1-27-1870)
Diggs, Elizabeth to James R. Vinson 1-31-1872
Diggs, Mintee to William Garner 11-4-1860 (not endorsed)
Diggs, Winney to Charles Dilday 8-5-1869
Dilday, Nancy to James W. Pruett 8-9-1865 (8-10-1865)
Dilday, Sarah to William S. May 2-10-1863
Dildy, A. J. to J. M. Eskew 11-1-1870
Dildy, Elizabeth to John Walker 1-30-1867 (no return)
Dilelay?, Ann to Wyley P. Gibson 3-12-1861
Dill, Eliza J. to James H. Noell 12-20-1865
Dill, Lucy to James Huffman 11-7-1866 (11-8-1866)
Dill, Lydia B. to Benager Stewart 4-4-1868 (4-5-1868)
Dill, Martha E. to Alphonzo Freeland 11-15-1865 (11-16-1865)

Dill, N. C. to John C. Laycook 12-31-1868
Dill, Sallie to J. J. Christerbery 2-7-1867
Dillion?, Catharine to Wiley Smothers 6-30-1869
Dodd, Elizabeth C. to James M. Tosh 1-9-1871 (1-10-1871)
Dodd, Rebecca F. to Robert C. Hill 3-27-1866 (3-29-1866)
Doherity, Nannie to James Haris 9-26-1870 (9-28-1870)
Doherty, Esther to Lewis Russell 6-1-1870 (6-5-1870)
Dolan, Mary J. to Robert Dolan 12-22-1866 (12-23-1866)
Dollar, S. C. to Asher Simpson 1-3-1871
Dollohite, Temperance to Josiah Cook 8-9-1860 (8-14-1860)
Dolron, Sarah E. to Ed Nesbett 1-25-1871 (1-26-1871)
Dougherty, Irene E. to R. G.? Cook 9-10-1867 (no return)
Dozier, Emma J. to T. A. White 6-12-1871
Drake, Eleira? to James Henderson 2-3-1868 (2-6-1868)
Drake, O. V. to J. F. Barksdale 2-20-1865 (no return)
Drewry, Florence A. to J. K. Kearney 12-27-1869 (12-28-1869)
Driggers, Penelopee L. to Worelson Clements 12-21-1860 (12-25-1860)
Drinkard, Sarah F. to Benjamin Todd 10-21-1865 (10-29-1865)
Dueley, Eliza C. to William P. Harrelson 10-18-1860
Duglas, Lucinda to Antina Pearson 6-14-1872 (no return) B
Duncan, Ellen to Adam Little 7-30-1870 (7-31-1870)
Duncan, Ellen to Thomas Franklin 9-23-1867 (9-24-1867)
Duncan, Susan F. to H. O. Park 3-30-1861 (4-5-1861)
Duning, M. L. to A. J. Rogers 12-2-1872 (12-5-1872)
Earls, Harriett F. to John L. Carter 1-28-1868 (1-30-1868)
Eason, C. J. to L. F. Butler 6-8-1867
Eason, Louisa to W. E. Mebane 1-29-1867 (1-30-1867)
Edmerson, N. C. to J. W. Mann 3-23-1872 (3-24-1872)
Edmison, Margaret to Joseph Mitchell 2-8-1869 (no return)
Edwards, Ann to James May 1-12-1863 (no return)
Edwards, Julie to N. J. Wren 11-18-1867 (11-20-1867)
Edwards, L. E. to J. H. Taylor 9-21-1871
Edwards, Lavina H. to H. C. Demoss 11-28-1866 (11-29-1866)
Edwards, M. E. to W. B. Briant 2-14-1870 (2-15-1870)
Edwards, Martha J. to H. J. Boren 12-26-1865 (12-28-1865)
Edwards, Nannie to Frank Prince 12-15-1872 B
Elenor, F. M. to A. H. Miller 9-25-1872 (9-26-1872)
Elkins, Mary E. to C. A. Rogers 1-22-1873 (1-23-1873)
Elliner, M. J. to J. G. Rust 7-27-1863 (7-27-1866?)
Ellinor, Martha J. to C. T. Rust 8-1-1867 (8-2-1867)
Ellis, Catharine E. to William Maynard 4-15-1870 (4-17-1870)
Ellis, Mary to John O. Keane 10-25-1860 (10-28-1860)
Ellmor, M. J. to John Y. Rust 7-27-1862 (no return)
Enloe, Mollie E. to William W. Deshong 6-8-1869 (6-10-1869)
Enochs, Martha F. to R. J. Hill 10-7-1872 (10-9-1872)
Enocks, Celia to John L. Cozart 12-23-1869 (12-26-1869)
Erocker, T. E. to J. R. Scott 12-14-1865 (12-21-1865)
Eskew, M. E. to H. H. Tosh 11-30-1871 (12-15-1871)
Eskew, S. J. to J. W. Adams 12-12-1872 (no return)
Eubanks, F. to Calvin King 2-12-1864 (2-14-1864)
Evans, Mary L. to J. H. McKiney 11-2-1865 (11-5-1865)
Evans, Mary L. to W. M. Warren 10-10-1860 (not executed)
Evans, Sally to G. Busbee 2-14-1870 (2-17-1870)
Everett, Elizabeth to Thomas Spears 3-22-1869 (3-23-1869)
Everett, M. C. to J. A. Hill 9-17-1866 (9-18-1866)
Everett, Margarett to Jas. H. Cannon 12-18-1872 (no return)
Everett, Mary M. H. to W. M. Cannon 12-19-1866
Everett, Rebecca to G. L. Lutsinger 11-26-1870 (11-27-1870)
Everett, S. A. to Wm. B. Everett 12-7-1860
Everett, Tempey to N. C. Tomlinson 7-17-1872 (no return)
Everitt, Sarah A. to William B. Everett? 12-7-1860 (12-13-1860)
Ezell, Caroline to E. D. Phipps 7-17-1860 (no return)
Ezell, Harriet to Harvy Gregory 2-20-1869
Ezell, Louisa to W. H. Cox 3-28-1865 (3-30-1865)
Falkner, Margarett to John Orr 10-18-1865
Felps, Elizabeth to Benjamin D. Vincent 1-29-1868 (no return)
Fergerson, Ann to Thomas Keirman 4-10-1869 (4-17-1869)
Field, S. B. to L. B. Listen 12-22-1870
Fields, Caroline to John Gray 2-17-1869 (2-18-1869)
Fields, M. E. to J. J. Fussell 4-22-1867
Fields, T. E. to John Gray 1-21-1871 (1-24-1871)
Finch, Flenda to John H. Park 2-9-1861 (2-10-1861)
Finley, M. J. to M. F. Roney 12-31-1862 (1-1-1863)
Finly?, Kezziah to Hadley Merritt 1-16-1861

Fish, Martha C. to Hance S. Eskew 12-?-1861 (12-22-1861)
Fisher, Fanny to Wm. Goodrun 4-1-1869 (4-27-1869)
Fisher, Julia A. S. to Z. R. Walker 4-21-1866 (no return)
Fite, E. J. to R. H. Bellew 9-17-1872 (9-18-1872)
Fite, H. E. to A. Davis 3-18-1871 (4-11-1871)
Flack, Mary E. to Hulon? W. Grizzard 11-20-1860 (11-21-1860)
Flake, Delpha A. to Henry C. Wall 10-20-1871 (10-22-1871)
Flake, Elizabeth to James Olive 9-9-1865 (9-13-1866?)
Flake, M. J. to L. H. Meals? 1-6-1873
Fletcher, Emma G. to F. H. Pate 5-15-1869 (5-17-1869)
Fletcher, L. A. to C. T. Allen 6-7-1865 (6-8-1865)
Fletcher, M. J. to Thos. D. Ingram 11-13-1866 (11-14-1866)
Fletcher, Mollie P. to E. L. Rice 2-6-1871 (no return)
Fly, Mollie D. to R. L. (Dr.) Bigham 5-22-1867 (5-23-1867)
Forluss, Mary J. to Francis M. Laycock 7-28-1860 (7-29-1860)
Forrest, Amanda to Monroe Lane 4-8-1869
Forrest, Eliza J. to Richard Lewis 1-28-1868 (1-30-1868)
Forrest, Martha E. to Joseph Dane 9-17-1868 (no return)
Forsheer, M. L. V. to Lewis K. Kee 8-6-1873 (8-7-1873)
Foshee, Lenora to Jesse Worrel 1-1-1870 (1-2-1870)
Foster, Elizabeth to James Webb 8-4-1865 (8-6-1865)
Foster, Lucy to James Madison 11-13-1871 (no return) B
Foster, Martha to Henry Webb 10-17-1867
Foster, N. M. to R. F. Webb 8-15-1871 (no return)
Fowler, Mattie H. to J. H. Coleman 6-24-1870 (6-28-1870)
Fowler, S. A. to Thos. L. Taylor 5-28-1873 (no return)
Fox, Agnus S. to E. Gustan 8-8-1865 (no return)
Fox, M. E. to J. H. Patton 1-23-1869 (1-26-1869)
Freeland, Ardella to John Dunn 4-5-1864 (4-7-1864)
Freeman, E. J. to H. P. Martin 6-19-1869 (6-20-1869)
Freeman, Mary E. to Milton H. Crider 1-16-1864 (no return)
Freeman, Mary E. to Milton H. Crider 1-26-1864 (no return)
French, Elizaeth C. to James G. Wilson 2-24-1870
French, Lovey A. to J. P. Medlin 11-11-1864 (11-12-1864)
French, Nancy to James S. May 3-5-1870
French, Nancy to Jarrett Taylor 6-4-1864
French, Sarah C. to Henry Carter 10-30-1869 (10-31-1869)
Frisbee, Sarah to Henry Hudson 10-22-1860
Fry, Emma J. to Johns W. Jolly 10-1-1861
Fry, Mollie B. to J. L. Montgomery 10-18-1870 (10-19-1870)
Fulks, Ann to Milton McDonal 3-12-1872 B
Fuller, Harriet to Columbus Carter 1-21-1870
Fuller, Lena to Andrew Barham 8-23-1871 (8-24-1871) B
Fuller, Levina to Wm. Richardson 4-9-1873 B
Fuqua, Elizabeth to R. A. Bellew 9-14-1866
Fuqua, Ellen to G. W. Boswell 1-23-1871 (no return)
Fuqua, M. M. to Clinton Adjn 5-28-1865 (6-8-1865)
Fuqua, Martha E. M. to T. J. Higgs 1-22-1870 (1-27-1870)
Fuqua, Sarah E. to C. L. Keaton 8-4-1868 (no return)
Fuqua, Virginia H. to J. A. Moss 1-18-1865
Furgerson, Lucinda to Isom Robinson 1-17-1871 (2-4-1871) B
Fussell, J.? A. to B. F. Arington 5-23-1861 (5-18-1861)
Fussell, Mary J. to W. A. Rogers 9-2-1861 (9-3-1861)
Fussell, N. E. to R. H. Surber 3-4-1872 (3-7-1870?)
Gaines, Emma to Alfred McNeill 4-20-1870 (4-21-1870)
Gallimore, Frances J. to F. L. Green 9-16-1865 (9-20-1865)
Gardner, Hester? B. to Samuel W. Hawkins 3-20-1867
Gardner, J. A. to W. B. Carroll 9-4-1871
Gardner, Mary J. to George White no date (with Feb 1863)
Gardner, Mary L. to J. W. Mitchell 1-21-1868 (1-22-1868)
Gardner, Saletha to Joseph Hester 9-11-1871 (9-12-1871)
Gardner, Susan M. to Thomas Rosebery 4-14-1866 (4-15-1866)
Garner, M. J. to W. T. Reynolds 6-22-1861 (8-1-1861)
Garrett, Amand to L. L. French 2-16-1871
Garrison, Mary E. to James D. Walker 2-?-1862 (no return)
Gateley, Sarah P. to E. H. Roaz 1-11-1865 (1-14-1865)
Gately, Mary to William R. Hampton 2-?-1866 (2-26-1866)
Gately, Sarah E. to Nelson Evans 1-3-1870
Gatland, Susan to E. W. Morgan 12-15-1862 (12-16-1862)
Gee, A. S. to Henry Comes 1-1-1873 (1-2-1873)
Gee, Eliza F. to Fleming C. Todd 10-21-1861 (10-22-1861)
Gee, Frances A. to N. G. Warbriton 12-12-1864
Gee, M. W. to J.H. Merrett 1-17-1871 (1-20-1871)
Gee, Matilda E. to Westly Brasier 1-1-1866 (1-4-1866)
George, Melvina to A. R. Hall 12-13-1870 (12-15-1870)

George, Sarah C. to J. W. Foster 12-11-1865 (12-31-1865)
Gibbons, Margarett L. to J. W. Mills 9-18-1865 (9-20-1865)
Gibbons, Virginia C. to Willie C. Richardson 11-29-1871 (11-30-1871)
Gibson, Jemima to James F. Hopkins 3-25-1868
Gibson, Milissia A. to A. A. O'Kane 8-8-1873 (9-3-1873)
Gilbert, Eliza to Joseph Moore 9-25-1868 (9-27-1868)
Gilbert, Ellen to Robert Gilbert 2-18-1870 (2-20-1870)
Gilbert, Emeline to Joseph Gilbert 1-21-1871 (no return) B
Gilbert, Esabella to George Drake 9-2-1868 (9-3-1868)
Gilbert, Vira to Carroll Moore 12-25-1871 (no return) B
Giles, Bettie (Mrs.) to John R. Rust 10-12-1867 (10-13-1867)
Giles, M. C. to J. C. McCollum 12-28-1872 (12-29-1872)
Giles, Susan C. to R. E. Bogle 12-27-1868 (12-28-1868)
Gilkey, E. J. to J. A. Harper 3-4-1869 (3-7-1869)
Gill, Mary C. to W. J. Johnson 3-12-1870 (3-13-1870)
Gist, Elizabeth to John Tesh 9-26-1861
Glancy, Julie to Patrick Johnson 9-24-1866 (9-28-1866)
Glover, E. A. to J. F. Lewis 12-2-1871 (no return)
Glover, Elizabeth to William H. Houston 3-17-1866 (3-18-1866)
Glover, Martha E. to William J. Boaz 2-7-1862 (no return)
Gooch, L. J. to J. G. Mebane 2-4-1868 (2-5-1868)
Gooch, Mary C. to Cannon Horn 12-23-1872 (12-24-1872)
Gooch, Sarah to Benjamin King 9-20-1871 B
Goodwin, Lou J. to Richard B. Moore 11-10-1870 (11-24-1870)
Gordan, Betsey to Pearse Gwinn 12-23-1871 (no return) B
Gorden, Mary to Rafe Dinwiddie 1-15-18?? (1-27-1870)
Gordon, Caroline to Jack Howard 2-27-1871
Gordon, Kandis to Jackson Gordon 4-5-1869
Gowan, M. J. to J. T. Turner 2-8-1873 (2-18-1873)
Gowan, Martha E. to George H. Martin 11-14-1868 (11-12?-1868)
Gowen, Mary F. to J. C. C. Thompson 12-12-1865 (12-14-1865)
Graham, Cintha J. to W. P. Woodard 1-8-1868 (1-9-1868)
Graham, Mary E. to J. M. Maynard 6-28-1871
Grant, Charlotte to William Widdis 4-12-1869 (4-13-1869)
Grant, H. L. to M. N. C. Robins 12-13-1867 (12-16-1867)
Graves, M. C. to A. M. Green 3-7-1867 (3-11-1867)
Graves, P. J. to J. F. Jarratt 1-16-1864 (no return)
Graves, P. J. to J. T. Jarrett 1-16-1864 (1-17-1864)
Gray, Margarett M. to George Taylor 1-21-1864 (no return)
Gray, Sarah T. to James T. Williams 1-29-1870 (2-3-1870)
Green, A. V. to J. D. Singleton 12-12-1871 (12-14-1871)
Green, Elizabeth to J. D. Abbott 9-5-1870 (9-6-1870)
Green, Emily M. to J. M. Manning 7-10-1871 (7-12-1871)
Green, Eveline to Solomon Hannings 12-2-1868 (12-6-1868)
Green, G. V. to T. L. Green 9-3-1870 (9-4-1870)
Green, I. J. to G. M. Holmes 12-23-1867 (12-25-1867)
Green, Louza to James Taylor 9-4-1865 (no return)
Green, Lucy to Henry Riggins 10-9-1872
Green, M. P. to David M. Butler 10-8-1870 (10-9-1870)
Green, Martha T. to Erasmus Piper 8-9-1860
Green, Mary A. to W. H. Palmer 11-1-1871 (no return)
Green, Mary Ann R. to S. Horn 5-18-1870
Green, Mary E. to Thomas Grooms 12-13-1869 (12-14-1869)
Green, Mary E. to W. R. Garrett 9-23-1862 (9-25-1862)
Green, Minnie to Joseph Hill 12-20-1871 (no return)
Green, Mollie to Nathan Piger 6-26-1869 (6-27-1869)
Green, Nancy A. to N. L. Rice 3-27-1868 (3-29-1868)
Green, Nancy C. to Miles J. Roberts 9-6-1860 (9-19-1860)
Green, Nancy J. to A. H. Holmes 10-19-1866 (10-21-1866)
Green, W. A. to W. P. Harness 10-23-1869
Greenwood, D. A. to James T. Lingo 9-11-1860 (9-13-1860)
Greenwood, D. A. to James T.? Lingo 9-11-1860 (9-13-1860)
Greenwood, Mary E. to Virgil R. Burk 6-12-1863
Greenwood, Mary E. to Virgil R. Burk 6-12-1863 (no return)
Greer, Eliza to Richard Clay 4-19-1870 (4-20-1870)
Gregory, Mattie to Jack Culp 10-25-1870 (10-26-1870) B
Gregory, Sina to Arch McCollum 2-3-1872 (no return) B
Gregory, Sinia to Arch McCollum 1-7-1870 (not endorsed)
Griffin, Adline to B. C. Clark 4-2-1867
Griffin, America to B. H. Looney 1-17-1870 (1-18-1870)
Grifin, Elzira to Moses Garrison 10-30-1865
Grisson, Mary Jane to J. A. W. G. Rogers 7-31-1861 (8-1-1861)
Grizzard, Mary to Pleasant Wright 8-23-1870 (8-24-1870)
Grogan, Elizabeth to J. B. Brandon 11-7-1872
Grogan, Martha J. to John O. Wall 1-6-1870 (1-7-1870)

Groom, Mary B. to Jesse P. French 1-6-1870
Groom, Mary F. to Thos. W. Groom 3-1-1871
Grooms, Louiza to James Angle 7-11-1871
Grooms, Susan A. to Wm. Cobb 9-27-1870 (10-16-1870)
Guffe, Amanda C. to John W. Tucker 1-2-1869
Guffee, Margarett to R. A. Clopton 3-4-1868 (3-15-1868)
Guinn, Eliza to Shad Cunningham 12-31-1869
Guinn, Victoria to Joseph Dinwiddie 12-29-1868 (1-2-1869)
Gullage, Elizabeth to Urias Springer 12-13-1870
Gullage, Martha C. to Newton C. Stanly 9-12-1860
Gulledge, D. J. to H. C. Scott 6-22-1867 (6-23-1867)
Gullet, A. E. to J. R. Hickman 1-11-1869 (1-14-1869)
Guthrie, Callie to L. T. Landrum 6-3-1872 (6-5-1872)
Guthrie, Corar to James W. Wilder 9-24-1867 (no return)
Guthrie, Jane to John Hines 1-15-1872 (no return) B
Gwinn, C. C. to J. J. Berryhill 10-11-1871 (10-12-1871)
Haines, Fannie to John D. Lush 12-11-1860 (12-13-1860)
Hall, Delia M. to James Stephenson 11-7-1868 (11-8-1868)
Hall, M. J. to E. T. McAuly 2-4-1868 (2-5-1868)
Hall, Martha to John Brown 9-6-1862 (9-8-1862)
Hall, Mary Ann to John F. Carlton 10-28-1861 (no return)
Hall, Mary E. to J. R. Hill 1-1-1873 (1-2-1873)
Hall, Mary E. to James B. McCally 2-13-1870
Hall, N. E. to J. L. Wood 12-12-1865 (12-15-1865)
Hall, Nancy E. B. to Thomas Butler 10-29-1860 (10-30-1860)
Hall, Nancy J. to William Baker 6-1-1870 (6-2-1870)
Hallmark, Mary A. to George Townsend 7-29-1871
Hallum, Emarilla J. to John D. Stroud 9-20-1869 (9-22-1869)
Hambleton, Susan to J. N. Freeman 10-8-1870 (10-9-1870)
Hamilton, E. J. to J. D. Thompson 10-17-1867 (no return)
Hamilton, E. T. O. to John Spelling 9-19-1867 (no return)
Hamilton, Edney S. to B. F. Garner 1-15-1872 (1-16-1872)
Hamilton, Elizabeth P. to Wilbron H. Graves 9-22-1858
Hamilton, Manerva to George W. Graves 6-6-1861
Hamilton, Martha F. to G. S. Gardner 2-12-1863
Hamilton, Minerva to George W. Graves 6-?-1861 (6-6-1861)
Hamilton, Nancy L. to J. H. Gardner 11-27-1860 (11-28-1860)
Hamilton, Nancy L. to J. H. Gardner 11-27-1863 (no return)
Hamilton, Narcissa H. to James W. Ozier 10-15-1867 (no return)
Hammer, Cordelia to S. E. Williamson 4-1-1871 (4-4-1871)
Hammett, Frances to Nelson Clark 10-26-1861 (10-30-1861)
Hammett, Martha to Jorden Jamison 7-6-1870 (7-10-1870)
Hammett, Mary C. to John C. Antry 2-26-1861 (no return)
Hampton, Edy to Andrew Flake 1-8-1872 (no return) B
Hampton, Harriet to Louis Gordon 3-21-1872 (no return)
Hampton, Lizzie to John Hart 3-7-1871 B
Hampton, Louisa to Henry Hargus 1-27-1869 (1-29-1869)
Hampton, Martha Ann to James Phillips 2-17-1866
Hampton, Mollie to Edward Barnett 10-2-1869
Hampton, S. A. J. to J. A. Brown 5-30-1864 (5-31-1864)
Hampton, Sarah E. to Benjamin Taylor Phillips 12-8-1866
    (12-12-1866)
Hampton, Sarah L. to J. M. King 3-21-1868 (3-22-1868)
Hanfred?, Frances E. to Jason Pritchard 3-24-1866? (3-25-1868)
Hanna, E. C. to N. W. Hanna 12-22-1864 (1-1-1865)
Hanna, S. J. to J. A. Crow 1-16-1869 (1-20-1869)
Hannah, Agness to G. W. Dismukes 12-10-1867 (12-11-1867)
Hannah, Bettie to G. B. Hrris 7-25-1868 (7-27-1868)
Hansbro, Callie T. to W. T. Younger 1-16-1869 (no return)
Harder, Lucy A. to Chas. M. Ross 4-22-1871 (4-27-1871)
Hardister, Addie T. to Joseph W. Felts 8-31-1865 (no return)
Hardister, D. P. to A. P. Felts 4-16-1866 (4-25-1866)
Hardy, Currillea J. to N. H. Belew 11-23-1870 (no return)
Hardy, Martha E. to Johnson Perrett 10-16-1872
Hardy, Martha E. to W. H. Rose 3-4-1861 (3-19-1861)
Hardy, Mary F. to Thomas H. H. Carter 12-18-1869 (12-19-1869)
Hardy, Verona A. to James R. Belew 12-22-1869 (12-23-1869)
Harman, J. A. F. to J. H. Garrett 9-21-1871
Harper, Allice to Richard Newbill 12-28-1872 (12-24?-1872)
Harper, Annie to Thomas Cruse 7-7-1865 (7-10-1865)
Harper, Elizabeth to Nimrod Burrow 11-15-1861 (no return)
Harper, Emily to Wm. Newbill 12-4-1863 (no return)
Harper, M. C. to P. W. Hester 8-6-1865
Harper, N. H. to J. J. Carroll 2-13-1873
Harper, Susan G. to W. R. Sparks 3-8-1873 (3-28-1873)

Harrell, M. J. to Wm. H. Vawter 1-2-1866 (1-3-1866)
Harrell, Martha S. to B. F. Woodall 9-16-1861 (no return)
Harrell, Molly to Wm. D. Lannum 11-28-1864 (no return)
Harris, Adaline to Ralph Davis 3-19-1869 (no return)
Harris, E. F. to J. W. Smith 5-29-1866 (6-3-1866)
Harris, Manerva to Lee Foster 12-24-1872 (12-26-1872) B
Harris, Maria to Robert Coleman 12-28-1869
Harris, Martha to Jacob Ross 5-13-1863 (5-16-1863)
Harris, Mary to B. F. Warbritten 12-21-1864 (12-22-1864)
Harris, Sarah to S. S. Nesbitt 12-26-1864 (12-27-1864)
Harris, Sarah to Samuel L. Swinney 4-17-1868 (no return)
Hart, Ginny to William Kates 7-23-1868 (no return)
Hart, M. T. to James K. P. Clements 8-31-1868 (9-3-1868)
Harvy, N. C. to Henry C. Stone 8-29-1866 (no return)
Hassell, Mary to Samuel McCollum 12-14-1869 (12-16-1869)
Hatch, Dillie to J. W. Evans 4-23-1872 (no return)
Hatch, Sopha A. to B. C. Smith 1-24-1872 (1-25-1872)
Hawkins, Flora A. to J. W. McCullough 9-25-1869 (9-26-1869)
Hawkins, Julia to Jasper Phillips 6-22-1872 (no return) B
Hawkins, Laura to Freeman Johnson 8-5-1870 (no return)
Hawkins, Margaret to Samuel Prince 12-25-1868 (12-30-1868)
Hayley, Louisa to J. H. Drummonds 10-30-1867
Haynes, Charity to Robt. Ridley 12-22-1870 (12-29-1870) B
Haynes, H. M. to T. W. Younger 2-10-1865 (2-12-1865)
Haynes, Mary F. to Thomas F. Diggs 10-3-1860 (no return)
Haynes, Mary Q. to J. M. Riggs 12-27-1869 (12-29-1869)
Haynes, Tabitha E. to J. M. Oliver 5-5-1866 (5-9-1866)
Haywood, Luisa to Presley King 12-8-1865 (12-10-1865)
Haywood, M. E. to A. G. Chamberlin 7-11-1872 (7-13-1872)
Haywood, _____ to Anderson Robinson 10-21-1866 (10-23-1866)
Haze?, C. A. to J. W. Rieves 5-29-1872
Hedgecock, Malinda to W. T. Thomas 10-9-1862 (no return)
Heelly, Martha J. to Wm. A. Thompson 1-6-1865 (no return)
Heflin, Laura to Thomas Lammond 11-16-1869 (11-17-1869)
Helms, Adaline to John Howard 1-30-1869 (1-31-1869)
Hempstead, Elizabeth to R. C. Brinkley 12-24-1860 (12-31-1860)
Henderson, Clary to Prince Henderson 12-13-1870 (12-12?-1870) B
Henderson, E. C. to J. F. Looney 12-19-1865
Henderson, Emma to Wade H. Nowlin 10-17-1870 (10-20-1870)
Henderson, Lucy to Jackson Cole 12-27-1870 (12-28-1870)
Henderson, Molly to Thomas Everett 12-24-1869 (12-25-1869)
Henderson, Susan A. to B. J. Brevard 12-8-1868
Hendly, Mary Margaret to John B. Todd 11-8-1867 (11-10-1867)
Henley, T. S. to G. M. Midlin 6-17-1870 (6-19-1870)
Henning, Hannah to Thomas Hamilton 3-12-1864 (3-16-1864)
Henning, Hannah to Thomas Hamilton 3-12-1864 (no return)
Henning, Julia A. (Mrs.) to John C. McKelsey 1-30-1861 (no return)
Henry, Laura E. to Francis M. Haflin 4-12-1866? (with 1862)
Herrell, Penny to Columbus Herrell 10-23-1868
Herron, Ella C. to John M. Lacy 11-20-1872 (11-21-1872)
Herron, Lizzy to King McLemore 4-16-1870 (4-17-1870)
Herron, Martha J. to Starkey Dawes 6-19-1869 (6-20-1869)
Herron, Martha to Henry Liles 12-9-1869
Herron, Mary M. to George B. Searingen 11-28-1866 (11-29-1866)
Herron, Milly to George Holland 8-1-1868 (8-2-1868)
Herron, Sally to Abram Banister 5-21-1869 (5-22-1869)
Herron?, Martha C. to J. F. Bellew 12-11-1865 (no return)
Hester, Fanny to John Davis 4-2-1865 (4-9-1865)
Hester, Mary E. to James M. Neely 10-25-1865
Hester, Mary E. to William H. Dotson 3-30-1862 (no return)
Hewey, Frances J. to John Evans 8-29-1866 (9-2-1866)
Hiatt, S. V. to J. R. Jones 1-3-1867
Hickman, E. J. to W. A. Porter 9-5-1870 (9-8-1870)
Hickman, M. E. to Nelson McAlexander 3-17-1871 (3-18-1871)
Hickman, Mary E. to David T. Spain 2-4-1869
Hickman, Rebecah F. to Jesse McAllexander 2-24-1868
Hicks, Lucinda to Henry C. Finch 8-31-1870 (9-1-1870)
Hicks, Savanah to Milton B. Kee 6-16-1866 (6-17-1866)
Higgins, Winney to Marion Coleman 4-1-1870 (4-2-1870)
Hill, Martha E. to Thompson Moore 10-5-1869
Hill, Mary J. to B. S. McAnley 12-17-1866 (12-20-1866)
Hill, Mollie E. to G. W. Fletcher 2-15-1873 (2-16-1873)
Hill, Sallie to Frank Denney 12-25-1871 (no return)
Hill, Sarah P. to Thomas Mitchel 3-30-1867 (3-31-1867)
Hilliard, Delia A. to John D. Crider 2-9-1865 (no return)

Hillman, Amanda to Mack Thomas 1-25-1873 (1-26-1873)
Hillsman, Caroline to George Atkison 12-30-1869 (1-9-1870)
Hillsman, Eliza to Daniel Hutcheson 6-28-1870 (6-30-1870)
Hillsman, Sally to Norvell Hillsman 8-29-1868 (no return)
Hinson, Martha J. to Joell W. Walters 2-1-1868 (2-5-1868)
Hodge, Mary E. to J. W. Lipe 11-30-1872 (12-1-1872)
Hogan, Mollie to Charles Weatherford 11-29-1866 (11-27-1866)
Hoggard, Rena to Green Coleman 12-9-1868 (12-10-1868)
Holcomb, Mary to Thomas Sullivan 9-20-1866 (9-3?-1866)
Holland, Caroline to Robert C. Browning 11-18-1861
Holloway, Sarah J. to William Cook 3-2-1867 (3-3-1867)
Holmes, A. E. to H. A. Walker 9-13-1866 (9-16-1866)
Holmes, Charlott to Wm. H. Scalbrough 8-9-1860 (8-11-1860)
Holmes, E. J. to J. A. Ingle 11-20-1868 (11-22-1868)
Holmes, Josie P. to Saml. T. Scott 2-13-1872
Holmes, M. A. to L. W. Pitman 3-31-1869 (4-1-1869)
Holmes, M. C. to W. H. H. Dysart 8-23-1870 (8-24-1870)
Holmes, M. J. to John F. Holmes 11-26-1872
Holmes, Margaret to A. E. Barnett 1-5-1869 (no return)
Holmes, Margarett to Jno. R. Sellers 1-18-1872 (1-19-1872)
Holmes, Mary A. to James R. Hodge 7-28-1866 (7-29-1866)
Holms, Arytine to J. C. Merrett 4-28-1873 (4-29-1873)
Holt, Callie to Nathan Mitchell 4-13-1869 (4-14-1869)
Hood, Harriet A. to James H. Box 9-25-1865 (10-18-1865)
Hooper, Mary to Pete Hamilton 12-30-1872 B
Hope, Josie (Mrs.) to James E. Totty 4-14-1873 (4-24-1873)
Hopper, Amanda to Elvis Perry 10-6-1870
Hopper, Dicey to Wesley J. Johnson 3-10-1864 (no return)
Hopper, Dicey to Wiley J. Johnson 3-10-1864 (3-12-1864)
Hopper, E. M. to Jesse Perry 9-1-1870
Hopper, Mary to Wm. B. Grogan 1-9-1873
Hord, Margaret J. to F. M. Kerby 3-29-1862 (3-30-1863?)
Horn, Alcy C. to P. B. Brewer 12-18-1865 (12-19-1865)
Horn, Frances to Ansil Linch 7-13-1863
Horn, Louiza to Tyson Autry 11-26-1861 (no return)
Horn, Mary J. to Austin Lovin 1-24-1872
Horton, Amada to James P. Park 3-1-1861 (no return)
House, M. R. to J. H. Spain 10-14-1871 (10-15-1871)
House, Mary T. to Daniel W. Nichols 11-9-1868 (11-12-1868)
House, S. C. to J. W. Leach 12-27-1870 (12-28-1870)
Houseman, Mary to Henry Vaughan 4-1-1866 (no return)
Houston, Mathe to J. W. Weams 1-20-1868 (1-21-1868)
Houston, Mattie J. to J. A. Adams 10-17-1871 (10-19-1871)
Howard, Mollie E. to Allen C. Hall 3-22-1864 (no return)
Howard, Sarah Ann to Jesse McCollom 12-21-1868 (12-22-1868)
Hubbard, T. C. to Thomas C. Calhoun 12-11-1860 (12-13-1860)
Huddle, M. J. to S. W. Williamson 9-15-1869 (no return)
Hudson, Allis to Louis Thomas 7-13-1871 (7-14-1871) B
Huffman, Ann to Lewis Fields 12-31-1868 (1-3-1869)
Huffman, Dilla to W. D. Owenby 8-14-1867 (8-15-1867)
Huffman, Jane to John Swayne 4-27-1872 (no return) B
Huffman, L. P. to W. A. Williams 1-24-1873 (1-30-1873)
Huffman, Nancy C. to G. H. Williams 7-14-1866 (7-15-1866)
Hughs, Allice to Milton Walker 12-23-1872 (12-26-1872) B
Hughs, Lou J. to Robert J. Baxter 8-1-1866 (no return)
Hull?, Elizaeth L. to James K. Rogers 8-8-1867 (8-9-1867)
Humphrey, Annie to Thomas Neely 8-5-1862 (no return)
Humphrey, Mary P. to James H. Rollins 2-10-1869
Humphreys, L. A. to John S. Vickers 4-9-1873 (4-10-1873)
Humphry, Catharine to William F.? Condray 3-10-1866 (3-11-1866)
Hurt, Ella to N. P. Barksdale 1-15-1872 (1-18-1872)
Hurt, Frances to J. C. Jones 2-19-1872
Hurt, Lear to Pett Harrell 9-27-1871 (9-28-1871) B
Hurt, Louisa to James Jones 12-19-1871 (no return) B
Hurt, Malissa A. to Thomas A. Leech no date (10-31-1865)
Hurt, Martha to John T. Fuqua 10-21-1867 (no return)
Hurt, Mary Jane to Hinton Chambless 10-11-1869 (10-13-1869)
Hurt, Mollie A. to Thos. A. Leach 10-27-1865
Hurt, Rachel to Silas Bigham 9-27-1871 (9-28-1871) B
Hurt, Sarah to C. A. Collins 12-19-1860 (no return)
Hutchison, Frances to Mitchell Quinn 3-6-1871 (no return)
Ingram, Martha L. to G. W. Housman 11-27-1867 (12-1-1867)
Jackson, Lucinda P. to J. M. Arnett 1-1-1869 (1-14-1869)
Jackson, M. A. to Wm. G. David 12-27-1868 (12-28-1868)
Jackson, Martha E. to William S. Lee 2-23-1867 (2-27-1867)

Jackson, Martha to William P. Quinn 2-24-1864 (no return)
Jackson, Martha to Wm. P. Quinn 2-24-1864 (2-26-1864)
Jacobs, America J. to Robert J. Mays 12-14-1866 (12-18-1866)
Jacobs, Louiza M. to Andrew M. Bugg 10-13-1866
Jacobs, M. S. to H. P. Reynolds 12-13-1870 (no return)
Jacobs, Malissa A. to James C. Fly 9-25-1865 (10-3-1865)
Jacobs, Sarah to J. P. Armstrong 6-7-1869
Jamerson, Frances to John Cawthon 11-22-1866
Jamerson, Victoria to John Burton 1-23-1861 (1-27-1861)
James, Fannie E. to John E. Waddill 10-6-1869 (10-7-1869)
James, G. W. to S. D. Parnell 12-19-1870 (12-21-1870)
James, J. B. to Wm. E. Jones 11-27-1871 (no return)
James, Marinda to Thomas H. Baker 4-22-1861 (no return)
Jamison, Jinnie to Peter Murry 6-24-1872 (no return) B
Jamison, Juda E. to Henry Harris 7-9-1870 (no return)
Jamison, Missouri to Charles Clark 1-8-1870 (1-9-1870)
Jarret, Mary J. to Mark Livingston 2-17-1860 (2-18-1860)
Jarrett, Parilla to J. C. Merrett 7-30-1869 (8-1-1869)
Jarrett, R. A. to T. J. Jones 7-22-1871 (7-23-1871)
Jarrett?, Martha E. to Joseph B. Fowler 10-21-1861 (no return)
Jenkins, Martha C. to Newton Finley 2-17-1863 (no return)
Jenkins, Mary Ann to Jacob Boston 6-30-1870 (7-2-1870)
Jenkins, Nancy E. to Patric Neenan 9-21-1861
Jenkins, Nancy E. to Patrick Newman 9-21-1861
Jenkins, S. E. R. to W. W. Jenkins 2-10-1867
Johns, Sarah E. to Asville P. Cribbs 4-28-1863
Johns, Sarah E. to Asville P. Cribbs 4-28-1863 (no return)
Johnson, E. T. to M. E. Lissenberry 2-1-1873 (no return)
Johnson, Edy to Nelson Allen 12-7-1872 (no return) B
Johnson, Jennie to Isaac Bell 12-24-1868 (12-28-1868)
Johnson, L. M. to R. L. Hart 5-10-1861 (no return)
Johnson, Lucinda to John T. Stell 4-1-1861 (4-2-1861)
Johnson, M. E. to Robert Jamison 11-14-1866 (11-15-1866)
Johnson, M. J. to Thomas Orr 1-13-1870
Johnson, Mary F. to James Scott 6-23-1866 (no return)
Johnson, Mollie C. to Benjamin A. Howard 7-4-1860
Johnson, Mollie to W. H. Gregory 10-6-1865 (no return)
Johnson, S. C. to J. D. McEwen 12-26-1872
Johnson, Sallie to J. R. McKinney 2-20-1867 (2-22-1867)
Johnson, Sarah C. to James M.? Brandon 12-28-1861 (1-6-1862)
Johnson, Sarah J. to J. M. Branch 12-23-1872 (12-24-1872)
Johnson, Tennessee to Joe Davis 9-30-1871 (10-9-1871) B
Johnston, Angeline E. to Calvin L. Thompson 2-8-1870 (2-9-1870)
Joiner, F. A. to J. T. Rogers 5-14-1864
Joiner, Martha E. to E. P. Owenby 1-?-1867 (1-23-1867)
Jolly, Martha G. to Robert Wright 9-21-1861 (no return)
Jolly, Nancy to William Corder 4-25-1861
Jones, Ann to George S. Moore 2-3-1869 (2-4-1869)
Jones, Ann to John Brand 1-4-1873 (1-5-1873)
Jones, B. E. to L. B. Barham 9-16-1871 (9-17-1871)
Jones, Beda A. to John D. Rogers 5-23-1865 (5-24-1865)
Jones, Dicie to Henry Anderson 2-2-1871 B
Jones, Dinarza M. to John Williams 9-2-1862
Jones, E.L. to H. V. McArthur 2-25-1867 (2-27-1866?)
Jones, Easter J. to J. R. Porter 12-6-1866 (12-5?-1866)
Jones, Fannie to J. C. Wilder 6-25-1872 (no return)
Jones, Harriet J. to Wiley M. Parnell 10-24-1860
Jones, Janie to Jessie White 9-4-1871
Jones, L. A. to Milton Morris 3-6-1871 (no return)
Jones, Laura to Wm. McAdoo 2-2-1866 (2-4-1866)
Jones, M. A. to L. B. Abbott 12-14-1866 (no return)
Jones, M. C. to W. T. Baird 2-4-1867 (2-12-1867)
Jones, M. L. J. to J. F. Allgee 1-1-1870 (1-2-1870)
Jones, Martha G. to Robert S. Boyd 7-17-1861 (7-18-1861)
Jones, Martha to James Parnell 9-29-1869 (9-30-1869)
Jones, Martha to John W. Abbott 12-7-1863 (12-18-1863)
Jones, Martha to S. N. J. Pope 7-19-1861 (no return)
Jones, Mary A. to J. W. King 1-1-1873 (1-2-1873)
Jones, Mary C. to William Capps 2-18-1869
Jones, Mary F. to Jas. W. Edwards 1-17-1871
Jones, Mary J. C. to T.? R. Wingo 2-18-1867 (no return)
Jones, Mollie to Jessie Palmer 6-22-1871
Jones, Mollie to R. A. Newell 1-7-1867 (no return)
Jones, Quixanna to Eli S. Metheny 8-31-1871 (9-3-1871)
Jones, Rebecca to H. H. Benton 8-15-1866 (8-16-1866)

Jones, Sarah to Poke Harrell 3-12-1872 (no return) B
Jones, Susan E. to James C. King 12-22-1866 (12-24-1866)
Jones, Varna to Henry Clay 7-22-1871 (7-23-1871) B
Jonett, Susan to T. M. Travis 12-30-1872 (1-1-1873)
Jordan, Ann to George Lipe 4-25-1871 (4-27-1871)
Jordan, F. A. to A. J. Pettyjohn 9-13-1864 (9-14-1864)
Jordan, Fannie R. to M. S. Martin 3-9-1869 (3-11-1869)
Jordan, Josaphine J. to John M. Rowe 10-1-1868
Jordan, July Ann to Silvestis Roberson 11-23-1870 (12-1-1870)
Jordon, A. P. to William Spellings 3-22-1871 (3-23-1871)
Joyner, Margaret M. A. to Zachary Barker 2-21-1861 (2-16?-1861)
Joyner, Mary E. to J. W. King 11-19-1866 (11-20-1866)
Kates, Rianna to Elijah Parish 12-18-1865
Keaney, Mary H. to D. J. Donavan 12-27-1869 (12-28-1869)
Keaton, Emily to B. F. Warpool 12-4-1865 (12-17-1865)
Keaton, Mollie A. to J. W. Keaton 1-30-1873 (1-31-1873)
Keaton, S. L. C. to S. C. Dowden 11-6-1869 (11-21-1869)
Kee, E. E. to James M. Hix 8-23-1866 (no return)
Kee, M. E. J. to John T. Blackwell 6-8-1872 (6-9-1872)
Kee, Mary L. to W. C. Blair 10-11-1866
Kee, Sarah M. to A. W. Dill 10-25-1860
Kee, Tensy E. to Walter C. Pugh 11-13-1860 (11-14-1860)
Kee, Winnie to James Flake 12-19-1872 (no return)
Kelley, M. A. to S. L. Jarrett 6-4-1873
Kelly, Ann to J. C. White 7-20-1872 (no return)
Kemp, Tabitha L. to W. H. Carter 12-26-1863 (no return)
Kenady, F. E. to W. T. McAlister 12-4-1868
Kennon, Louisa A. E. to Allen K. Brandon 12-2-1869
Kennon, Nancy to John W. Adams 12-19-1868 (12-20-1868)
Kerby, D. P. to Richard Carigton 3-27-1867 (3-28-1867)
Kerby, Susan A. to G. A. Jones 11-22-1868 (12-10-1868)
Kerly, Polly Ann (Mrs.) to Enoch Brewer 12-28-1867 (1-2-1868)
Kerr, F. M. to W. G. Gray 1-21-1871
Kesbitt, G. A. to F. M. Moore 3-24-1866 (3-29-1866)
Keting, Lydia to Garland Sneed 6-21-1869 (6-22-1869)
Key, Mary to Leonedas McAdoo 12-3-1864
Key, Nancy C. to Bemin Pritchard 12-26-1869
Key, Nancy Parale to John G. Lawrence 11-14-1869
Killan, Fannie to Godfrey Donaldson 5-25-1872 (5-26-1872) B
Killbreath, Matilda to Napoleon B. Pinckston 12-31-1869 (1-4-1870)
King, B. L. to James Pruett 3-8-1871
King, C. W. to N. L. Joyner 7-6-1865
King, Cardilea A. to John C. Haywood 11-22-1866 (11-24-1866)
King, Catharin to D. R. Adams 5-14-1866 (5-17-1866)
King, Everline to L. C. Robison 12-5-1871 (no return)
King, Frances to Richardson Harris 12-31-1868 (1-1-1869)
King, Julie E. to Z. B. Rose 1-2-1867 (no return)
King, L. D. to S. B. Gilkey 7-2-1863 (no return)
King, M. C. to L. C. Kyle 2-6-1873
King, M. E. to W. A. Hall 2-11-1867 (2-12-1867)
King, Mary A. to T. L. Tayler 6-18-1873
King, Mary E. to Samuel P. Reece 1-7-1861 (1-9-1861)
King, Mary H. to Elwood Moore 9-25-1861 (9-29-1861)
King, Maryann to C. K. Thompson 12-16-1865 (12-18-1865)
King, N. C. to B. F. Ellender 9-15-1860 (9-16-1860)
King, Nancy C. L.? to John Collins 8-2-1865 (8-4-1865)
King, Susan E. to J. P. Laster 1-24-1863 (1-25-1863)
King, Susan to H. Laster 6-23-1863
King, T. J. to J. D.? Sugg 9-7-1866 (9-9-1866)
King, Tenness to N. M. Moore 12-3-1866 (11?-6-1866)
King, Winnie to John G. Blount 2-24-1869
Kirk, Dorthy to Isaac N. Brewer 10-25-1865 (10-31-1865)
Kirk, Mary Jane to James G. Hamilton 7-22-1869
Kirk, Milly to Harry J. Hatch 2-12-1861 (no return)
Kirk, Vilet to Daniel Darnall 12-27-1870 (12-29-1870) B
Kirkland, Ann T. to George S. Jones 5-13-1868 (5-17-1868)
Kirly, Elizabeth to J. W. Pendergrass 3-27-1872
Knuckles, Frances to Jacob Fuqua 8-5-1872
Kyle, M. J. to J. R. Fuller 1-25-1871 (1-26-1871)
Kyle, Pinkey to G. W. Butler 10-29-1867
Lacy, Margaret A. to G. W. Wilk 1-4-1866 (1-14-1866)
Lacy, Mary to Wm. D. Jarrett 12-22-1871 (12-23-1871)
Lafloore, Ann E. to John T. Smith 12-11-1868 (12-13-1868)
Lammond, Sarah to D. L. Rigsby 12-5-1868 (12-7-1868)
Lane, Bell (Mrs.) to Jefferson Malone ?-?-1863 (with Aug 1863)

Langlie, Mary to Johnathan Mann 3-28-1872 (no return)
Lanier, Annie W. to W. A. Ellis 12-19-1865 (no return)
Lanier, Jennie to T. J. Alexander 9-2-1865 (9-3-1865)
Lankford, Julia to Humphrey Herrell 8-19-1871 B
Lankford, Lucy J. to R. W. Ramsey 10-16-1860 (10-15?-1860)
Lankford, Margaret to Ross Sparks 1-18-1869 (1-21-1869)
Lansden, Amanda to Elzey Dudley 7-17-1869 (no return)
Lansdon, Alice to W. H. Roach 9-23-1867 (10-1-1867)
Larance, M. J. to J. W. Eskew 11-15-1871 (11-16-1871)
Lawrance, Elizabeth to R. K. Pinckley 10-13-1865 (10-15-1865)
Laws, M. E. to J. M. Springer 11-13-1867
Lay, Elizabeth J. to James M. Johnson 8-28-1864 (9-4-1864)
Lay, Elizabeth J. to James M. Johnson no date
Laycock, E. J. to James S. Bates 12-5-1872
Laycock, L. F. to G. W. Kee 10-27-1872
Laycock, Nancy C. to Joseph C. C. Rhodes 1-5-1870
Laycock, Sarah E. to Sebrom Smothers 6-11-1870 (6-12-1870)
Laycook, L. V. to J. B. Dill 2-13-1873
Leach, Ardina to John jr. Briant 10-18-1870 (10-23-1870)
Leach, Elizabeth Ann to W. F. Seymore 2-23-1863 (no return)
Leach, Elizabeth ann to W. F. Seymore 2-23-1863
Leach, Josephine to J. J. Cuningham 1-31-1871 (2-2-1871)
Leach, M. T. to Z. T. Browning 8-5-1872 (8-8-1872)
Leach, Martha E. to Benjamin C. McCollom 12-29-1868 (12-31-1868)
Leach, Mary A. to J. R. Jones 10-27-1866 (no return)
Leach, S. E. to J. R. McAlexander 2-5-1866 (2-8-1866)
Ledsinger, M. C. to J. P. Shaw 12-21-1869
Ledsinger, M. J. to G. W. Williams 10-7-1871 (10-8-1871)
Lee, Cynthia to John M. Bigham 9-29-1865 (10-1-1865)
Lee, M. J. to J. A. R. Utley 11-24-1870
Leech, M. A. to T. K. Harvy 2-3-1866 (2-5-1866)
Leech, Martha to G. N. Carter 3-14-1861 (no return)
Leigh, Lowtica? to James C. Lurence 12-19-1867
Leigh, Lucy to John Bush 11-24-1861
Leigh, Nancy C. to Thomas W. Stacy 8-23-1871 (8-24-1871)
Leigh, Sarah A. Barbrey to Isarah Morris 11-3-1866
Lemmons, Frances to Edward Smith 6-7-1867 (6-9-1867)
Lemmons, Julia N. to J. M. Johnson 2-14-1867 (no return)
Lemons, Mary J. to J. W. Lee 10-2-1865 (10-3-1865)
Lenea?, E. J. to B. D. Mills 10-7-1871 (10-9-1871)
Leshlie, M. R. to Jerome Bevell 12-21-1872 (12-25-1872)
Leslie, Mary J. to Henry P. Smith 11-9-1872 (11-10-1872)
Lett, Malinda to Stephen Dunkin 12-24-1866 (12-27-1866)
Lett, Mary A. to Newton P. Berry 2-10-1862 (2-11-1862)
Lewellen, Elizabeth to Quincy J. Mathews 3-11-1862
Lewis, M. J. to L. L. Martin 8-5-1868
Lewis, R. J. H. to V. H. Kelley 1-4-1871
Liffsy, Eliza to Shadrick Pearson 9-19-1864 (9-21-1864)
Lightle, Frances to William Arvinshire 7-15-1864 (7-17-1864)
Liles, Eliza to James M. Rogers 8-27-1860 (9-7-1860)
Liles, Elizabeth J. to Wm. T. Cagle 4-14-1860 (4-29-1860)
Liles, Elizabeth to J. D. R. Green 4-16-1864
Liles, Elizabeth to T. H. H. Presson 12-?-1861 (12-15-1861)
Liles, Sarah M. to John F. Phelps 11-25-1864 (11-26-1864)
Liles, Susan to Marvell Butler 8-6-1860
Linch, Mary A. to E. W. Haywood 11-10-1871
Linzy, Milly to Thomas Brewer 11-24-1870 (no return)
Lipe, Lucinda F. to John H. Edwards 9-14-1871
Lipe, M. F. to J. T. Hensler 9-1-1870
Lipe, M. J. to James M. Hodge 8-14-1863 (no return)
Lipe, Martha J. to James M. Hodge no date (with Aug 1863)
Liston, M. F. to F. M. Patterson 12-23-1868
Litle, Georgiann to James K. P. Rogers 8-3-1869
Little, Amanda to David Phillips 7-3-1864
Little, Mary Susan to J. M. Scott 2-2-1867 (2-4-1867)
Lodgins, Louisa C. to James N. Malone 4-28-1865 (4-29-1865)
London, Jane V. to Almus Grooms 1-24-1872 (1-25-1872)
Long, Martha to James Walker 6-30-1866 (7-1-1866)
Long, Parlee to Peyton Gregory 12-24-1869 (no return)
Long, Salenia to Joe Denton 1-18-1873 (no return) B
Longmyre, Leanna to Norwood Roper 8-14-1868 (8-16-1868)
Longworth, Mary E. to George W. Walker 1-2-1861 (1-3-1861)
Looney, C. A. to J. H. Claiborn 4-21-1865 (no return)
Lorance, Agnes to James H. Green 11-14-1866 (11-16-1866)
Lorance, Ellen to Orange Chambliss 1-10-1873 (no return)

Lorance, Lavina C. to J. M. Cross 12-20-1869 (12-23-1869)
Lorance, Sophia to George W. Boaz 10-13-1866 (10-14-1866)
Lorate, Harriett to Isah Briant 1-1-1872 (no return) B
Louis, L. J. to L. M. Tosh 3-11-1868
Louis, M. E. to J. W. Kelly 1-2-1873
Love, Mattie E. to N. C. Howard 1-30-1865 (no return)
Loveall, Martha C. to W. L. Pinson 11-2-1870 (11-6-1870)
Loveland, Mattie J. to William L. Dorsey 5-14-1861
Loving, Ella to B. G. Ezzell 5-4-1872 (5-5-1872)
Loving, Mary to L. C. Robison 4-22-1866 (no return)
Lowell, Sarah Ann to Thomas Smith 1-?-1862 (1-13-1862)
Lowery, Rosella to Newton Cox 6-16-1860 (6-24-1860)
Lowery, Sarah A. L. to Erasmus J. Hutchins 7-7-1866 (7-8-1866)
Lowery, Susan R. to David McMackins 3-18-1863 (3-19-1863)
Lucas, Amy to Ned Utley 1-4-1869 (1-8-1869)
Lusk, Amanda L. to Henry D. Featherston 5-12-1862 (no return)
Lusk, L. H. to J. A. Lorance 1-11-1867 (1-16-1867)
Luter, Amy to George Greer 4-3-1869 (4-4-1869)
Mabon, Wiry? to Case Johnson 2-13-1870 (no return)
Malcar, Orpha J. to Cahl P. Owenby 12-13-1866
Malone, Jane to James Mullin 7-1-1861 (7-7-1861)
Malone, Susan E. to R. Phelps 1-27-1869 (1-30-1869)
Mann, Dicey H. to Thos. J. Mann 8-7-1862
Mann, Esper An T. to Joseph Mitchell 11-12-1870 (11-13-1870)
Mann, Julie E. to C. G. Mann 5-19-1860 (5-20-1860)
Manning, Emily to W. B. Nevill 12-20-1869 (12-23-1869)
Manning, Texanna to Jefferson Brinkley 4-28-1868 (5-3-1868)
Manuel, Serrilda to E. W. Melton 8-2-1872 (8-3-1872)
Marris, Julia to Frank Elgin 10-1-1870 (10-2-1870)
Marshall, Rebeca (Mrs.) to Norwood Scarlott 7-18-1860
Martin, L. E. to Samuel A. Robinson 2-2-1870 (2-13-1870)
Martin, Martha M. to James F. Martin 11-20-1866 (11-21-1866)
Martin, Mary S. to J. W. Pritchett 5-20-1869
Martin, Szieber? C. T. to Wm. H. Green 1-21-1862 (no return)
Martin, V. V. to B. F. Chambers 11-1-1871 (no return)
Massey, Adaline to Moses Rowland 1-23-1869 (1-27-1869)
Massey, Martha to Thomas W. Pinson 10-24-1860 (10-25-1860)
Massey, Mary E. to James H. Rhoads 11-30-1870 (12-1-1870)
Massey, Mary L. to Thomas L. Stanford 10-8-1865 (10-12-1865)
Massey, Mary to B. B. Simmonds 11-9-1863 (11-10-1863)
Massey, Mary to Thomas A. Turner 10-10-1868 (10-11-1868)
Matheny, E. C. to J. E. Everett 4-26-1867 (5-2-1868?)
Matheny, M. M. to D. J. Green 4-23-1869 (4-25-1869)
Matheny, Mary P. to J. W. Cox 1-24-1870 (1-27-1870)
Mathewson, Henrietta to Dick Johnson 12-23-1872 (12-27-1872) B
Mathis, Elizabeth to Sanford Tippitt 12-14-1866 (12-16-1866)
Mathis, M. C. to S. A. Miller 1-24-1867
Mathis, Mahala to Wm. McAdoo 8-6-1864 (no return)
Mathis, Mary P. to Pleasant G. Morgan 8-1-1866 (8-2-1866)
Mathis, Mary to Felix G. Morgan 10-15-1861
Mathis, Nancy to John Steel 6-14-1860
Mathis, Sallie to T. R.? Blow 2-?-1868 (2-6-1868)
Mathis, Ursul M. to James F. Hickman 5-23-1866 (5-3?-1866)
Maxwell, M. J. to J. R. King 7-30-1873 (7-31-1873)
Maxwell, S. A. to W. M. Burk 2-29-1872
Mayar, Cornelia A. to J. P. Shaw 12-24-1866 (12-26-1866)
Mayberry, Caroline to Maston Randle 4-11-1865 (4-12-1865)
Maynard, M. Jane to W. H. Pope 9-21-1870 (9-22-1870)
McAdoo, America J. to Quincy A. Harper 2-13-1866
McAdoo, C. T. to L. N. Drewrey 8-2-1871 (8-3-1871)
McAdoo, Harriet to Wm. C. Peeples 10-26-1863 (no return)
McAdoo, Mary A. to John Cannie 3-18-1868
McAnley, Mary A. to John M. Sanders 4-10-1867
McArthur, Mary A. to P. T. Butler 7-21-1862 (no return)
McAskille, Mary to E. S. Thomas 2-26-1873 (2-27-1873)
McAuley, J. J. to W. H. Bailey 7-24-1869 (7-25-1869)
McAuley, M. E. to E. W. Autry 11-21-1868 (11-22-1868)
McAuley, M. J. to James Lesslie 9-6-1871 (9-7-1871)
McBride, M. E. to J. L. Cockrell 2-10-1873 (2-11-1873)
McCain, Elizabeth to Benjamine Bennett 12-6-1872 (12-7-1872)
McCall, C. J. to L. F. Williams 11-16-1866 (11-21-1866)
McCane, Lucinda to H. W. Wright 11-16-1865
McCarter, Harriet L. to T. E. Jones 1-13-1866
McCaslin, Mary E. to John C. McKiney 12-17-1866 (12-18-1867?)
McCaslin, Mary E. to Thomas J. Vickers 12-7-1867 (12-12-1867)

McClame, Sallie Ann to H. M. Pritchard 8-12-1873
McClintock, Rachel to Geo. Seymore 11-17-1863 (no return)
McClure, Mary E. H. to John N. Williamson 1-6-1868 (1-7-1868)
McCluskey, Issabella to Michael Brandon 11-2-1864 (no return)
McCollum, J. M. to J. F. Leach 1-?-1867 (1-15-1867)
McCollum, L. B. to J. M. Roberts 8-10-1872 (8-13-1872)
McCollum, L. F. to B. T. Frost 3-4-1872 (3-5-1872)
McCollum, Mahala to John H. Wright 11-10-1863 (11-12-1863)
McCollum, Martha to G. T. Belew 5-25-1870 (5-26-1870)
McCollum, Mary J. to J. M. Williamson 4-26-1866
McCord, Martha H. to A. P. Arington 8-5-1873 (8-6-1873)
McCoy, Frances to Sebron Smothers 12-18-1868 (12-22-1868)
McCracken, Paula A. to James M. Gibson 3-24-1863
McCracken, Sarah to Oscar McCargo 1-22-1869 (1-28-1869)
McCrackin, Eliza A. to John M. Cannon 12-26-1864 (12-27-1864)
McCrackin, Fanlee A. to James M. Gibson 3-21-1863 (no return)
McCullough, R. J. to J. N. Reaves 10-18-1870 (10-19-1870)
McCutchin, Martha to Jerry Mitchel 10-23-1872 (10-24-1872)
McDonald, Jinnie to Joseph Carter 9-15-1869 (9-20-1869)
McDonald, Mollie to Ezekiel Barham 12-8-1869 (12-9-1869)
McDougal, Kate to Bennett Downing 8-25-1869
McHood, N. M. to J. P. Peel 2-12-1872 (2-14-1872)
McKiney, Amanda J. to James H. Burns 11-28-1866 (12-2-1866)
McKinney, Frances E. to L. D. Cook 1-16-1865 (1-17-1865)
McKinney, Harriet A. to H. T. Harper 1-24-1870 (1-26-1870)
McKinney, Margaret to C. G. Giles 3-28-1868 (3-29-1868)
McKinney, Sarah J. to Allen jr. Johnson 9-20-1871 (9-21-1871)
McKinzie, Narcissa C. to J. M. McClintock 8-11-1866 (no return)
McLemore, Dora to Joseph Haley 10-5-1869 (10-7-1869)
McLemore, Elizabeth to Hudson Strayhorn 10-7-1871 (no return) B
McLemore, Elizabeth to R. D. Fry 6-13-1860 (6-14-1860)
McLemore, Mary J. to James Cook 10-5-1869 (10-7-1869)
McLemore, Mary L. to Daniel M. Briant 11-10-1866 (11-11-1866)
McLemore, Mattie E. to Thomas B. Manning 4-13-1870 (4-24-1870)
McLune?, Julie A. to Jesse J. H. Jordeen? 4-2-1866 (no return)
McMacken, Maria J. to William White 9-21-1869 (9-23-1869)
McMackens, Angeline to Allen Martin 12-25-1868 (12-27-1868)
McMackens, Nancy Ann to John W. Jenkins 10-4-1869 (10-28-1869)
McMackin, Elizabeth to F. H. Grissom 7-16-1873 (7-17-1873)
McMackin, Lucinda to Andrew McMackin 10-9-1867 (10-10-1867)
McMackins, Elizabeth F. to Robt. N. Rowland 11-25-1872 (11-26-1872)
McMackins, Lucinda to Eli S. Moss 3-28-1870 (3-31-1870)
McMackins, Mary M. to William A. French 9-12-1865 (9-14-1865)
McMullin, Margrarett? J. to F. P. Tarply 9-24-1860 (9-25-1860)
McNamara, Ann to Jeremiah FitsJerrel 1-7-1873 (1-28-1873)
McNeill, Angeline to William Trotter 9-4-1871 (9-7-1871) B
McNeill, Irene? to W. B. Grizzard 1-19-1871
McNeill, Parlie to Dennis Grizzard 2-6-1872 B
McNight, Martha A. to A. V. Hyatt 4-27-1867 (4-28-1867)
McRea, Eliza to Duncan Hopper 12-11-1869 (12-12-1869)
McVey, Mary to Berry Kirby 8-24-1870 (8-25-1870)
Mebane, Eliza E. to Charles Y. Gooch 10-31-1866
Mebane, Letha to Wiley Sutton 10-24-1868
Mebane, M. E. to T. T. Williams 10-26-1870
Mebane, Martha to Doremus N. Young 9-26-1865
Mebane, S. F. to N.? B. Nesbitt 2-27-1867
Mebene, Elizabeth F. to W. S. Adams 4-23-1864 (4-24-1864)
Medearis, Mary A. to T. A. Huffman 10-6-1861
Medearis, Susan H. to H. H. Butler 9-12-1860 (no return)
Medley, Jane to Gideon Faray? 2-11-1867 (2-12-1867)
Melton, Fanny to Beverly J. Crews 7-30-1870 (8-7-1870)
Meritt, Lidy J. to J. S. Bullington 12-15-1870
Merrett, M. A. to G. M. Little 12-7-1872 (12-8-1872)
Merrett, Martha to Alonzo McAdoo 1-13-1872 (no return)
Merritt, J. C. to D. W. Gee 12-11-1866
Merritt, Nancy to J. C. Merritt 4-28-1866 (4-29-1866)
Messer, Elizabeth to John Brown 7-16-1873 (7-17-1873)
Milam, Harriett to Jerry Nesbitt 2-3-1873 (2-6-1873) B
Milam, Rachael L. to James J. Carnal 1-26-1870 (1-27-1870)
Miller, Millie to Rewbin Belerford 4-27-1873 B
Miller, P. F. to W. C. Colvitt no date (8-6-1873)
Miller, Sarah A. to G. F. Parish 9-17-1872 (9-19-1872)
Miller, Sarah Jane to William O. Davis 3-11-1869
Mills, Caroline S. to A. M. Adcock 5-13-1863 (5-14-1863)

Mills, Harriet A. to Wm. A. Threadgill 11-28-1860 (no return)
Mills, Martha J. to Banks M. Burrow 10-1-1867 (no return)
Mills, Mollie A. to S. S. Hayley 12-5-1865 (12-14-1865)
Milon, L. E. to Peter Pearson 10-6-1866 (10-11-1866)
Milum, Mary Ann to T. A. Hollaway 1-4-1872 (no return)
Mitchell, Alice to George W. Walker 3-12-1870 (3-13-1870)
Mitchell, Ardell to J. M. Cotton 8-14-1866
Mitchell, Jinnie to Sidney B. Nesbitt 9-12-1872 B
Mitchell, Joann to Geo. Baucom 8-31-1872 (9-1-1872)
Mitchell, Julia A. to E. B. Wilks 3-25-1869
Mitchell, M. F. to J. N. Brewer 1-20-1872 (1-22-1872)
Mitchell, M. J. to B. H.? Jones 1-1-1868 (1-2-1868)
Mitchell, M. L. to Richard H. Briant 2-20-1861 (2-21-1861)
Mitchell, M. L. to Richd. H. Briant 2-20-1861 (2-21-1861)
Mitchell, Mainard to John G. Ballew 10-23-1860 (10-24-1860)
Mitchell, Mamaret? to John G. Belew 10-?-1860 (10-24-1860)
Mitchell, Mary L. to R. H. Crider 3-6-1869 (3-7-1869)
Mitchell, Ridley J. to Geo. T. Hatch 1-16-1872 (no return)
Mitchell, Sophronia E. to J. N. Cotton 3-29-1870 (no return)
Mitchell, Sophronia E. to J. N. Cotton 7-25-1870
Mitchiner, M. E. to P. D. Warlick 7-15-1867 (no return)
Mitchum, Elizah to R. E. Bumpass 11-18-1870 (11-22-1870)
Mitchum, M. to James Johns 5-10-1872 (5-12-1872) B
Mizell, L. S. to Jacob Turner 5-21-1873 (5-22-1873)
Mizzell, Perina J. to James A. McGill 10-16-1869 (10-20-1869)
Monroe, Lucinda to Wm. H. Lawrence no date (with 10-1867)
Monroe, Rebeca to William Francisco 11-21-1861 (no return)
Montgomery, Eliza J. to Syron? Parrish 12-10-1866 (12-13-1866)
Montgomery, Victoria to V. S. Birdwell 1-8-1872 (1-10-1872)
Montgomery, Zora to Elizah Piggue 7-14-1871 (7-15-1871)
Mooney, Lucy to William May 2-16-1871
Moore, Araminta B. to Simpson Pinckley 3-9-1870 (3-10-1870)
Moore, Canellis E. to B. J. Perry 11-21-1867 (11-22-1867)
Moore, Easter to James Herron 3-12-1873 (3-13-1873) B
Moore?, Fannie E. to W. R. Christain 11-20-1866 (11-23-1866)
Moore, Filbis to Walton Warlick 1-5-1871 B
Moore, G. A. to John S. Steele 10-4-1869 (10-6-1869)
Moore, Harriett to S. P. Woods 12-31-1868 (1-1-1869)
Moore, I. N. to A. J. Walters 2-19-1873 (2-20-1873)
Moore, Jane to J. J. Downing 7-6-1867 (7-11-1867)
Moore, Margaret C. to Jas. J. Porter 2-25-1873 (2-26-1873)
Moore, Margarett to Andrew Vinson 1-17-1872 (1-18-1872)
Moore, Martha J. to H. A. Traywick 1-6-1867
Moore, Mary A. to Henry T. Jones 2-6-1866 (2-8-1866)
Moore, Mary E. to Martin Pierce 4-20-1867 (4-21-1867)
Moore, Mary J. to Clinton King 10-24-1871 (10-25-1871)
Moore, N. A. to J. R. Ozier 3-21-1871
Moore, Nancy A. to John M. Rowland 4-25-1861
Moore, Nancy to Columbus Wright 2-24-1869
Moore, S. C. to A. B. Gibbons 2-13-1863 (no return)
Moore, Susan A. to William B. Kennon 9-14-1866 (no return)
Morgan, Margaret to J. K. Everett 1-1-1867 (not executed?)
Morgan, Martha to Richard Key 3-20-1865 (3-22-1865)
Morgan, Sarah J. to George Owens 11-29-1871 (11-30-1871) B
Morris, Angeline to William Mitchell 9-5-1868 (9-6-1868)
Morris, Christiana E. to John H. Pounds 12-24-1866 (12-25-1866)
Morris, Frances L. to A. H. Spain 11-26-1869 (11-28-1869)
Morris, Louisa to H. D. Brawner? 1-23-1869 (1-24-1869)
Morris, Lucy J. to E. Marshall Joyner 2-27-1866 (3-1-1866)
Morris, Margarett to S. Y. Bigham 5-14-1860 (5-16-1860)
Morris, Mary to Wm. A. Sayles 2-14-1865 (2-15-1865)
Morris, N. A. to Green C. Pinckston 4-15-1872 (no return)
Morris, Susan to R. A. Deleny 12-20-1860 (12-23-1860)
Morris, Susan to Walter S. Fuqua 11-17-1868 (11-18-1868)
Morris?, Harriett to James Barnes 3-16-1866 (no return)
Moss, Elizabeth to William Cain 12-2-1865 (no return)
Moss, Elizabeth to William Kain 5-2-1866 (5-3-1866)
Moss, Emma to Joseph Morgan 1-20-1872 (1-21-1872)
Motion, Malinda to Benj. Alexander 12-18-1872 (12-19-1872) B
Mount, Lavenia to Marshall Thomas 3-3-1863 (no return)
Mount, Levinia to D. M. Thomas 10-9-1862 (no return)
Mullin, Jane to Thomas Higdon 11-7-1866
Mullin, Perneta A. to A. J. Fields 12-4-1867
Mullins, M. A. to G. W. Bouldin 4-13-1870 (4-14-1870)
Munn, L. A. to J. E. Sanders 1-21-1872

Murphy, Margaret E. to W. F. Cooper 7-4-1870 (7-5-1870)
Murphy, Mary to William Pendigrass 1-27-1866 (1-28-1866)
Murphy, Nancy A. to Joseph C. Kirby 5-15-1862 (5-18-1862)
Murray, Josephine to Robert B. Graves 2-9-1870 (2-10-1870)
Murry, Ann to James Mohan 5-15-1861 (5-16-1861)
Murry, Cilla to James Mull 5-4-1872 (no return) B
Nannie, Adaline to Nathaniel Brown 3-30-1869
Nannie, Catharine to John W. Crews 11-4-1865 (11-5-1865)
Nease, Elizabeth to John Grissom 9-9-1868 (9-17-1868)
Neely, Adaline to John L. Murray 8-28-1869 (8-29-1869)
Neely, E. R. to W. H. Clark 1-16-1871 (no return)
Neely, L. A. to S. J. Montgomery 1-13-1869
Neely, M. E. to James C. Grun? 10-14-1864
Neely, Sarah to James C. Green 10-18-1860
Neigbors?, Rebecca to Jesse L. Sellers 8-?-1867 (8-11?-1867)
Neighbours, Nancy A. to Jas. E. Carden 12-18-1865 (12-19-1865)
Nelson, L. M. to W. J. Suiter 11-1-1871 (11-2-1871)
Nelson, M. C. to G. A. McBride 1-4-1872 (no return)
Nelson, Mary F. to William A. Mann 8-10-1870 (8-11-1870)
Nelson, Permelia J. to W. R. J. Carroll 7-6-1867 (no return)
Nesitt, Mollie to William Mitchell 2-4-1869
Nevills, Permelia C. to J. A. Russell 8-27-1869 (8-29-1869)
New, Fanny to Robert Bigham 12-10-1868 (12-11-1868)
Newbill, A. to J. R. McCrackin 12-15-1864 (no return)
Newbill, Alice H. to H. C. Burns 12-19-1864 (no return)
Newbill, Eliza to Anderson Jones 9-28-1869 (9-30-1869)
Newbill, Elizabeth to William Jones 3-7-1866 (no return)
Newbill, Harriett to Bowlen Clark 7-4-1870 (7-7-1870)
Newbill, M. A. to J. M. Mitchum 2-9-1871 (no return)
Newbill, M. A. to W. E. Landrum 12-3-1870 (12-6-1870)
Newnan, Julia A. to Wm. P. Pinkstone 6-23-1865 (6-25-1865)
Newnan?, Tamar to William Coulter 12-27-1869 (12-28-1869)
Niceler, Elizabeth to Archa B. Chandler 6-22-1860 (no return)
Nichols, Cathorin to L. H. Carter 7-14-1873
Nichols, Elizabeth to Jackson Bashen? 4-10-1862 (no return)
Nichols, Ellen to James M. Carnal 6-28-1869 (6-29-1869)
Nichols, Mary J. to John L. Barton 10-30-1867 (10-31-1867)
Nichols, Sarah A. to Joseph Barham 5-4-1863 (5-7-1863)
Nichols, Susan F. to Davis J. Pugh 9-6-1867 (9-11-1867)
Niederegger, Rosalia to Samuel C. Clancy 1-18-1868 (1-19-1868)
Noell, M. E. to T. J. Briant 6-14-1866
Norman, Mary A. to W. B.? Hartman 10-1-1860 (10-2-1860)
North, Tamer J. to Thomas A. Younger 10-1-1860 (no return)
Norvell, Canely? M. to John J. Williams 3-27-1864 (3-27-1864)
Norvell, Matilda to Henry Russel 1-7-1870 (1-8-1870)
Norvell, Susan to Jackson Dinwiddie 8-4-1870
Norwood, Martha E. to H. F. Abbott 10-8-1869 (10-10-1869)
Null, Louiza M. to Wm. P. Hill 2-24-1866
Null, Mary E. to George H. Rogers 10-13-1863 (no return)
O'Conner, Mary B. to Charles H. Gray 2-6-1869
O'Conner, Susan to Henry Murphy 4-8-1868
O'Neill, Pining B. to Jas. M. Younge 11-7-1865 (11-9-1865)
Oliver, Anna E. to Smith Lankford 9-10-1872 (9-11-1872)
Oliver, H. M. to J. M. Johnson 12-27-1871 (no return)
Oliver, Martha to Wiley Britt 9-9-1864 (9-11-1864)
Oliver, Martha to Wily Britt 9-9-1864
Oliver, N. L. to C. H. Ridley 3-7-1870 (3-9-1870)
Oliver, Sarah E. to James H. Britt 10-?-1861 (10-20-1861)
Oliver, Sarah to A. J. Haynes 10-19-1869 (10-20-1869)
Oliver?, Elizabeth to Edward Thompson 1-1-1866
Orr, Elen to Alex Johnson 11-28-1865 (11-29-1865)
Owen, Angeline to Andrew Humble 6-7-1873 (6-8-1873) B
Owen, Victoria to H. K. Manuel 3-15-1869 (3-16-1869)
Owenby?, Martha L. to Hezekiah Coble 9-20-1866 (10-3-1866)
Owens, Amanda to G. H. Wilson 2-15-1865 (2-20-1865)
Owens, Arabella C. to Patrick Newson 9-19-1860 (9-20-1860)
Owensbey, Rebecca to M. Livingston 12-1-1863 (no return)
Ozier, E. A. to T. T. Cooper 7-12-1867 (no return)
Ozier, F. C. to E. N. Royall? 8-15-1867
Pace, Elizabeth to Wm. Bennett 3-30-1871
Pace, Mary A. N. to James A. Chandler 7-27-1860
Pace, Mary A. N. to James A. Chandler 7-?-1861 (7-7-1860?)
Pace, Mary J. to John Offenshine 4-14-1869 (4-15-1869)
Page, Mary C. to Archibald Grant 12-19-1864 (no return)
Palmer, Elizabeth to Joseph A. Williams 2-3-1863 (2-4-1863)

Palmer, Ellen to Washington Johnson 7-23-1868 (no return)
Palmer, Ellen to Wilson White 7-2-1869 (7-4-1869)
Palmer, Lutitia P. to George W. Bennett 12-19-1860 (12-20-1860)
Palmer, M. B. G. to A. C. Tucker 12-7-1864 (12-8-1864)
Palmer, Martha D. to William S. Hightower 4-28-1866 (5-14-1866)
Palmer, Mary E. to J. L. Horton 7-29-1871
Palmer, Mattie to George W. Brown 10-5-1864 (10-7-1864)
Palmer, N. C. to G. W. Wood 2-20-1869 (2-21-1869)
Palmer, Orfrey M. to William C. Ross 12-8-1860 (12-9-1860)
Palmer, Saphrona to Robert Barnhart 7-2-1866 (7-4-1866)
Palmore, Nancy G. to Silas D. Witt 2-23-1861 (2-24-1861)
Parish, Arminta to J. T. Rust 9-10-1870 (9-11-1870)
Parish, Elizabeth A. to S. W. Roberts 9-17-1861 (9-18-1861)
Parish, Jane to Jacob Butler 2-8-1873 (2-9-1873) B
Parish, Louisa to J. W. Thomason 12-24-1869 (12-28-1869)
Parish, Martha J. to W. P. King 11-3-1868 (11-4-1868)
Parish, Rianna to William Bateman 3-2-1871 (3-5-1871)
Park, Eliza A. to Eben Rowland 3-13-1866
Parker, Amanda to Wm. F. Cooper 9-17-1862 (9-18-1862)
Parker, Eviline to John Pearson 1-25-1865 (1-26-1865)
Parker, L. E. to J. M. Carnal 3-13-1867 (3-15-1867)
Parker, Rebecca J. to John W. Watson 12-18-1860
Parker, S. E. to W. L. Carnall 1-23-1873
Parnell, Mattie V to B. L. Ellsberry 10-31-1870 (no return)
Parsons, Elizabeth to John A. Young 4-10-1866
Parsons, Mary to John W. King 11-5-1869 (11-9-1869)
Parsons, Sarah F. to James S. Whitehorn 11-27-1869 (11-28-1869)
Parsons, Sarah P.? to W. H. Harris 11-8-1869 (11-9-1869)
Pasteur, G. A. to J. R. Simpson 2-19-1866 (2-20-1866)
Pate, Ann to Walter S. Fuqua 5-20-1863
Pate, Ann to Walter S. Fuqua 5-20-1863 (no return)
Pate, Ashley? W. to David W. Henry 7-29-1861 (no return)
Pate, Catherine to Richard Dudley 7-18-1872 B
Pate, Elizabeth to Richd. Simmons 12-11-1870 (12-15-1870) B
Pate, Martha to P. T. Walton 5-23-1865 (no return)
Pate, S. V. to J. K. Pate 2-27-1873 (3-2-1873)
Pate, Tennessee to John W. Rushing 9-25-1865 (9-28-1865)
Patten, L. E. to R. F. Elder 1-1-1866 (1-7-1866)
Patten, Sally to J. M. Delany 12-6-1865
Patterson, Amanda to John Scales 2-26-1872 (2-27-1872)
Patterson, Amanda to John Scates 3-4-1870 (no return)
Patterson, Caroline to Jack Kile 12-31-1869 (1-1-1870)
Patterson, Eliza J. to Isaac Harlin 5-25-1863 (5-27-1863)
Patterson, Eliza Jane to Isaac Harlin 5-25-1863
Patterson, Eliza to Adam Fowler 11-25-1865 (4-14-1866)
Patterson, Emma A. to John M. Dickson 12-18-1866 (12-20-1866)
Patterson, Hellen to Harvy Mitchum 6-1-1866 (6-7-1866)
Patterson, Lucinda to John Culee? 2-12-1867 (2-13-1867)
Patterson, Martha to Sancho Clay 9-21-1868
Patterson, Molba? to Gip Jones 2-28-1871 (3-2-1871)
Patterson, Parilee to Milton Hart 11-19-1860
Patterson, Parilee to Milton J. Hart 11-19-1860 (11-20-1860)
Patterson, Telia to Alfred Reives 9-7-1872 B
Patterson, Tilia to John Hart 8-31-1870 (no return)
Pattison, Mary to Plase Ezzell 5-19-1873 (5-29-1873) B
Patton, M. E. to W. P. Wilkins 10-12-1869 (10-13-1869)
Patton, Rosy to A. G. Love 11-22-1870 (11-24-1870)
Pearce, Dulla to John Crafton 8-14-1871 (8-17-1871)
Pearce, F. A. B. to T. D. Foresyth 1-15-1873
Pearce, M. A. to Andy Hamett 4-17-1872 (no return) B
Pearce, Sarah to John A. Newbill 12-8-1869 (12-9-1869)
Pearcy, Julia A. to Wm. M. Meals 7-22-1865 (7-25-1866?)
Pearman, M. A. F. to A. T. Crossett 2-17-1866 (2-20-1866)
Pearman, M. A. to J. B. Crossett 1-8-1864 (no return)
Pearman, Mary Jane to Walter C. Crewes 10-24-1860 (no return)
Pearman, Susan A. to D.? Marshall 1-5-1863 (1-7-1863)
Pearman, Susan A. to M. D. Marshall 1-5-1863 (no return)
Pearmon, M. A. to J. B. Crossett 1-8-1864 (no return)
Pearson, Effarilla to Jery Murphey 5-25-1872 (5-26-1872) B
Pearson, Fredonia to Peter Britt 5-29-1871 (5-30-1871)
Peler, M. B. P. to James M. Williams 11-10-1870
Pendygrass, J. E. to S. H. Butler 9-28-1871
Penick, E. J. to Eli Compton 2-18-1867 (2-19-1867)
Penick, Sarah A. to Marion Wood 12-18-1866 (12-19-1866)
Peoples, Harriet to Alge Jamison 12-13-1871 (no return)

Perkins, E. J. to N. J. Dunlap 2-3-1872 (2-5-1872)
Perkins, Harriett to W. H. Pope 2-28-1866 (3-1-1866)
Perkins, Mary E. to George W. Gallimore 8-15-1870 (8-16-1870)
Perkins, Molly to William S. Johnson 7-17-1868 (no return)
Perkins, Reny to Andrew Taylor 10-31-1871 (no return) B
Perkins, Sarah to E. E. B. Brown 12-24-1866 (1-1-1867)
Perrett, Eliza to William Webb 9-27-1860
Perritt?, Mary to J. M. Reynolds 5-15-1869 (5-16-1869)
Persons, Anna T. to James M. Towns 4-5-1865 (no return)
Persons, Medora Alice to John E. Gwinn 1-6-1868 (1-8-1868)
Petty, Martha J. to Fantry Roberts 12-12-1867
Petty, Rutha A. to Israel E. Mainard 8-7-1866
Petty, Vina A. to J. L. Snowden 11-14-1867
Pettyjohn, N. P. to J. T. Berryhill 2-20-1869 (2-21-1869)
Phelps, Elizabeth to Sherwood L. Liles 7-3-1866 (12-27-1866)
Phelps, Hanna R. to Moses M. Rigsby 8-12-1862 (no return)
Phelps, Sarah E. to N. J. Rogers 5-15-1873
Phillips, Mary F. to J. W. Bowelen 1-2-1867
Phillips, Susan H. to John L. Bellew 2-9-1862 (no return)
Phillips, U. J. to R. J. Bell 11-27-1868 (11-29-1868)
Philps, Wilmoth C. to Harrison Simpson 12-11-1860
Phipps, Jane to Joseph Cooper 11-20-1865 (11-31?-1866?)
Phipps, Narcissa A. to James S. Reece 5-7-1867 (no return)
Pickett, Eliza to William Hampton 10-21-1865 (no return)
Pickett, Fanny A. to Thomas Y. Haynes 12-21-1869 (12-22-1869)
Pickler, Any (Mrs.) to Latent Pearce 8-20-1860 (8-24-1860)
Pickler, Mary J. to J. W. Allen 7-30-1863
Pickler, Nanc S. to John N. Freelin 12-7-1867 (12-15-1867)
Pickler, Susan J. to W. B. Bradberry 1-27-1864 (1-31-1864)
Pickler, T. P. to George W. Freeland 8-27-1869 (8-29-1869)
Pickles, Mary J. to J. W. Allen 12-5-1863
Pierce, Marry E. to John J. Henslee 3-6-1868 (no return)
Pigel, Silvia to Robert Hudgen 12-26-1872 B
Pinckley, M.J. to Wm. C. Chambers 2-2-1871
Pinckley, N. C. to James W. Belew 11-9-1870 (11-10-1870)
Pinkston, Elizabeth to Thos. Norwood 1-2-1866
Pinkston, Emily M. to Jabez T. Boyd 8-25-1868 (8-26-1868)
Pinkston, Martha to John Hutchison 12-1-1871 (no return)
Pinkston, Mary A. to Wm. C. Newman 8-6-1861 (8-9-1861)
Pinkston, Melissa J. to Edmond Finch 10-25-1869 (10-28-1869)
Pinson, Martha J. to Samuel V. Fields 11-28-1865 (no return)
Pinson, Matilda D. to Newton H. Martin 2-20-1865 (2-25-1865)
Pinson, P. C. to J. R. Massey 2-25-1870 (2-28-1870)
Plummer, Jennie to J. W. White 7-25-1871 (7-13?-1871)
Poindexter, Evalin to S. M. Hayley 3-21-1871 (no return)
Polston, Martha J. to J. B. Bateman 6-22-1869 (6-23-1869)
Pope, B. F. to J. F. Brown 4-9-1866 (no return)
Pope, Darthula to Richard H. Byrns? 1-19-1869 (1-24-1869)
Pope, Laura A. to M. T. Kernan 5-28-1872 (no return)
Popkins, Nancy to Nathaniel Newbill 7-26-1866 (no return)
Porter, Amand to Ed White 2-21-1873 (2-23-1873)
Porter, Catharine S. to William R. Gardner 11-26-1866 (12-2-1866)
Porter, E. F. to A. T. Burns 12-16-1872 (12-19-1872)
Porter, J. A. to W. D. Jones 11-6-1861
Porter, M. T. to J. H. Spain 2-19-1873
Porter, Martha to Perry Porter 2-14-1870 (2-15-1870)
Porter, Persia M. to John C. Hawkins 5-27-1863
Porter, Rebecca T. to H. C. Hale 10-14-1864 (10-16-1864)
Porterfield, E. J. to W. E. Burrow 3-2-1871
Powel, Mary E. to William Barnhart 8-19-1871 (8-21-1871)
Prewitt, Elizabeth R. to W. R. Bateman 6-25-1870 (6-26-1870)
Price, A. C. to J. G. Arnold 10-15-1870 (10-16-1870)
Price, Amanda C. to James M. Felts 3-11-1862
Price, Elizabeth to Joseph N. Phelps 12-15-1870 (no return)
Price, Mollie to George McDonald 1-19-1871 B
Price, Rebeca to A. Arrington 7-3-1865 (7-6-1865)
Prichard, Mary Ann to Dennis McCain 8-21-1869 (8-22-1869)
Priest, Anna E. to F. G. Williams 10-19-1871 (no return)
Priest, Caroline to Joe Hawkins 12-30-1871 (no return) B
Priest, Elen to Thomas D. Vauters 1-18-1865
Prince, Emma E. to W. D. Baker 12-10-1864 (12-14-1864)
Prince, Fannie to Berry Carter 12-14-1872 (12-19-1872) B
Prince, Lucy A. to Adolphus Briant 11-19-1868
Prince, Susan E. to A. G. Hawkins 11-10-1869 (11-11-1869)
Pritchard, Cordelia E. to James A. Burton 6-19-1871 (no return)

Pritchard, Eliza C. to Joseph W. Grogan 1-12-1869 (1-13-1869)
Pritchard, Elizabeth to Thomas G. Roper 7-15-1868 (7-16-1868)
Pritchard, M. J. to D. H. Williams 1-28-1868 (1-30-1868)
Pritchard, Mary M. to Josiah Anderson 2-?-1862 (no return)
Pritchard, Mourning E. to William Phillips 9-11-1860
Pritchard, Susan E. to Thomas L. Kee 8-12-1868 (8-13-1868)
Province, B. A. to S. A. Dinwiddie 8-29-1871 (8-31-1871)
Pruett, Catharine A. to Jasper N. Cole 11-15-1865 (11-19-1865)
Pruett, Eliza J. to W. T. Haywood 12-7-1865 (12-10-1865)
Pruit, Mary V. to Wm. D. Dilda 10-20-1864
Pruitt, Mary V. to W. D. Dilda 10-20-1863 (10-25-1863)
Pruitt, Mary V. to William D. Dilday 10-20-1863 (no return)
Pucker, Susan A. to Samuel Williams 8-19-1867 (8-20-1867)
Pugh, Mary E. to Littleton O. Gooch 3-16-1869 (3-17-1869)
Pugh, Nancy T. to N. C. Joiner 11-5-1867
Purdy, Lizzie to G. M. Graves 12-16-1865
Purslay, Elnora to William D. Newlett? 11-8-1865 (11-11-1865)
Purvis, Sarah J. to Charles P. Briant 12-31-1868
Putman, Mary M. (Mrs.) to Jesse McCollum 7-3-1860 (7-5-1860)
Putman, Mary M. to Jessy McCollum 7-3-1860 (7-5-1860)
Quinn, Alethia M. to A. D. Bryant 10-15-1866 (no return)
Quinn, F. M. to John H. Green 1-19-1869 (1-22-1869)
Quinn, M. F. to J. W. Hedgecock 7-2-1866 (no return)
Quinn, Martha to H. S. Flippin 1-6-1866 (no return)
Quinn, V. A. to W. H. Holmes 9-8-1871 (9-9-1871)
Ragland, Fanny to John B. Norman 10-31-1865 (11-1-1865)
Ragland, Lila to Nathan H. Grogan 5-21-1869
Rainey, E. C. to Wm. B. Richardson 8-9-1864 (8-12-1864)
Ramsey, Loucy to Thomas F. Collins 12-27-1866 (no return)
Randall, Amanda M. to Thomas E. Jones 9-30-1861 (10-1-1861)
Randle, Patience to Abraham McNeill 1-20-1871 (1-22-1871) B
Raney, Nancy to H. M. Hill 5-28-1864 (no return)
Ray, Martitia to Livra? Williams 2-28-1868 (3-1-1868)
Ray, Susan to T. C. Smith 10-17-1868 (10-21-1868)
Ray?, Sarah A. to J. R.? Mitchell 12-6-1860
Read, Dorothy A. to Henry C. Taylor 2-16-1864 (no return)
Read, Winny to G. V. Enochs 12-28-1869 (12-30-1869)
Reader, Mily A. to W. T. J. Melton 12-27-1867 (12-28-1867)
Reaves, Elizabeth to J. J. Porter 1-17-1871 (1-18-1871)
Rece, Mary Ann to J. H. Beavers 6-27-1863 (7-5-1863)
Redden, Paralee A. to William Finley 12-31-1869 (1-5-1870)
Reddick, Sarah E. to John T. Burks 7-17-1869 (7-19-1869
Reece, Norah J. to J. R. McHood 9-5-1872
Reed, Caroline to William King 12-14-1860 (12-19-1860)
Reed, Elizabeth to G. V. Enochs 9-11-1865 (9-12-1865)
Reed, Mary J. to James Johnson 6-12-1867 (6-13-1867)
Rees, M. E. to William R. Williams 7-27-1863 (7-28-1863)
Rees, Martha E. to William R. Williams 7-27-1863
Revel, C. S. to Wm. S. May 8-29-1864 (9-1-1864)
Revel, R. E. to W. F. Simpson 11-8-1866 (11-9-1866)
Reynolds, Elizabeth Ann V. to James M. Reynolds 2-18-1864
Reynolds, Elizabeth Ann V. to James M. Reynolds 2-18-1864 (no return)
Rhodes, A. J. to R. L. Vawton 11-15-1869 (no return)
Rhodes, Adaline to Henry Perminter 9-20-1867 (9-22-1867)
Rhodes, Eviline to Wilson King 5-11-1865 (5-14-1865)
Rhodes, Frances P. to A. J. Vawter 1-2-1866 (no return)
Rhodes, Harriet to Henry Clark 12-20-1869 (12-22-1869)
Rhodes, Mary E. to Yancy E. Wilks 12-16-1869
Rice, Martha to T.J. Barton 11-23-1872 (11-26-1872)
Rice, Nicie to Green Crews 8-28-1871 (8-31-1871)
Rice, Parthena to Harris Akers 1-20-1872 (1-23-1872)
Rice, Sarah to Robert Hagler 12-17-1868 (12-18-1868)
Richardson, Mary to Robt. H. Burrow 5-1-1873 (no return) B
Richardson, Nancy A. to S. T. C. Gibbons 12-15-1869 (12-16-1869)
Richardson, Sarah J. to Charles W. Tidwell 3-26-1868
Richars?, Caroline to Thomas J. McCaslin 12-18-1866 (12-19-1866)
Ridley, Adelia C. to T. J. Oliver 10-17-1866 (10-18-1866)
Ridley, Matilda to Edom Keys 6-14-1868
Ridley, Sallie to W. M. Carson 1-14-1862 (no return)
Riggs, Latitia to W. C. Rossom 10-17-1861 (10-11?-1861)
Ritchie, Mary Jane to Samuel Maynard 7-21-1869 (7-22-1869)
Roach, Cora A. to W. M. Shephard 4-26-1872 (no return)
Roach, Lenora M. to D. S. Ezzell 12-31-1872 (1-1-1873)
Roach, Mary to John Craig 3-15-1864 (3-16-1864)

Roach, May to John Craig 3-15-1865 (no return)
Roach, S. A. to H. B. Thomas 10-31-1867 (11-5-1867)
Roach, Tisha to Henry Alexander 5-3-1869 (no return)
Roaney, Candas M. to Albert Finley 2-3-1864 (no return)
Roark, Elizabeth J. to Abner T. Scott 1-8-1870 (1-9-1870)
Roberson, Ann to W. P. King 12-16-1872 (12-17-1872)
Roberson, T. J. to J. J. Bateman 4-4-1867
Roberts, A. E. to J. M. Kirk 9-16-1869
Roberts, Della to Thomas Carray 6-1-1867 (no return)
Roberts, Elizabeth to Saml. R. Graham 10-22-1866 (10-23-1866)
Roberts, Harriet A. to John N. Roberts 5-19-1871 (5-21-1871)
Roberts, Louisa to L. D. Williams 1-8-1865
Roberts, Margarett to George Hollowell 10-23-1864 (10-26-1866?)
Roberts, Narcissa to Thomas P. Williams 9-25-1861 (no return)
Roberts, Rebeccah to John Williams 8-21-1866
Robertson, D. to James McHood 1-1-1866
Robertson, Eliza J. to Haywood Hampton 1-4-1862 (1-5-1862)
Robertson, N. P. to E. F. Stayton 3-1-1873 (3-3-1873)
Robeson, Emeline C. to Wm. Montgomery 1-28-1864 (2-1-1864)
Robeson, Emeline C. to Wm. Montgomery 1-29-1864 (no return)
Robeson, Lidia J. to William N. Hammett 11-16-1865
Robeson, Louisa to M. M. Morris 3-31-1865 (4-6-1865)
Robey, Mary to J. G. French 10-20-1868
Robinson, E. J. to J. A. Zellner 2-26-1872 (2-27-1872)
Robinson, Margaret to Amos McCane 12-25-1860 (12-27-1860)
Robinson, Martha Ann to N. M. Morris 1-22-1864
Robinson, Martha Ann to N. M. Morris 1-22-1864 (no return)
Robinson, Mary to Wm. F. Cunningham 10-1-1860 (10-2-1860)
Robison, America P. to William T. Boyd 4-29-1870 (5-1-1870)
Robison, Eliza to Henry Williamson 5-3-1870 (no return)
Robison, Frances E. to Robert F. Knight 5-25-1869
Robison, Mary A. to G. W. Parker 1-13-1868 (1-14-1868)
Rochell, Nancy to M. S. Berry 11-21-1868 (11-22-1868)
Rochell, Sarah to Wilson Barns 10-31-1862 (no return)
Rodgers, E. Y.? to J. R. Rodgers no date (with Aug 1866)
Rodgers, N. A. to G. D. Moore 1-23-1867
Rogers, Amanda J. to A. J. Mizell 11-28-1867 (1-6-1868)
Rogers, Amea? E. to William Roberts 1-2-1862 (no return)
Rogers, Anna E. to William Roberts 1-1-1862 (1-2-1862)
Rogers, Anna to William Roberts 12-31-1861 (1-1-1862)
Rogers, D. A. to C. A. Bridges 4-1-1865 (no return)
Rogers, Elizabeth to Samuel Stone 8-3-1863 (no return)
Rogers, Frances to Joel A. Butler 1-1-1868 (1-5-1868)
Rogers, Judiath S. to John Massey 4-22-1871 (4-26-1871)
Rogers, M. C.? to A. T. M. Woolen 4-2-1860 (4-10-1860)
Rogers, Margaret to Saml. McCracken 7-25-1868 (7-28-1868)
Rogers, Martha J. to Alexander Manuel 4-21-1864 (4-23-1864)
Rogers, Mary A. to Wm. P. Martin 12-15-1860 (not endorsed)
Rogers, Mary E. to G. W. Malear 1-20-1866 (3-4-1866)
Rogers, Mintie S. to A. R. Carnes 3-5-1862 (3-6-1862)
Rogers, Nancy E. to F. M. Bilbrey 1-17-1865
Rogers, Nancy R. to Wm. F. Garner 6-10-1861 (not endorsed)
Rogers, Rilley to S. W. Autery 12-21-1863 (12-23-1863)
Rogers, Sarah P. to Henry N. Moore 11-14-1868
Rogers, Winna R. to J. A. Wright 8-22-1864 (8-25-1864)
Rogin, Nancy to W. L. Gooch 10-18-1869 (10-20-1869)
Rollens, Elizabeth A. to James J. Thompson 7-13-1863 (no return)
Rollins, Ellen H. to James D. Carlton? 2-8-1871 (2-9-1871)
Rollins, Emily D. to J. H. Davis 2-28-1870 (2-29?-1870)
Rollins, Manerva F. to Richd. T. Partete 9-24-1861 (9-29-1861)
Rollins, Marassela C. to John Baxter 8-5-1865 (8-6-1865)
Rollins, Mary E. to Cyrus Smith 8-5-1865 (8-6-1865)
Rome, M. M. to Wm. M. Pearce 1-4-1862
Roney, N. A. to J. C. Buchanan 8-6-1872 (no return)
Roper, Mary Ann to H. C. Cox 10-24-1866 (10-25-1866)
Rose, M. L. to A. A. Pinckley 7-12-1872 (no return)
Ross, Betsy to William Hillsman 11-29-1869 (no return)
Ross, E. P. to R. P. Scarbro 12-3-1866 (12-5-1866)
Ross, Martha A. to Tilson Murphy 6-24-1870 (6-25-1870)
Ross, Martha J. to Jesse W. Palmer 11-14-1867 (11-17-1867)
Rothrock, Margaret D. to W. J. Fields 5-6-1864 (5-7-1864)
Rothrock, Susan A. to Lycurgus McCracken 11-10-1863
Row, M. C. to W. M. Frinch 2-10-1865 (3-12-1865)
Rowe, Elizabeth M. to B. Z. Haywood 1-21-1868 (1-28-1868)
Rowe, Mary S. to Ferrell Pruett 12-6-1870 (12-8-1870)

Rowe, Nancy A. to James C. Bilbry 4-17-1871 (4-20-1871)
Rowe, Nancy C. to Robert M. Pruett 10-2-1865 (10-8-1865)
Rowe, Sarah to W. T. Higdon 5-27-1867 (5-29-1867)
Rowland, Anne E. to sJ. T. Boswell 3-20-1861 (no return)
Rowland, Elizabeth to J. M. Grooms 2-19-1866
Rowland, Ella to Levi Butler 8-24-1870
Rowland, Ennis to W. H. Lowrey 12-31-1872 (1-1-1873)
Rowland, Josephine to John Cooper 1-11-1872
Rowland, M. F. (Mrs.) to Lagrand P. Phillips 8-25-1860 (8-26-1860)
Rowland, Malissa Jane to E. B. Wilborn 8-14-1868 (8-16-1868)
Rowland, Margaret C. to J. C. Barnhart 4-?-1867 (4-21-1867)
Rowland, Margaret to J. M. Pickler 12-29-1866 (12-31-1867?)
Rowland, Nancy to T. B. Rowland 1-24-1867
Rowland, Sarah E. to G. N. Dillon 2-3-1868 (2-5-1868)
Rowland, Sarah H. to J. W. Groom 12-1-1860 (12-2-1860)
Rowland, Sarah H. to James W. Grooms 2-22-1870
Rowland, Sarah P. to Benjamin Boswell 12-12-1860
Rowland, Sarrah E. to James Moore 10-6-1870
Rowland, Synthia A. to Phineous Gray 1-28-1870 (2-1-1870)
Royall, Nannie to W. A. McCall 10-?-1867 (10-29-1867)
Rual?, Ana Liza to Thomas Little 12-26-1861
Ruce?, Nancy L. to G. W. Wright 1-31-1870 (2-10-1870)
Ruff, Amanda to David McMackin 12-24-1866
Ruff, Clarkie to T. J. Rial 12-29-1868 (12-30-1868)
Rumage, Sarah L. to P. B. Caps 9-13-1870
Rumley, Nancy to Sal W. Haynes 11-14-1872
Rumley, Permelia to William Sherwood 12-14-1871 (5-23-1871?)
Rumly, Nancy to Wilson B. Rhodes 11-16-1861 (11-11?-1861)
Ruse, R. C. to W. M. Taylor 10-7-1862 (10-12-1862)
Rushin, Sarah E. to Thomas C. Brown 12-3-1860 (12-9-1860)
Russ, C. A. to J. R. Hall no date (with Mar 1866)
Russel, Mary E. to W. H. H. Massey 9-26-1870 (9-28-1870)
Russell, Martha E. to J. W. Gunter 8-20-1862 (no return)
Russian, Marilda Jane to Thos. Grooms 9-5-1867
Rust, A. S. to Robert H. Hall 4-18-1864 (4-20-1864)
Rust, Deliar A. to Isaac Shoffner 9-5-1871 (9-6-1871) B
Rust, Randy J. to L. F. McMackins 12-23-1869 (12-29-1869)
Rust, Rowann to E. W. Haywood 3-24-1869
Rust, S. J. to S. T. Johnson 5-31-1867 (6-2-1867)
Sampson, Bettie to T. T. Morgan 1-3-1872 (no return)
Sampson, J. P. to R. S. Walker 11-7-1861
Sampson, Sarah to W. B. Rhoads 10-27-1870
Sayles, F. J. to C. Wilder 1-11-1867
Scales, Sarah to John Williams 12-24-1868 (12-25-1868)
Scarbrough, Sarah E. to S. E. Smith 2-4-1865
Scarlett, Mary E. to N. J. Peel 1-12-1871 (1-13-1871)
Scates, Marsha to Nelson Mitchum 12-5-1870 (no return)
Scoby, M. E. to W. J. Scott 10-25-1860
Scoby, Mary to John H. Barlow 2-1-1864 (2-11-1864)
Scoby, Mary to John H. Barlow 2-1-1864 (no return)
Scott, Bettie A. to Elijah Falker 2-13-1872
Scott, Evaline to R. H. Tosh 12-11-1870 (12-13-1870)
Scott, Frances to J. G. Tosh 3-1-1866
Scott, L. A. to D. P. Jenkins 1-21-1861 (1-24-1861)
Scott, Mary A. to Granvill H. Butler 2-6-1872
Scott, Mary to John Ballew 3-2-1863
Scott, Mary to John Ballew 3-2-1863 (no return)
Scrobrough, Mary J. to G. L. Smith 8-4-1866 (8-5-1866)
Scruggs, M. P. to J. B. Utley 5-30-1873 (no return)
Sellars, Nancy E. to H. T. Simpson 12-7-1871 (no return)
Sellers, Clementine to R. B. Springer 12-9-1865 (12-19-1865)
Sellers, Henrietta L. to James Townsend 6-3-1871 (6-11-1871)
Sellers, Henrietta to William Simpson 1-29-1861
Sellers, Isabel L. to R. H. Davis 12-11-1868 (12-15-1868)
Sellers, Martha E. to Nick G. Joyner 2-7-1866 (2-8-1866)
Serconas, W. C. to J. H. Ethridge 10-8-1864
Settles, Nancy C. to Hosea Springer 11-8-1865 (11-8-1865)
Seymore, Nannie to G. G. Walker 12-21-1868 (12-22-1868)
Seymore, Ritter to Adam Brown 2-22-1869 (2-28-1869)
Shad, Mattie to Hiram Richardson 12-15-1869 (12-16-1869)
Shad, Rachel to Nelson Caldwell 5-10-1870 (5-14-1870)
Shadwick, Mary to P. McShane 11-7-1868 (11-8-1868)
Shankle, Mary E. to William White 3-3-1869
Shaver, Eliza to Amos Roberts 8-26-1868
Shaver, Nancy to W. H. Caudle 1-11-1867 (1-17-1867)

Shaw, Jane to Isaac Lawhorn 1-3-1872 (no return)
Shaw, Rebecca to E. White 2-22-1861 (no return)
Shay, Joanna to Lackey Brandon 12-23-1868 (12-24-1868)
Shelly, Ellen to Alexander Shawl 10-3-1865
Shepherd, Molly to Jacob Algea 2-14-1870 (2-15-1870)
Shepherd, Virenna to James Massey 12-17-1868 (12-18-1868)
Sherfield, Ruth to A. T. Butler 3-28-1870 (3-30-1870)
Sherrell, Martha A. to M. A. Fields 7-13-1872 (no return)
Shipman, Charlott to E. H. Derryberry 8-?-1860 (8-14-1860)
Shipman, M.A. to E. W. Derybery 1-8-1868 (1-9-1868)
Shoeterick?, Elizabeth to John Sayles 3-16-1866 (3-23-1866)
Shoffner, Eveline to Beverly Townes 8-1-1868 (8-3-1868)
Shoffner, Mary Ann to Andrew Nesbitt 2-19-1870 (2-20-1870)
Shofner, Dosha to Cain Shofner 10-9-1869 (10-10-1869)
Shofner, Eliza to Isaac Pinson 11-7-1864 (11-8-1864)
Shofner, Elizabeth M. to R. D. Bell 1-10-1866
Shofner, Lettie to Levin Palmer 12-20-1869 (1-10-1870)
Shofner, M. Ella to E. A. Thomas 2-17-1873 (2-19-1873)
Shofner, Mary Ann to Marion Edwards 3-16-1864
Shofner, Maryann to Marion Edwards 3-16-1864 (no return)
Shofner, Sarah to Andrew Jackson 2-25-1870 (2-26-1870)
Shuford, Susan A. to James E. Woodard 3-17-1868 (3-18-1868)
Simmons, N. L. to H. G. Duffer 1-26-1871 (1-29-1871)
Singleton, Caroline to Josiah Bateman 9-23-1867 (no return)
Singleton, Emeline to M. W. Johnson 11-12-1869 (11-18-1869)
Slaton, Elizar O. to Marion Cobb no date (8-22-1869)
Smith, Ama to George Moore 12-25-1872 (12-26-1872) B
Smith, Ann to Jesse Williamson 12-11-1869 (12-12-1869)
Smith, Artamissa J. to William B. Wilson 9-18-1865
Smith, Cordelia C. to W. F. Bridges 5-25-1865 (5-30-1865)
Smith, Elizabeth A. to W. M. Waddle 2-8-1868
Smith, Elvora to Ed Williamson 11-27-1868
Smith, Emeritter to James D. Leigh 3-13-1867 (3-14-1867)
Smith, F. P. to E. A. McMackins 1-5-1872 (1-7-1872)
Smith, H. R. to A. B. Christian 6-24-1868 (6-25-1868)
Smith, Harriet Jo to Benj. F. Smith 5-20-1868 (5-24-1868)
Smith, Laura to Benjamin Herron 3-23-1869 (3-24-1869)
Smith, Louiza to L. G. Parham 5-27-1871 (6-7-1871)
Smith, Lucy Jane to James M. Woodard 8-3-1869 (no return)
Smith, Marry (Amey?) to Jordan Burrow 5-19-1871 (5-20-1871)
Smith, Martha J. to Green C. Rogers 7-31-1866 (8-2-1866)
Smith, Martha J. to Samuel L. Chilton 2-16-1870
Smith, Mary A. to Robert Wren 8-1-1865 (no return)
Smith, Mary J. to John T. Steele 5-29-1867 (5-30-1867)
Smith, Mary to Joseph Kirby 12-14-1871 (12-15-1871)
Smith, Nancy J. to P. W. Gorden 1-1-1866
Smith, Nancy to Lawson Quinn 4-12-1861 (no return)
Smith, Selah Ann M. to John H. Connell 3-14-1864 (no return)
Smith, Selahann M. to John H. Connell 3-14-1864 (no return)
Smoot, M. A. to R. D. Carr 10-14-1866 (no return)
Smothers, Martha to Bery Blakeny 3-9-1861 (3-10-1861)
Snead, Janie to W. T. McCall 5-20-1872 (no return)
Snead, S. A. to J. F. Baker 1-6-1873 (1-7-1873)
Sneed, Elizabeth to A. J. Sneed 1-11-1871 (1-12-1871)
Sneed, Ellen to W. H. H. Thompson 1-19-1871 (1-20-1871)
Sneed, Frances to Richard Wilson 3-4-1870
Snowden, Ritter K. to W. S. B. Lacy 4-4-1866 (4-5-1866)
Southerel, Harriet A. to J. W. Porter 8-29-1868 (8-30-1868)
Spain, D. M. A. to A. W. M. Martin 8-7-1871
Spain, Eliza to F. M. Logue 12-15-1869 (12-22-1869)
Spain, Elizabeth F. to William J. Northcut 7-16-1868
Spain, Harriet to W. J. Linsey 11-22-1871 (no return)
Spain, M.L. to W. B. Montgomery 2-8-1873 (2-9-1873)
Spain, Nancy E. to D. G. Porter 12-10-1868 (12-11-1868)
Sparks, Ann to M. S. Dinwiddie 11-2-1863 (11-5-1863)
Sparks, Betty to James Price 9-16-1869 (9-18-1869)
Sparks, Frances to Julius Ridley 12-31-1868 (1-7-1869)
Sparks, Margarett to Steward Carson 11-21-1872 B
Sparks, Mattie to J. T. Grundy 7-26-1871 B
Sparks, Nelly to Samuel Baucum 3-8-1870
Sparks, Sallie E. to R. T. Fowler 2-4-1867 (2-14-1867)
Spears, Sallie to John H. Pickler 7-11-1871 (no return)
Spellings, E. T. to Robert D. Shoffner 9-20-1869 (9-23-1869)
Spellings, Martha A. to A. M. Bennett 12-31-1872 (no return)
Spellings, Mary F. to Nathaniel J. Edwards 10-6-1865 (10-8-1865)

Spillings, Rebeca A. to Thomas E. Enboe? 9-6-1865 (9-8-1865)
Spoon, Sarah A. to W. G. Palmer 1-14-1870 (1-16-1870)
Springer, Burnetta to Scott Pinckley 3-29-1869 (3-31-1869)
Springer, Susan E. to M. R. Browning 1-21-1868 (no return)
Springer, Triona L. to Andrew Stewart 12-5-1865 (12-6-1865)
Springer, Triona L. to Andrew Stewart? 12-5-1865 (12-6-1865)
Stafford, Jennetta to Moses Jones 1-2-1869 (1-3-1869)
Standfield, J. B. to R. J. Woods 7-27-1871
Stanfield, Jerleen to Wm. J. Berryhill 8-?-1863 (no return)
Stanfield, Jerlien to W. J. Berryhill 8-9-1863
Stanford, Ann to Stephen Hillsman 12-20-1871 (12-21-1871)
Stanford, Louisa to Jobe Hill 8-28-1869 (9-1-1869) B
Stanly, Fannie to George S. Jones 12-19-1867 (no return)
Steel, Linda Ann Eliza to W. G. Carver 3-5-1870 (3-9-1870)
Steel, M. A. to H. C. Crdier 12-26-1871 (no return)
Steele, Jinnie to Carroll Humble 6-20-1868 (6-21-1868)
Steele, Martha L. to James B. Arnold 11-5-1867 (11-7-1867)
Steele, Melvina to G. W. Kile 12-6-1869
Stewart, Louisa to Thomas J. Morris 2-26-1862 (2-27-1862)
Stewart, M. J. to J. T. Bridges 12-11-1872
Stewart, P. C. to H. A. Chambless 1-18-1870
Stewart, Sarah E. to John R. Murphy 9-14-1868 (9-20-1868)
Stoker, Florida Ann to James R. Hodge 7-4-1872 (no return)
Stokes, California to Pinkney Wyatt 12-28-1866 (12-29-1866)
Stone, A. A. to Z. R. White 11-7-1866 (no return)
Stone, Cyntha C. to Jas. A. Williamson 4-21-1863 (no return)
Strange, Mary Henry to W. W. Murray 1-4-1869
Strayhorn, Deliah to Abriham Moore 3-10-1873 (3-13-1873) B
Strayhorn, Esther to Hardy Herron 1-19-1869 (1-21-1869)
Strayhorn, Julia to Richard Elem 7-26-1872 (no return)
Strayhorn, Silvey to Toney Nesbitt 2-27-1869
Striblin, Parlee to Add Cuningham 1-14-1873
Stribling, Nancy J. to M. L. Bullington 12-19-1871 (no return)
Stroud, M. S. to S. B. Shaffin 3-29-1869 (3-31-1869)
Strouse, C. A. to J. W. Jackson 12-12-1865 (12-16-1865)
Stubbs, Martha G. to B. F. Gibson 11-15-1863 (no return)
Stubbs, S. C. to M. A. Crawford 1-6-1868 (1-9-1868)
Stubbs, Susan L. to Joseph G. Milam 9-3-1870 (no return)
Sugg, Nancy E. to J. W. King 12-3-1868 (12-6-1868)
Suggs, Caroline to Thomas King 2-20-1864 (2-22-1864)
Suggs, Clery? A. to Janes Kee 11-10-1860 (11-17-1860)
Suggs, Lucinda to James A. Hatch 4-5-1861 (no return)
Suggs, Mary A. to J. W. Horn 1-11-1867 (1-13-1867)
Suggs, Winnie C. to Granvil L. Hatch 4-7-1873 (4-9-1873)
Sugs, Eveline to J. C. King 2-20-1866 (2-25-1866)
Sullivan, Margaret T. to Zachariah Wyatt 5-20-1869 (no return)
Surber, Rebeca to J. H. Watson 12-20-1867 (12-22-1867)
Swain, Martha to Josiah Billberry 1-1-1866 (1-10-1866)
Swarigen?, Lucie to Sidney Broach 9-12-1867
Swayne, Ellen to Elijah Hannah 1-6-1871 B
Swayne, Nannie to Mitchel Sparks 12-23-1872 (12-24-1872) B
Swayne, Virinda C. to Phillip Myers 9-7-1862 (9-8-1862)
Sweaney, W. C. to J. H. Etheridge 10-8-1863
Sweaney, W. C. to J. H. Etheridge 10-8-1863 (no return)
Sweany, Caroline E. to N. T. Newbill 6-23-1866 (no return)
Sweargim, Earline to Ned Bledsoe 7-23-1868 (7-29-1868)
Sweney, Rebecca to James F. Sloan 12-29-1869 (1-6-1870)
Swift, Corsicana? to G. M. Parkinson 12-8-1863 (no return)
Swindle, Sarah L. to Josiah C. Abernathy 5-26-1866 (5-7?-1866)
Swinney, Martha to T. H. French 1-17-1872 (no return)
Swinney, Mattie L. to L. M. Walton 1-1-1866 (1-4-1866)
Swinney, Sallie to William French 8-10-1871
Swinney, Tenney C. to W. M. Harrell 7-27-1872 (7-28-1872)
Tarply, Susan C. to N. C. Giles 11-7-1860
Tate, E. A. to James H. Ozier 11-25-1862
Tate, Parisett to James H. Davis 1-8-1861
Tayler, Martha to John H. Briges 2-16-1864 (no return)
Tayler, Mary to B. B. Jamerson 4-15-1861 (4-17-1861)
Taylor, Adaline to C. K. Jameson 2-24-1863 (no return)
Taylor, Adaline to C. K. Jamison 2-24-1863 (no return)
Taylor, Bethe to R. T. Williams 12-25-1861 (no return)
Taylor, Catharine T. to John T. Wood 2-5-1869
Taylor, D. A. to J. H. Bethewen 1-9-1873 (1-12-1873)
Taylor, Jarusha Jane (Mrs) to James D. Stewart 11-3-1867
Taylor, L. F. to Wm. D. Sellers 5-24-1873 (5-25-1873)

Taylor, Louisa K. to James J. Webb 8-23-1867 (8-25-1867)
Taylor, M. L. to W. E. Hilliard 3-6-1872 (3-7-1872)
Taylor, Martha E. to Levi Ozier 11-5-1870 (11-6-1870)
Taylor, Martha to John H. Bridges 2-16-1864 (no return)
Taylor, Mary J. to Sugars McLemore 7-28-1862 (no return)
Taylor, Mary to R. B. Jamerson 4-15-1861 (4-17-1861)
Taylor, Nancy C. to R. C. A. Thomason 2-13-1861 (2-16-1861)
Taylor, R. E. to T. H. Cooper 10-14-1868
Taylor, Susan to Calvin Jones 8-15-1860 (8-16-1860)
Taylor, Zelvey E. to Whitley A. Haywood 11-1-1866
Terry, C. P. to Wm. E. Warner 5-8-1863 (5-10-1863)
Terry, C. R. to Wm. E. Warner 5-8-1863 (no return)
Terry, E. V. to T. C. McKinney 6-27-1868 (7-1-1868)
Terry, Molly to Thomas M. Patton 12-18-1866 (no return)
Thogmortin, Manda to Robert Barlow 12-24-1867 (1-16-1868)
Thomas, Alabama to James Coleman 12-24-1867 (1-5-1868)
Thomas, Amanda J. to William Howard 1-10-1872 (no return)
Thomas, America to Isaiah Hunter 2-4-1869
Thomas, Arabella to James R. Thompson 12-30-1868 (12-31-1868)
Thomas, C. M. to Jonathan Pritchard 5-4-1867 (5-8-1867)
Thomas, Martha L. to William L. McCracken 10-22-1861
Thomas, Susan to Wm. J. Bryant 12-20-1870 (12-22-1870)
Thomason, Mary M. to J. M. Roberts 8-23-1864 (8-24-1864)
Thompson, B. L. to L. F. Deshony 10-28-1872 (10-29-1872)
Thompson, Harriett to J. C. Pearce 12-18-1866 (12-20-1866)
Thompson, Mary C. F. to A. J. Thompson 12-19-1871 (no return)
Thompson, Sarah D. to Charles G. Brown 10-19-1869 (10-21-1869)
Thorn, Sarah E. to John H. Jones 7-5-1866
Threadgill, Harriet E. to George W. Haley 9-20-1867 (no return)
Threadgill, Sarah F. to W. W. Mills 11-18-1865 (no return)
Thredgill, Martha A. to W. T. Oliver 12-2-1867 (12-4-1867)
Tiles, Elizabeth to T. H. W. Presson 12-13-1861 (12-15-1861)
Tilmon, Nancy to J. P. Wright 3-5-1867 (3-10-1867)
Todd, Amanda to George N. Wilson 8-5-1868
Todd, E. F. (Mrs.) to W. T. Thomas 10-19-1869
Todd, Martha to Newton Henley 1-11-1872
Tomblinson, Mary to Wm. Akins 5-16-1871 (5-17-1871)
Tomlinson, Margaret M.J. (Mrs.) to S. T. Boaz 11-13-1867
    (11-14-1867)
Tosh, Emeritta to William A. Williams 12-11-1865 (12-12-1865)
Tosh, Nancy to John Z. Kelly 1-10-1866
Tosh, Z. L. to J. M. Kelly 12-19-1872
Towery, Hariet J. to W. C. Hutchins 4-4-1868 (4-6-1868)
Townes, Amanda M. to W. J. Kerr 12-17-1867 (12-19-1867)
Townes, Mary to J. Dennis Moore 5-4-1866 (5-6-1866)
Towns, E. C. to J. C. Trainer 3-7-1871 (3-8-1871)
Towns, Mollie E. to C. C. Harris 12-25-1865 (no return)
Towns, Virginia C. to P. M. Wallick 10-14-1867 (10-16-1867)
Towns, W. F. to W. G. Richardson 11-26-1872 (11-27-1872)
Townsel, M. A. to W. W. Stoker 2-8-1867
Townsend, Amanda to George W. Towsend 4-8-1864 (4-9-1864)
Towsend, Elizabeth to Wm. B. Spoon 1-2-1866 (1-5-1866)
Travis, S. E. to T. D. McKinzie 10-20-1868 (10-22-1868)
Travis, Susan E. to John Reece 1-26-1867 (1-30-1867)
Traylor, Tilda to H. C. Adkins 7-30-1870 (7-31-1870)
Traywick, Jane to Samuel Neal 5-18-1869 (5-20-1869)
Traywick, Manerva C. to Sidney A. Johnson 9-26-1866 (10-4-1866)
Traywick, S. F. to J. N. Warbritton 2-5-1870 (2-6-1870)
Tucker, Caroline to John B. Lissey 5-3-1860
Tucker, Elizabeth A. to J. H. Fuqua 12-13-1869 (12-15-1869)
Tucker, P. A. to W. A. Matheny 9-29-1868 (10-1-1868)
Turner, E. C. to L. H. Malone 10-4-1867 (10-6-1867)
Turner, M. E. to R. A. Presson 10-9-1871 (no return)
Turner, Margarett to G. W. Yarbrough 5-13-1873 (5-14-1873)
Turner, Martha L.? to James L. Childress 12-16-1867 (12-18-1867)
Turner, Mary E. to John Chandler 4-9-1866 (4-12-1866)
Turner, Mary Jane to C. H. Wright 8-30-1860 (9-4-1860)
Turner, S. V. to J. D. Pate 10-8-1867 (10-10-1867)
Turner, Sarah Ann to W. J. Yarbrough 12-18-1865 (12-20-1866?)
Tynes, Elnore A. to Samuel J. House 1-9-1871 (1-10-1871)
Upton, Bettie S. to R. A. Newbill 8-26-1868 (no return)
Utley, Martha to W. S. Cooper 5-22-1865 (no return)
Utley?, Martha to B. A. Denny 10-15-1866 (10-17-1866)
Vancleave, Elizabeth to W. D. Myrack 3-22-1867 (3-24-1867)
Vancleive, Sallie to Bevily Bates 3-8-1872 (3-10-1872)

Vaughan, Emeline to W. R. Gardner 6-11-1861 (6-13-1861)
Vaughter, M. A. to G. L. Roper 5-18-1868 (5-19-1868)
Vaughter, M. E. to W. H. Algee 6-28-1867
Vawter, Susan A. to Silas R. Wyatt 1-13-1866 (1-15-1866)
Vickers, Andromedia to Z. H. Berry 12-24-1872
Vincent, Mary J. to Wm. K.? Williamson 7-9-1861 (7-10-1861)
Vinson, Manerva F. to Thomas T. Gatland 12-8-1866 (no return)
Vinson, Martha to Robt. Moore 2-19-1872 (2-20-1872)
Vinson, Susan to Manuel Parker 12-25-1869 (no return)
Wadkins, Nancy R. to W. H. Bilbrey 12-29-1870
Walker, Clary to Charles Cuningham 12-29-1871 (11-30-1871) B
Walker, Dora to A. White 3-18-1861
Walker, Elizabeth to J. N. Prewett 12-8-1871 (no return)
Walker, M. J. to A. J. Little 5-14-1864 (no return)
Walker, M. to John W. Towson 2-2-1865 (2-6-1865)
Walker, Mary J. to John Crab 3-29-1873 (3-30-1873)
Walker, Polly to John Long 3-8-1865 (3-10-1865)
Wall, Mary L. to A. C. Holmes 5-1-1873
Wallace, Araminta to Barney Mack 10-27-1860
Wallace, Elizabeth to George Parrish 11-3-1863
Waller, S. A. to T. B. Carter 2-28-1866 (3-1-1866)
Wallice, Arenia to J. B. George 4-28-1860
Walls, Elizabeth to L. T. Williams 8-13-1872 (8-15-1872)
Walpole, M. F. to J. T. Younger 7-21-1864 (7-25-1864)
Walter, Martha S. to E. J. Jackson 12-3-1868
Walters, J. N. to J. W. Smith 12-2-1869
Walton, M. A. to John L. Jones 7-21-1864 (7-23-1864)
Warbrittan, Mary F. to Samuel S. Hane 10-7-1865 (10-8-1865)
Warbritton, Emma C. to James R. McArnally 3-11-1867 (3-13-1867)
Warbritton, Mary Jane to Nathan Kirk 1-24-1870 (1-29-1870)
Ward, Drucilla to Robert H. Elmore 2-25-1863
Ward, Drucilla to Robert H. Elmore 2-25-1863 (2-27-1863)
Ward, J. R. to M. B. Flippin 4-7-1866 (4-8-1866)
Ward, Mary C. to David D. Murphee 9-23-1867
Ware, Susan A. to J. P. Pace 2-15-1866 (no return)
Warpooll, Ellen to John H. McCollum 1-?-1867 (1-16-1867)
Warren, Frances E. to William Clark 9-25-1867 (no return)
Wassey, S. A. to W. T. King 10-17-1871 (10-19-1871)
Waters, Mary V. to T. E. Freeman 11-7-1866
Watkins, Nancy to Anderson Edwards 8-9-1860 (no return)
Watson, Tabitha to C.? M. Hutchins 1-22-1868
Weatherford, M. C. to H. J. Hansbro 2-4-1861 (2-7-1861)
Webb, Caroline to Daniel Burrow 2-13-1871 (2-16-1871)
Webb, Lucinda J. to Henry C. Balinger 11-21-1865 (no return)
Webb, Martha M. to Franklin Conley 12-30-1869
Webb, Mary to H. S. Brandon 10-17-1866
Webb, S. E. to B. F. Thompson 12-20-1871 (no return)
Webb, S. E. to L. M. jr. Jones 1-7-1873 (no return)
Webb, Susan to W. G. Webb 12-12-1860 (12-13-1860)
Webb?, Susan to W. Z.? Wiles? no date (with 12-1860)
Westmoreland, Clarissa L. to Moses B. Swindle 9-11-1868 (9-12-1868)
White, Bhethsheba? to J. A. Cox 12-17-1872 (12-19-1872)
White, Elizabeth E. to J. Ezzell 7-17-1860 (no return)
White, L. F. to W. C. Lemons 4-4-1872
White, Manerva to William Hunt 6-21-1869
White, Margarett to Frank Irvine 2-26-1866 (no return)
White, Martha R. to John Carter 11-14-1865 (11-15-1865)
White, Martha to David McCloud 1-31-1870 (no return)
White, Mary to A. H. Lemmons 2-11-1867 (2-12-1867)
White, N. S. to H. C. Lemons 12-7-1871 (no return)
Whitehorn, Paralle to Alfred Devine 8-19-1868 (8-21-1868)
Whitley, Artimisa F. to Jordon Butler 3-2-1869 (3-10-1869)
Whitten, Carrie to James M. Gilbert 5-18-1869
Wiggins, Mariah to John Gilbert 1-9-1871 B
Wiggins, Narcisa to Thos. Gilbert 1-9-1871 B
Wilcox, N. J. to J. M. White 11-9-1870 (11-10-1870)
Wilder, Frances A. to A. H. Patterson 10-3-1864 (no return)
Wiles, Mollie A. to W. S. Gardner 5-16-1873 (no return)
Wiley, Aramissa to E. H. Smith 2-17-1868 (2-19-1868)
Wilkins, Mary L. to Christopher C. Crane 11-3-1860 (11-4-1860)
Wilks, |illy E. to John S. Laycock 12-27-1866
Williams, A. P. to Elvis B. Whitehorn 8-10-1867 (8-11-1867)
Williams, Caroline to Robt. C. Barnhart 1-22-1872 (no return)
Williams, D. M. to Thomas Dewhitt 12-31-1866 (1-1-1867)
Williams, E. B. to A. T. Jamison 3-13-1869 (3-14-1869)

Williams, Eliza to Alexander Bratton 8-18-1860 (8-19-1860)
Williams, Ellen to Alexander Duke 12-4-1869 (12-5-1869)
Williams, F. E. to M. J. C. O'Malley 3-7-1870 (3-8-1870)
Williams, Funtrey? to B. D. Hatch 8-?-1861 (no return)
Williams, Julia Ann to William Russell 2-17-1870
Williams, M. M. to J. T. Hopper 5-22-1871 (no return)
Williams, Mahulda A. to Basey D. Kemp 3-17-1869
Williams, Marry to Alvert Gibson 6-19-1873
Williams, Marth to Henry H. Haywood 11-14-1866 (11-18-1866)
Williams, Martha A. to Samuel H. Bennett 10-29-1868
Williams, Mary E. to James M. Joiner 9-17-1860 (9-18-1860)
Williams, Mary to William Little 4-7-1866 (4-15-1866)
Williams, Nancy A. to H. C. Petty 12-26-1865 (12-27-1865)
Williams, Nancy C. to Harvy T. Little 1-12-1867 (1-13-1867)
Williams, P. L. to R. B. Reynolds 5-14-1870 (5-15-1870)
Williams, Rachel to Luke Thomas 12-16-1870 (12-28-1870) B
Williams, Roxanna F. to R. G. Moore 2-9-1864 (3-10-1864)
Williams, Roxanna F. to R. G. Moore 2-9-1864 (no return)
Williams, Sallie to Rye Hayns 1-2-1871 B
Williams, Sarah C. to L. G. Giles 11-12-1872
Williams, Sarahann M. to J. F. Rogers 6-16-1871 (6-18-1871)
Williams, Tabitha A. to A. C. Edwards 11-8-1871
Williams, Tennessee to R. W. Jones 1-22-1866 (1-25-1866)
Williamson, Addie to B. Ezell 9-21-1870 (9-22-1870)
Williamson, Elizabeth J. to G. W. Williamson 9-7-1864 (no return)
Williamson, H. J. to John T. Ragland 2-14-1861
Williamson, Lenora to W. H. Ragland 4-27-1870 (4-28-1870)
Williamson, M. D. to J. W. Carter 1-14-1867 (no return)
Williamson, S. A. to B. A. Jones 1-7-1867 (no return)
Willis, Nancy to Joseph Branch 1-7-1864 (no return)
Willson, Louiza J. to Robert P. Woods 12-31-1861 (1-5-1862)
Wilson, Agnes to Caroline Covington 9-16-1869 (9-18-1869)
Wilson, Caroline to D. A. Buchannon 12-7-1864 (12-8-1864)
Wilson, Caroline to D. A. Buckannan 12-7-1864
Wilson, Frances P. to G. W. Edwards 10-15-1866 (10-16-1866)
Wilson, H. E. to J. T. Crumb 1-18-1871 (1-19-1871)
Wilson, M. J. to R. B. F. Carter 12-10-1868
Wilson, Margaret C. to Murray A. Brandon 2-2-1869
Wilson, S. L. O. to L. P. Allen 1-12-1861
Wilson, Silvia to Andrew Walker 1-4-1873 (1-9-1873) B
Winberg, Elizabeth to Abrom Hay 10-14-1866 (no return)
Wingo, Eliza to Foster Meadows 12-24-1870 (12-27-1870)
Wingo, Elizabeth to Martin Gilbert 1-4-1871 (1-5-1871)
Wingo, Harriet to Isham Everett 4-28-1870 (5-1-1871?)
Wingo, Jenny to Armstead Dammond? 2-1-1870 (2-2-1870)
Wingo, Sallie E. to R. L. Holt 8-29-1871 (9-3-1871)
Winn (Norrod), Sarah P. to James S. Capps 8-28-1868
Winn, M. E. to F. A. Williams 8-10-1867 (8-11-1867)
Winters, Mary to T.? Roach 1-21-1862
Wolff, Cordelia to R. H. Rawls 2-11-1869
Wood, Alice B. to E. G. Rowe 3-29-1869 (3-30-1869)
Wood, Elizabeth J. to E. A. G. Hall 1-15-1873 (1-16-1873)
Wood, Mary J. to Robt. L. Harris 1-18-1873 (1-19-1873)
Wood, Nancy E. to Henry A. Hampton 7-17-1869 (7-18-1869)
Wood, Sarah A. to R. S. Carter 10-14-1862 (10-16-1862)
Woodard, Mary L. to John K. Dunning 8-28-1864 (no return)
Woods, Ellen to Hail Gossett 5-7-1870 (5-8-1870)
Woods, Martha E. (Mrs.) to R. M. Hurt 4-24-1860
Woods, Mary to Wm. Har 5-12-1865 (6-1-1865)
Woods, Mary to Wm. Hurt 5-12-1865 (no return)
Woods, Susan Y. to T. A. Duke 7-15-1868
Woollen, L. L. to W. C. O'Neill 10-25-1870 (10-26-1870)
Worlds?, Polley to J. W. Polston 12-22-1866 (12-23-1866)
Worrell, Mary J. to J. C. Hill 5-14-1870 (5-15-1870)
Worsham, Amanda to Robert T. Key 3-25-1869
Wray, M. E. to H. R. Parnell 12-19-1868 (12-20-1868)
Wren, S. A. to F. W. Turner 6-27-1870 (6-29-1870)
Wright, Harriett to Sim Barham 8-5-1873 (8-6-1873) B
Wright, Jobie A. to Benjamin A. Williams 6-26-1861 (6-27-1861)
Wright, M. N. to R. N. Enocks 12-17-1872
Wyatt, Lydie A. to Felix H. Brackens 7-16-1869 (7-17-1869)
Wyatt, S. C. to R. H. White 11-28-1870 (11-30-1870)
Yancy, L. D. to J. B. Moore 2-5-1868 (1?-11-1868)
Yonger, Mary A. to G. W. Nowlin 1-5-1867 (no return)
York, Mary to Robert Hutchins 8-6-1868

Young, Ann to Charles Harris 1-22-1870 (2-13-1870)
Young, L. D. to J. T. Crawford 12-20-1869 (12-22-1869)
Younger, Caroline to Ralph Morgan 12-16-1868 (12-17-1868)
Younger, Dollie to R. C. Gelby 8-13-1866 (no return)
Younger, Kate to E. J. Coleman 11-14-1865 (11-15-1865)
Younger, L. A. to L. S. Howard 7-8-1867 (7-10-1867)
Younger, L. E. to J. C. Roach 5-20-1872 (5-21-1872)
Younger, Mary J. to Benjamin Watts 10-16-1860 (10-6?-1860)
Younger, Mattie to J. A. Oneil 2-28-1871
Younger, Nancy M. E. to John N. Viar 10-24-1860 (10-25-1860)
Younger, Vina to Spencer Jones 1-31-1871 (2-2-1871)
_____, N. to J. H. Key 2-?-1860 (no return)
_____, _____ to James Allen 9-29-1871
_____, _____ to William J. Edwards 12-8-1866 (12-11-1866)

www.ingramcontent.com/pod-product-compliance
Lightning Source LLC
La Vergne TN
LVHW061341060426
835511LV00014B/2062